Drink Water, but Remember the Source

The publisher gratefully acknowledges the generous support of the Asian Studies Endowment Fund of the University of California Press Foundation.

Drink Water, but Remember the Source

Moral Discourse in a Chinese Village

Ellen Oxfeld

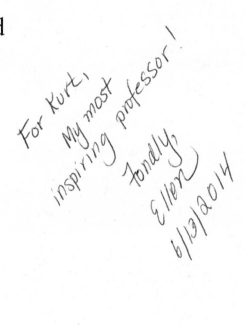

For Kurt,
My most inspiring professor!
fondly,
Ellen
6/13/2014

UNIVERSITY OF CALIFORNIA PRESS
Berkeley · Los Angeles · London

University of California Press, one of the most distinguished university presses in the United States, enriches
lives around the world by advancing scholarship in the
humanities, social sciences, and natural sciences. Its
activities are supported by the UC Press Foundation
and by philanthropic contributions from individuals
and institutions. For more information, visit
www.ucpress.edu.

University of California Press
Berkeley and Los Angeles, California

University of California Press, Ltd.
London, England

Library of Congress Cataloging-in-Publication Data
Oxfeld, Ellen.
    Drink water, but remember the source : moral
discourse in a Chinese village / Ellen Oxfeld.
        p.   cm.
    Includes bibliographical references and index.
    ISBN 978-0-520-26094-8 (cloth : alk. paper)
    ISBN 978-0-520-26095-5 (pbk. : alk. paper)
    1. Meixian Shi (China)—Moral conditions.
2. Meixian Shi (China)—Social conditions.   3. Village
communities—Moral and ethical aspects—China—
Meixian Shi.   4. Country life—Moral and ethical
aspects—China—Meixian Shi.   5. Conduct of life.
I. Title.
HN740.M45O94   2010
170.951'27—dc22   2010011949

Manufactured in the United States of America
19   18   17   16   15   14   13   12   11   10
10   9   8   7   6   5   4   3   2   1

This book is printed on Cascades Enviro 100, a 100%
post consumer waste, recycled, de-inked fiber. FSC
recycled certified and processed chlorine free. It is acid
free, Ecologo certified, and manufactured by BioGas
energy.

For Frank

Contents

Illustrations

Tables

Notes on the Text

ROMANIZATION

Most Chinese words and phrases in the text are written in Mandarin and romanized according to the pinyin system. The glossary at the end of the book provides the Chinese characters for these words. Occasionally a phrase is spelled out in Hakka. When this is the case, it is noted in the glossary.

PERMISSION TO REPRINT MATERIAL

Grateful acknowledgment is made for permission to reprint revised versions of the following material: Ellen Oxfeld, "Chinese Villagers and the Moral Dilemmas of Return Visits," in *Coming Home? Refugees, Migrants, and Those Who Stayed Behind,* edited by Lynellyn D. Long and Ellen Oxfeld, 90–103, © 2004 University of Pennsylvania Press, reprinted by permission of the University of Pennsylvania Press. Ellen Oxfeld, " 'When You Drink Water, Think of Its Source': Morality, Status, and Reinvention in Rural Chinese Funerals," *Journal of Asian Studies* 63, no. 4 (November 2004): 961–90, © 2004 Association for Asian Studies, reprinted with the permission of Cambridge University Press. Ellen Oxfeld, "The Man Who Sold the Collective's Land: Understanding New Economic Regimes in Guangdong," *Taiwan Journal of Anthropology* 2, no. 1 (June 2004): 11–40, © 2004 Academia Sinica, reprinted by permission of the Institute of Ethnology, Academia Sinica.

Preface and Acknowledgments

This book is based on fieldwork conducted in a village in Meixian (Mei County), Guangdong Province, southeast China. I first visited this village, which I call Moonshadow Pond, in the summer of 1993 and subsequently returned to conduct fieldwork in 1995 through 1996, in the summer of 1997, for a short visit in the summer of 2006, and again for five months in the spring of 2007.

My focus is on the moral discourse of the residents of this village. All of us have to make decisions every day about how to live in our immediate environment, how to conduct ourselves within our families, with friends and acquaintances, in our economic transactions, in our spiritual and religious lives and in reference to the structures of power in which we live.

In rural China, as elsewhere, such decisions about how to act are influenced by both practical and moral considerations. But how do people themselves understand and explain their own actions or make judgments about others? And what portion of these decisions is understood in moral terms? This is a world that has undergone revolutionary transformation in just a few decades. I was curious to know how people in this context spoke about their obligations and articulated ideas about what they regarded as good versus bad actions—both interpersonally and with regard to the wider society.

To be clear from the outset, the realm of the "moral" in rural China cannot be ascertained with reference to a great text or unyielding set of rules. Rather, the realm of the moral in this book refers to people's ideas about their basic obligations and about what we might colloquially say is "doing the right thing." These ideas are worked out in the course of issues they face in their ongoing lives. As we shall see, there *are* some underlying principles that inform people's thinking and actions. However, decades of tumultuous political change as well as differences in individual personalities and circumstances also result in a complicated mix of ideas about morality in specific contexts.

Such ideas are hard to learn about through questionnaires, one-time interviews, or other methods that are divorced from the actual circumstances in which people live their lives. In this case, the most fruitful approach was the traditional anthropological method of "participant observation"—slowly acquiring an understanding by living with people over an extended period of time.

Social and cultural anthropologists from East Asia, North America, and Europe have steadily produced work on rural China since Fei Xiaotong published his path-breaking studies in the late 1930s and 1940s. While the practice of anthropology in mainland China was suspended during the Mao era, the ethnography of rural China flourished during that time based on fieldwork in Hong Kong's New Territories and in Taiwan. With the Reform and Reopening in 1980, the discipline of anthropology was revived in China, and both Chinese and foreign anthropologists returned to work.

With the ongoing economic changes in China fueling massive migrations of young people to the cities, some might question the usefulness of another book whose focus remains "a village in rural China." Certainly, there is a great need to look at the interconnections between China's rural areas and the world beyond. Nonetheless, I would argue that for the purposes of understanding moral ideas, concentrating on one village makes sense, even while the village is connected in a myriad of ways to the outside world. People come and go, as migrants to cities or as émigrés returning from abroad. And like any other village in China, Moonshadow Pond has been changed by both the revolutionary reordering of life in the collective era and the subsequent introduction of a market economy and opening to global economic forces. But "the village" is still a real place where people have to make sense of these diverse influences.

Finally, as previously indicated, people's moral ideas are worked out over time with respect to their fellow villagers, and to really understand these, there is no substitute for sustained fieldwork in one small place.

In my case, such fieldwork would not have been possible without the help of many people. First and foremost, I would never have found Moonshadow Pond if my good friend from Hong Kong, whom I call Ruolan in this book, had not introduced me to her relatives there. I am also more than grateful for the help of the Guangdong Academy of Social Sciences and particularly General Secretary Li Jiangtao, who enabled me to secure permissions and visas to study in Meixian from 1995 through 1996 and again in the summer of 1997. Without the initial introduction of Professor Thomas Chan of Hong Kong Polytechnic University, this affiliation would also not have been possible. Professor Fang Xuejia of the Hakka Research Institute of Jiaying University was a wonderful intellectual resource on Hakka culture. He also generously helped me to secure affiliations and official permission to start a new round of research in the spring of 2007. Whenever I traveled to Meixian, I usually passed through Hong Kong, where many wonderful friends and their families were generous hosts, especially Rose and Thomas Chan, and Nancy and Michael Ling. My own institution, Middlebury College, supported me through several sabbaticals, and without these breaks from teaching, it is doubtful that this manuscript would have seen the light of day. My research in the spring of 2007 was also supported by a Fulbright Fellowship.

Earlier versions of some chapters in this book were published in journals or edited volumes. I benefited greatly from the comments and criticisms of anonymous reviewers for all these publications, as I also gained immensely from the comments of two anonymous reviewers for the University of California Press. Weihe Xu helped me to felicitously translate a number of Chinese proverbs. My husband, Frank Nicosia, and my late father, Emil Oxfeld, consistently encouraged me to forge ahead, and my mother, Edith Oxfeld, assiduously edited my final revisions, contributing greatly to the readability of the final manuscript. For all this I am deeply grateful!

Finally, and most importantly, I must thank the residents of Moonshadow Pond. I have used pseudonyms for all the individuals I discuss in the book, so I cannot thank them by name here. Nonetheless, without them there would not only be no book, but I would not have learned what I did. They were patient with my unceasing, often repetitive questions and were understanding when matters that were quite obvious to them took me a much longer time to comprehend. During the time I conducted this research, some people in Moonshadow Pond celebrated weddings, births, and economic success, but they also had to contend with two major floods, and some also experienced family tragedies and economic hardships. Despite all this, they were generous and helpful throughout my stay. To the residents of Moonshadow Pond, therefore, I owe my everlasting thanks, and I will consider myself a success if I can attain even a fraction of their fortitude and resourcefulness.

ANTHROPOLOGIST'S LANDLORD AND LANDLADY:

Songling and Baoli:
- Their married daughters, Meiying and Fengying
- Their son, Yanhong, and his wife, Lianfang

OTHER MEMBERS OF TEAM 2 (ALL ARE ALSO MEMBERS OF LINEAGE BRANCH OR *FANG* 2):

Aihua, former team leader of Team 2:
- Her husband, Uncle Wei, general secretary of the Production Brigade from the late 1960s to the late 1970s
- Their married sons, Guofei (who slaughters pigs and sells pork for a living) and Guobin (who raises pigs and fish)
- Their nephew "Ironpot" (the gambler)

Skinny Hong and Yuelan:
- They have five sons and a daughter, Ailing

Red Chong:
- Lives next door to Songling and Baoli; does not believe in a spirit world

Miaoli and her husband, Wentong:
- Miaoli's life is characterized by discord with her mother-in-law

Weiguo (older brother) and Jieguo (younger brother):
- Both are successful and well-connected residents of Moonshadow Pond who have recently retired from their jobs. Jieguo was a police officer and Weiguo was a security officer in a cigarette factory. They have houses in Moonshadow Pond, as well as apartments in the county capital. But they frequently come back to their village homes.

Jiawen, the village doctor:
- Guizhen, his wife and also a midwife
- Chunyu, Jiawen's mother, also a midwife

OTHER RESIDENTS OF MOONSHADOW POND, WHO ARE NOT IN TEAM 2:

Big Gao, former village head:
- His daughter, Small Gao, who is in business with Baoli and was leader of Team 4
- His son, Zhide, married to Baoli's eldest daughter

Slippery Cheng:
- Village resident who "sells" the collective's land

Sneaky Tao:
- Former member of the local Party Branch Committee

Bright Ling:
- College-educated and unmarried woman who is serious about Buddhism

PART ONE

Morality in Rural China

Contexts and Categories

CHAPTER I

Moonshadow Pond

Moral Expectations and Daily Life

Mountains provide for the population; water brings them
wealth. *(Shan guan rending, shui guan cai.)*

—Chinese proverb

In Moonshadow Pond, as in many other villages in southeast China, the
front doors of the old houses face south or east, but never toward the
harsh north winds or to the inauspicious west.[1] A river runs past fields
and through the center of the village; the ancestors' graves lie nestled in
the mountains above. Like the houses beneath them, the graves are carefully placed to guard against misfortune according to the principles of
"wind and water," or *fengshui.*[2]

Once a year, during the two-week period following the Lunar New
Year holiday, the descendants of Jianxigong, the common ancestor of all
those born in Moonshadow Pond, climb the slopes on both sides of the
village to "sweep the graves" of their ancestors. After cleaning the grave
area, they lay out offerings of fruit, homemade New Year's treats and rice
wine, packaged biscuits, tea, and the "three kinds of sacrificial offerings"
(san sheng)—cooked chicken, pork and fish. They burn spirit money (paper representations of real money) for their ancestors' use in the spirit
world and finally set off firecrackers to ward off dangerous spirits. These
efforts to commemorate their ancestors are testimony to a quality of character that the villagers call *xiuxin,* which roughly translated means "a
cultivated heart and mind." Those who are *xiuxin* remember to do the
right thing, and by giving offerings in this way ensure their ancestor's
continued goodwill.

Indeed, the idea that there is never closure to any human relationship
is a basic assumption for village residents and it sets the context for this

book, an exploration of moral culture in contemporary rural China. As we shall see in subsequent chapters, there is a lively debate about the nature of moral ideas in reform-era China. Contemporary accounts of China in the Western media often concentrate on rapid economic expansion, political corruption, human-rights violations, and environmental degradation. In scholarly literature, some authors raise questions about whether, in the wake of the demise of the collective order and the rise of global capitalism and consumerism, there is any moral code in China at all. Amidst all these changes it is fair to ask whether ordinary citizens have any readily available moral compass to live by. While I cannot answer such questions for a country so vast, I do hope that through this study I can shed some light on how the residents of at least one small corner of rural China have spoken about moral obligations in relationship to the circumstances of their daily lives during a time of comprehensive cultural, social, and political transformation.

As subsequent chapters will illustrate, in Moonshadow Pond today, one's debt to one's parents, as well as one's ancestors, is viewed as a prototype of all reciprocal transactions in society. Acting upon one's memory of past help is a central element of the notion of what it means to be a good or "moral" person in many domains. The connection between memory and morality is summed up by a commonly quoted maxim, which I refer to in the title of this book: "When you drink water, remember the source."[3] It refers to the necessity of remembering who helped you, and it is a principle that is deeply rooted; it is both consciously articulated and unconsciously assumed. Yet the rapid changes in Chinese society, as well as to some degree the nature of social life itself, which inevitably involves choices, means that even as people continue to employ ideas about moral debt in their relationships, there is much to disagree about when evaluating specific situations.

My exploration of moral concepts in Moonshadow Pond will focus on the way they are used in ordinary discourse. " 'Moral discourse,' " says the sociologist Richard Madsen, "attempts to understand the nature of moral responsibilities, to evaluate the nature of oneself or others in the light of such understandings, and to persuade others that one's understandings and evaluations are correct."[4] Madsen himself wrote an important study of moral discourse in a Mao-era village, focusing on the way local officials used different kinds of moral claims to bolster their own power. In this book, however, my focus is not so much on the use of moral discourse as a way of gaining political leverage as it is on its use by villagers to evaluate an array of actions and decisions that they and their fellow villagers undertake in their everyday lives.[5] As such, I have chosen to examine moral discourse in areas of daily life that are important to Moonshadow Pond residents and about which not all people agree or are even internally consistent in their judgments.

After laying out the context and key concepts in the first two chapters, my examination of moral discourse will begin with a focus on the way villagers articulate ideas about moral obligation within the family. As stated earlier, family life and its obligations serve as a metaphor in Moonshadow Pond for moral debt in other domains of social life; for most rural Chinese, family is still one's most immediate set of relations. So issues of moral debt are most constantly posed within the family. Relations with ancestors and geographically distant kin are viewed as extensions of family relations, and therefore chapters on moral discourse regarding death ritual and relations with overseas kin follow naturally from the chapter on family. The latter parts of the book turn to an investigation of moral discourse as it relates to villagers' experiences of economic and political transformations. To a certain extent, these chapters are also extensions of the chapters on family. Since Moonshadow Pond is a single-lineage village, in which residents conceive of themselves as descended from a common ancestor, local economic and political relationships may also be experienced as relations amongst kin. Yet the enormous economic and political changes that all Chinese have lived through over the last several decades have called for a continuous need to reframe ideas about what constitutes a "right" or "wrong" action within these domains of action. In particular, villagers need to contend with the way economic inequalities or power differences amongst them affect their social obligations toward one another based on common ancestry.

Beginning with moral discourse as it applies to the most intimate relationships within the family and moving outward to incorporate villagers' ideas about the moral implications of their relationships with the world beyond, my chapters are therefore ordered to take account of an expanding circle of social relationships. At the conclusion of each chapter, we turn our attention to an individual whose situation or ideas illustrate some of the elements of moral discourse discussed in that chapter. I should also point out that while one can certainly find extended studies of many of the specific areas dealt with in this book—such as gender and family in rural China, or changes in property relations—my aim is not to replicate these studies. Rather, my purpose is to examine villagers' ideas about moral obligation with reference to these different domains—and, indeed, to show that there is a vibrant moral discourse regarding these many areas of social life.

ARRIVING IN MOONSHADOW POND

I first arrived in Moonshadow Pond in the summer of 1993 and returned for several stays thereafter; I lived there from 1995 through 1996, during the summers of 1997 and 2006, and finally for five months in the spring of 2007. I was introduced to Moonshadow Pond by Song Ruolan, the sister of a good friend from the Chinese community in Calcutta, India, where I had undertaken previous research. Ruolan's father was born in Moonshadow Pond and emigrated to India in the 1940s. In 1962, when Ruolan was just a teenager, China and India went to war. Most of Ruolan's family members in India were deported to China, along with other Indian Chinese, because the government accused them of disloyalty during wartime. When the Cultural Revolution broke out throughout the country in 1966, Ruolan was a student in the city of Guangzhou. Two years of intensifying violence followed in which bands of young Red Guards roamed the country attacking "class enemies" and relics of the old society, ranging from temples to private libraries. Teachers, party cadres, factory managers, and ordinary citizens that the Red Guards identified as being from the wrong "class" or holding a counterrevolutionary point of view would find themselves surrounded by a mob and even beaten to death.

Mao's call for continuous revolution had been the initial spark that unleashed the chaos, but in the midst of its most destructive moments, a new initiative was launched. Young urban youth were called upon to resettle in the countryside and learn from the peasants. Although couched in revolutionary terms, it is probable that by that point sending the youth to the rural areas was the only way to quell the urban factional violence that had spun out of control.

Ruolan was one of millions of high school students whom this decision would affect. While the majority of her classmates in a high school for returned overseas Chinese in Guangzhou were sent to Hainan Island off the coast of south China, Ruolan petitioned for permission to live with her own relatives in Moonshadow Pond. The permission was granted, and she lived there from 1968 until 1972, before legally immigrating to Hong Kong by means of marriage to another Indian Chinese with Hong Kong residency papers.

Because she was from the city, Ruolan's rural relatives in Moonshadow

Pond did not expect her to be able to do the work that they did and they allowed her to buy her provisions from the collective without laboring in the fields. Indeed, as an overseas Chinese who had only recently arrived in China, Ruolan did not bring revolutionary idealism to the village and she was happy to leave for Hong Kong as soon as possible. Nonetheless, Ruolan remained in contact with the village after she left, and she traveled there frequently after the reforms of the late 1970s made it easier for Hong Kong residents to visit their kin in China.

Ruolan accompanied me to Moonshadow Pond for a brief introductory visit in the summer of 1993, and when I returned for a longer period of fieldwork in 1995 and 1996, she arranged for me to live with her closest relatives in the village. In 1995, her relatives Songling and Baoli were a couple in their late fifties with two married daughters and an unmarried adult son (for this and subsequently referenced villagers, see figure 1, page xix). Like many middle-aged couples in Moonshadow Pond, Songling and Baoli had stayed in the village while their grown children had moved to the county capital or even further away. Songling worked on the family's rice-paddy land and vegetable plots and Baoli ran a village rice-threshing operation. For a village couple of their age, both Songling and Baoli were quite well educated. Songling had completed the first few years of high school and Baoli had graduated from high school. Over the years, they became an invaluable resource for me and shared information about the village as well as much traditional lore.

On the day of my arrival in Moonshadow Pond in 1995, Songling and Ruolan took me to the lineage halls at the center of the village and to the altars to popular gods that guard the village borders. There, we made offerings and asked both the deities and ancestors to ensure that my stay in Moonshadow Pond would be safe and that my research would succeed. Ruolan sternly warned me that these precautions were important and that launching into my work without first paying the proper respects was not wise. However, our trip to acknowledge these deities was questioned by Baoli. "She's an intellectual," he said about me, "and intellectuals don't believe in gods." If I needed an introduction to the heterogeneous nature of belief and opinion in Moonshadow Pond, this was certainly a good one.

VILLAGE IDENTITY: LINEAGE, PLACE, AND ETHNICITY

Moonshadow Pond is in Mei County, or Meixian, one of six counties in an area of Guangdong Province now called Meizhou.[6] The residents

MAP 1. People's Republic of China. Inset: Meizhou area of Guangdong Province.

of the Meizhou area are Hakka, a distinct ethnic and linguistic group in southeast China who are nevertheless considered to be ethnic Chinese or Han. They believe their origins were in north central China many hundreds of years ago. According to their own history, when they migrated to southeast China they received their name from the Han who already resided there (see map 1). Indeed, *Hakka* means "guest people" in Cantonese.

Recently there has been renewed interest in the Hakka on the part of both academic historians and the Hakka themselves, who have also migrated overseas and forged links based on Hakka identity in the diaspora. A number of theories have been promulgated and debated about the origins of Hakka identity. One of the most respected historians of the Hakka, S. T. Leong, contends that they first gained a sense of themselves as Han in the course of ethnic squabbles between themselves and aboriginal peoples called the She. The Hakka ultimately defeated the She in the sixteenth century and occupied the area that is contemporary Meixian.[7]

"Eight parts mountain, one part water, and one part fields" *(Ba shan, yi shui, yi tian)*. This phrase is how schoolchildren learn to characterize Meixian. Although it is now called the Hakka heartland, Meixian was originally a peripheral and mountainous area not associated with any major commercial center. Over time the Hakka began to migrate from Meixian to other peripheries, rather than to the economically abundant lowlands that were already occupied. The Hakka never existed on subsistence agriculture alone, but traded agricultural, forest, and industrial products such as tobacco, sugar cane, and iron ore with the lowland groups. During more prosperous eras there was reasonably little conflict, but ethnic skirmishes and even serious ethnic wars did occur during economic downturns and in the nineteenth century the Hakka and the Cantonese often entered into violent conflicts over land.[8] Leong has suggested further that it was these conflicts between Hakka and Cantonese that lead Hakka to think of themselves as a distinct group. All Han Chinese in the south migrated from north central China at some point or other, but it was only the Hakka who became "guest people."[9]

Although the Hakka resided in mountainous and peripheral areas, this did not mean they valued such topography. Mountains are associated with the strength of the family line in traditional thought and *fengshui* principles, but in ordinary discourse mountains are more commonly associated with poverty. On a day trip in 1996 with some of the teachers from the village elementary school to the neighboring Hakka county of Dapu, I gasped in admiration at the scenery and frantically tried to shoot some good photographs. But my travel companions saw things in a different light. As they looked out the windows of the bus at the villages we passed, they sighed sympathetically: "What a bitter life." The steep mountain slopes, they implied, made agriculture more difficult and strenuous.

For these young schoolteachers, the landscape was viewed in terms of the human labor needed to eke out an existence. This view is reflected in both past and present practices in Moonshadow Pond. Men who come from more mountainous areas have always been considered less desirable marriage partners, while women who marry into Moonshadow Pond from mountain communities are seen as marrying "up."[10] As people prosper now, they build their new homes closer to the highway rather than nestled into the hills like their original village homes. The highway, after all, brings people that much closer to the outside world and its economic opportunities.[11]

Indeed, traveling to Moonshadow Pond today from the county capital is an easy matter. One takes a bus, taxi, motorcycle, or bike on the increasingly congested highway that begins in the capital and runs north past Moonshadow Pond, through another Hakka county, Pingyuan, and finally to the neighboring province of Jiangxi. This route, like so many other things in Moonshadow Pond, bears the marks of several eras. It was paved in the 1990s, replacing a dirt road that had been built after Liberation (1949), when the Communists established the People's Republic of China (PRC). Prior to that, one entered and left Moonshadow Pond on a footpath, a narrow vein that connected the village to the outside world through the exhausting work of men and women carrying buckets of goods hung from sturdy bamboo poles strung over their shoulders.

Before the 1950s, men from Jiangxi Province to the north carried packs filled with tobacco and soybean to Meixian. In Moonshadow Pond and other villages along the route, they met Hakka women traveling in the opposite direction weighed down with sacks of salt. Somewhere along the way, they would exchange their loads and return to their points of origin. Moonshadow Pond also had some leather tanneries at this time, and women would haul the finished leather from the village to the county seat, returning with more raw hides to be processed.

In Meixian, it has always been women who were largely responsible for both agricultural work and much of the physical labor of hauling goods. Hakka women never bound their feet as did women in many other areas of China, and the energy and involvement of women in economic activities is still referred to by Hakka in communities throughout the world as a unique aspect of their identity.[12] More than one historian of Hakka identity has speculated that the Hakka may have been influenced by the aboriginal people who inhabited Meixian before them. But once borrowed, these gendered practices were highly adaptive. As Hakka men began to migrate throughout southeast China and abroad, it became even more important for women to hold down the agricultural economy at home.[13]

Even now, a brief stroll through the village testifies to the extraordinary importance of Hakka women in their families' economic lives. Walking through the village, one still sees women washing laundry in the stream, building new houses, working in rice fields, tending to vegetable gardens, or hauling heavy loads of agricultural supplies.

Many Hakka men left to go overseas before Liberation, leaving their wives to raise their children in their family homes. If their husbands did not return from abroad, some women even adopted heirs. They contributed greatly to the work effort of their in-law's families, and while some of their husbands remitted funds from abroad and returned home to retire, others were never heard from again. Before Liberation, those men who did not emigrate worked at the peripheries of the agricultural economy—tending water buffalos or finding work in construction or village industries such as tanning. A few men prospered as landlords, overseers of the coolie laborers who carted goods, or managers and owners of village tanneries.

At present, the approximately eight hundred residents of Moonshadow Pond are divided into 198 households.[14] In 1997, only 10 percent of households earned their living entirely from agriculture, while 14 percent of Moonshadow Pond families did not farm at all, with the remainder relying on a mixture of agriculture and wage labor. But by 2007 the number of families who did not farm at all had grown to 33 percent, while the number who earned their living only from agriculture had dropped to 6 percent. The majority of families still fall between these two options. They use the land allocated to them to provision themselves with rice and vegetables, but they also rely on wage labor or small business activities of some family members to augment their livelihoods.

Many of Moonshadow Pond's young people have now migrated to large cities, such as Shenzhen and Guangzhou, which are hundreds of miles away, to earn money (which is then sent home) as factory workers, cooks, drivers, or hostesses in restaurants. By 2007, about 24 percent of all households had one family member who had migrated beyond Meixian for work.[15] Other villagers work nearby in road and home construction, or they earn their living in the village itself by cultivating fruit trees or raising fish, poultry, or pigs for sale. Some individuals operate small stores, butcher and sell fresh pork, or produce value-added agricultural products such as tofu. Two families run small health clinics to treat minor ailments, and there is even one family that has achieved financial success by making paper offerings for use in seasonal and life-cycle rituals. A few villagers have also prospered in the ranks of the bureaucracy or in business in the nearby county capital, a growing metropolis of over three hundred thousand residents.

Wherever residents of the village ultimately disperse, however, those born in Moonshadow Pond are members of one patrilineage—tracing their ancestry through the male line to an ascendant ancestor. Like many lineages in south China, the Songs of Moonshadow Pond possess an official written genealogy *(zupu)*. Historians contend that many such accounts, especially the records of the most distant times, are apocryphal and inevitably glorify the earliest ancestors. But whatever their actual historical validity, these records serve as important social charters.

The Song lineage history traces ancestry to an official named Ganggong, who was born in the year 1083 in the neighboring province of Jiangxi and served in the imperial government. The *zupu* tells us that fifteen generations after Ganggong was born (in the year 1408), one of his descendants moved to Mei County. Thirteen generations later, *his* descendant moved to Moonshadow Pond. This man is the village founder Jianxigong, and, according to the genealogy, he had three sons, each of whom started a branch (or *fang*) of the main lineage. The dates are rather murky here, because the official history gives us none. But the grave of the village founder's second son tells us that he died thirty-three years after the beginning of the Wan Li Emperor's reign in the Ming dynasty— that would be in 1606 (see figures 2 and 3).

Almost every man in Moonshadow Pond can situate himself within this lineage history and knows in which branch, sub-branch, and so forth he belongs. During the New Year's holiday, as described at the chapter's beginning, villagers visit the graves of the lineage branch founders (see photograph 1). Most of the participants in these rituals are men. Since women customarily join their husband's families at marriage and leave their natal villages, they do not necessarily share equally strong feelings about the lineage. Daughters are not included in the genealogy at all, since they will marry out, and wives in the lineage history are identified only by their surname group. Indeed, at one point during my research, while I was enmeshed in an investigation of the lineage history, my landlady Songling dismissively told me that such things were "men's concern."

However, while women may express little interest in some of the more remote ancestors of the lineage, the Lunar New Year holiday is also the time when both men and women return to the graves of their immediate relatives, those with whom they had personal connections. This activity is of equal interest to women and men. Furthermore, during this time, young people who have left the villages in order to labor in larger

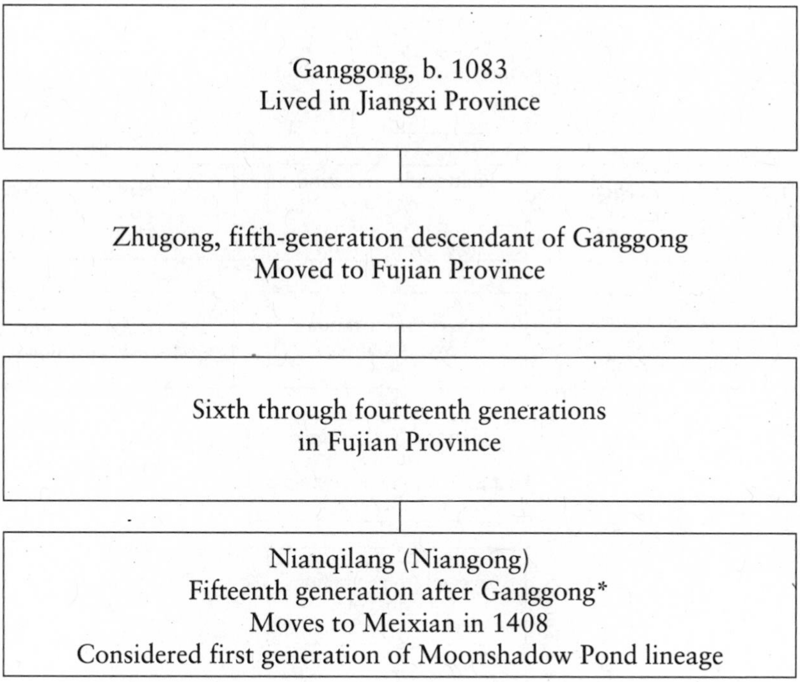

| Ganggong, b. 1083 |
| Lived in Jiangxi Province |

| Zhugong, fifth-generation descendant of Ganggong |
| Moved to Fujian Province |

| Sixth through fourteenth generations |
| in Fujian Province |

| Nianqilang (Niangong) |
| Fifteenth generation after Ganggong* |
| Moves to Meixian in 1408 |
| Considered first generation of Moonshadow Pond lineage |

* Niangong, Zhugong, and Changgong are all posthumous titles.

FIGURE 2. The Song lineage of Moonshadow Pond, earlier generations.

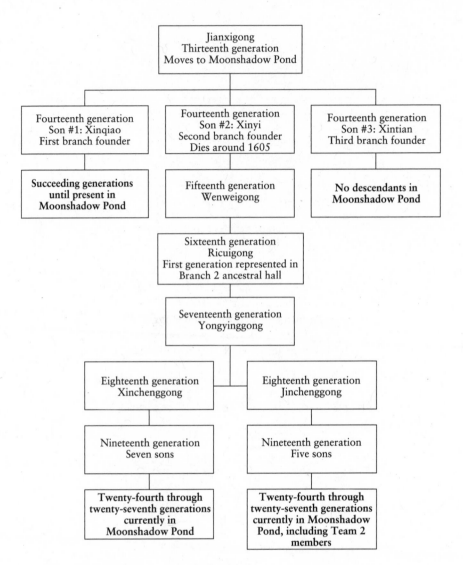

FIGURE 3. The Song lineage in Moonshadow Pond.

PHOTOGRAPH 1. Annual worship at grave of second lineage branch founder, spring 2007.

cities also return to take part in the festivities. On New Year's Eve, young and old, migrants and those who stayed behind, also make offerings and set off fireworks at the geographical and psychological center and symbol of the village—the two lineage halls at the site of the first village settlement (see photographs 2 and 3). One hall commemorates the village founder and all subsequent descendants; the other celebrates his second son and all his descendants. This second son is the founder of the second lineage branch (or *fang*), which today is the largest lineage branch in the village. Its central altar contains wooden ancestral tablets painted in red, each one with the name of a deceased member of this lineage branch inscribed in gold. Although hidden away during the Cultural Revolution, these tablets were returned to the temple at the beginning of the reform period. All living members of this lineage branch can find their immediate and more distant male ancestors recorded here. When a male baby is born to a member of the lineage, he is taken by his parents to the lineage hall during the Lunar New Year and a lantern is hung to mark the addition of a new lineage member (see photograph 4).

Ancestors therefore reside at the center of Moonshadow Pond. The

PHOTOGRAPH 2. The original village area, 2007.

PHOTOGRAPH 3. Second lineage branch temple, Chinese New Year's Eve, 2007.
Note the fireworks in front of the hall; in the foreground are fishponds.

original village boundaries are marked by bridges over the river at the
northern and southern ends of the village and guarded by local gods.
These are the gods I visited on my arrival in the village. These gods include gods of the bridges at the formal village entrance (Qiao Baigong),
as well as Gong Wang, a village guardian who can ease communication

PHOTOGRAPH 4.
Hanging a new
lantern. The parents
of a baby boy bring a
lantern to the lineage
temple during the
Lunar New Year to
mark the birth of a
new lineage member.

between the underworld of ghosts and the human world, and Sheguan
Laoye, the god of earth and grain. This arrangement, gods at the periphery
to protect the village and ancestors at the center, is common to many
Hakka villages (see photograph 5 and map 2).

But we should also note that not all Hakka villages are single-surname
villages like Moonshadow Pond. This attribute, in fact, meant that they
were considered relatively "strong" in comparison with neighboring villages before Liberation. Even now, old people from other villages say that
during the old society Moonshadow Pond youths were more likely to
"bully" them, because they had an entire village to back them up. And
the Songs, like other southeast Chinese lineages, owned some land corporately. The income from these lands was used to support lineage-based
rituals such as the yearly ancestor worship, a symbolic statement of lineage unity that helped to reinforce their stronger image as opposed to
neighboring villages.

PHOTOGRAPH 5.
Offerings for village
guardians. Villagers
and returning urban
migrants give offerings
to village guardians
on Chinese New
Year's Eve, 2007.

REMEMBERED TIME AND HISTORICAL TIME

While it is a commonplace to observe that China is a society undergoing rapid transformation today, one should keep in mind that dramatic change has occurred in China in almost every decade for the last one hundred years. The first half of the twentieth century in China was a violent and unsettled time marked by the end of the dynastic system, economic crises, Japanese invasion, civil war, revolution, and finally "Liberation" in 1949 *(jiefang)* with the victory of the Communists in the civil war.

After the founding of the PRC in 1949, the term "old society" *(jiu shehui)* was coined to refer to culture and society before the Communist victory. When the elders of Moonshadow Pond speak about their memories of the "old society" today, it is usually in reference to oppressive poverty, most frequently articulated in terms of food. "All we ate was sweet potatoes" or "We never ate meat" are frequent refrains. During this time, many

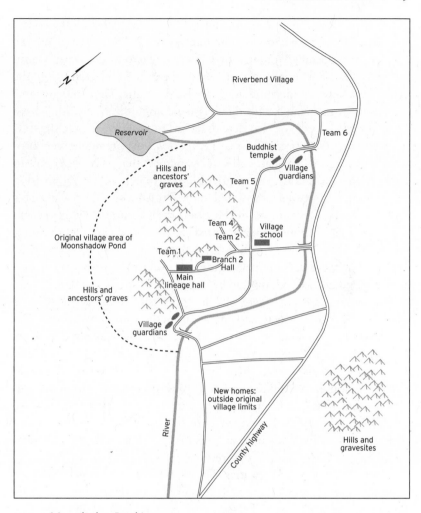

MAP 2. Moonshadow Pond in 2007.

families in Moonshadow Pond gave their daughters away as infant brides who would later marry the brothers they were raised with, thus avoiding the expense of a formal wedding on both sides.[16] Other daughters were sent to work as servants in wealthy families, or if they were lucky, to monasteries where, unlike other girls, they would learn to read and write. in order to become nuns. Many adult men also left home, migrating to Southeast Asia, India, or Mauritius, where they could find work. Sometimes they never returned, leaving their wives as virtual widows.

Of course, as time passes, when people in Moonshadow Pond speak about earlier eras, they refer not to the "old society," but to the collective period—the time between the founding of the PRC in 1949 and the "reform and opening" initiated by China's de facto leader Deng Xiaoping in 1978.[17] For those who remember the era of collectivization, the differences between then and now are also dramatic. The economic mismanagement associated with the massive communization of the Great Leap Forward (1958–61) led to widespread food shortages and the starvation of millions. After the Great Leap Forward, communes were broken down into smaller-scale collective structures that were better able to motivate people and organize agricultural production, but progress on the economic front was interrupted in the late 1960s by the social chaos of the Cultural Revolution. In the cities, the Cultural Revolution was marked by violent internecine warfare between rival gangs, each claiming that it was the true revolutionary. But even in rural areas such as Moonshadow Pond, the impact of the Cultural Revolution was felt, and some individuals were victimized by its politics of struggle and revenge.[18]

Meanwhile, although there was never a return to the deprivation of the Great Leap, frugality remained the rule in the 1960s and 1970s. Food that is on the daily menu now, such as meat and fruit, was saved for New Year's gatherings. People had only a few items of clothing that they would wash again and again until threadbare. Several separate families would share one house, each taking one or at most two rooms within it. Family members often huddled together on winter nights to keep warm, since blankets and heavy clothes were scarce. (Although Moonshadow Pond is in southeast China, its mountainous location means that winter temperatures can hover around the freezing mark.)

The reform and opening initiated in 1978 generated dramatic changes in material life. Beginning in 1985, village residents started to build new houses, and many of the old structures have now been abandoned. The diet is more abundant and varied than ever before, and meat is now a daily rather than a yearly item. Provisioning for daily needs has also become easier. Gathering wood in the hills for cooking was replaced by buying fuel in the mid-1970s (first blocks of coal and now gas). Water, which women once hauled from streams, was accessed through wells in the late 1980s and finally with modern plumbing in the 1990s. Consumer goods have multiplied in each subsequent decade. In the 1980s, watching television replaced nighttime chitchat in village lanes, although gossiping still continues with neighbors who invade each other's living rooms. In the 1990s, telephones eased communication with relatives beyond the village, while a decade later cell phones have become ubiquitous and Internet cables have been installed. Although bicycles never went out of style, motorcycles gradually replaced them for trips to the county capital or to work, and by 2007 a few of the wealthiest families had bought cars. Economic numbers also provide evidence of significant change. In the county where Moonshadow Pond is located, the cash income of farmers increased more than tenfold between 1965 and 1987.[19] Equally impressive increases in farmers' incomes continued through the mid-1990s before leveling out in the first decade of the twenty-first century.[20]

Despite such dramatic developments, certain continuities in the daily schedule and yearly agricultural calendar also provide a sense of continuity with the past. One still sees women washing their laundry in the river every morning and the agricultural cycle of rice planting and harvests still creates the framework for the yearly ritual cycle, with the Spring Festival (Lunar New Year) marking a period of feasting and visiting before the hard work of the first of two rice harvests. Further, while the old society inspires no longing, the new insecurities and tensions of the reform era create a more complicated memory of the collective period for those who lived through it. There is satisfaction in the greater comforts of today, and no one expresses a desire to return to the material level of the collective era. Yet some people express nostalgia for what seems, at least in retrospect, to be a less corrupt and simpler time, when activities like building the local reservoir or improving the irrigation ditches were visible achievements in which everyone could take a measure of pride. The collective system also provided minimum subsistence (except during the Great Leap Forward) by allocating everyone a basic grain ration, and there was also some help in medical emergencies. Middle-aged people, who were only children during the collective era, express a different kind of nostalgia. They recall evenings of play in the public spaces outsides their homes without the contemporary distractions of television or phones.

Memories of these earlier periods are of course affected by differing individual experiences. From 1949 to 1978, a new class system prevailed in China. Each person was given a label based on his or her father's class, and this class status would continue to be passed down patrilineally. This occurred in the context of a revolutionary overturning of preexisting social and property relations. But it meant that the descendants of landlords and rich peasants lived with these labels long after land had been collectivized, and the descendants of capitalists continued to be called capitalists even though they no longer had any capital.

At the time of Liberation, all but four of the almost two hundred families in Moonshadow Pond were categorized as either tenants (no land), poor peasants (little land), or middle peasants (families with enough land to get by, but who did not hire workers).[21] There were also a few families who received "good" class labels as far as their relationship to land was concerned, but who were placed in suspect categories for other reasons, such as those who had a family member who had been in the Nationalist Army. The minority who lived in such stigmatized families experienced hardships and even cruelties. Lineage unity counted for little in this politically changed and charged atmosphere. In Moonshadow Pond, one landlord committed suicide during the land reform and his son fled to Taiwan. Others caught on the "wrong" side during this era spent time in jail or labor camps, or they were shunned or excluded from possibilities to better themselves because of their class backgrounds. The most truly horrible event occurred during the first two years of the Cultural Revolution (1966–68), when an angry mob attacked and beat to death a young man who was returning to the village after a dam he worked on broke and caused a flood. Later, many people said that his fate was sealed because he was from a "landlord" family.

Neither stories about the worst of these times nor nostalgia for its achievements or pleasures is a subject of daily conversation. But memories still come to the surface in the context of contemporary events. For instance, imagine that during the collective period you had declined to criticize someone who was the object of a "struggle" meeting, or perhaps you had simply helped a person find more provisions to feed his family. If such a person slights you now, it matters little how long ago or in what situation you provided help. You will certainly find fault with his or her failure of memory in the present. Obligations and debts from the past are not dissolved or forgotten just because the era of Mao has ended, and political leaders with different policies are installed far away in Beijing.

Events from one's own past or references to earlier political eras can be invoked in the ongoing discourse of the present in Moonshadow Pond. Hence, when I refer to historical time from the viewpoint of Moonshadow Pond residents, I will refer to three eras: "the old society," "collective" or "Maoist," and "reform." In this case, old society refers to anything that happened before the Communist Party came to power in 1949. Collective or Maoist refers to the era between 1949 and the formal acceptance of Deng Xiaoping's reform agenda in 1978. Reform refers to everything that occurred after this date.

While village residents usually talk about these periods of time in this way, and it is a useful form of shorthand, we need to keep in mind that historically speaking these categories are certainly oversimplified. For starters, the old society that Moonshadow Pond residents can actually remember is what historians would call the Republican era, the period between the end of the Qing dynasty in 1911 and the Communist victory in 1949. While Moonshadow Pond residents use old society to simply refer to pre-Communist times in a general way, it certainly would be hard to argue that this is an actual historical period, since it refers to all of China's pre-Communist history. Nonetheless, since villagers often use this term, and since the Communists did explicitly forge a policy that advocated change in culture as well as politics and economy, I will use the label old society when discussing the prerevolutionary time period before Liberation from the point of view of Moonshadow Pond residents.

Of course, by categorizing time we can be blinded not only to significant transformations within the historical eras we create through simple labels, but also to important continuities between the periods of time marked differently. But we should also note that these categories stay with people for good reasons as well. The eras denoted by the labels old society, collective or Maoist, and reform undeniably distinguish critical political shifts that have affected the lives of all Chinese living today in tangible ways.

RESEARCHING LOCAL MORAL CONCEPTS

We have already seen that the contemporary lives of Moonshadow Pond residents (like those of all of us to some extent) are never lived solely in the present. But if the ability to remember and reciprocate past assistance figures importantly in the notion of how one should be a good person, this hardly means there is agreement about how to act in specific situations. As I learned during my many visits to Moonshadow Pond, not only do individuals disagree with one another, but it is not uncommon for one person to express contending views about the proper course of action. In these cases, ambivalence often mirrors conflicting ideas and pressures in the social world. When it comes to making judgments in any given case, people may draw upon ideas from the old society, the collective era, and the present in justifying their own actions or criticizing others.

Further, there is not necessarily agreement on the boundaries of the moral community. In most societies, moral strictures are not applied equally to all persons, even in those societies that claim that their ideologies of right and wrong are based on universally applicable and context free principles.[22] For instance, in recent Chinese history, the revolutionary fervor created during the Cultural Revolution was able to motivate some people to abandon very basic controls on reciprocal thinking when it came to people defined as class enemies, even if they were village and lineage mates.

The next chapter looks more closely at the issue of which particular relations are actually covered by the ethos of remembrance and reciprocity. But first, we need to ask how one actually investigates moral culture in a Chinese village. An initial assumption is that ordinary people sort out their ideas of right and wrong, should and should not, by confronting everyday dilemmas and challenges. In examining notions of morality in culture, most ethnographers would agree with Arthur Kleinman's categorical distinction between "ethical discourse" and "moral processes."[23] Ethical discourse is identified by Kleinman as the province of elites who conduct it as a commentary that is "principle based." It is philosophical and abstract. Moral processes, in contrast, are characterized as "practical engagements in a particular local world, a social space that carries cultural, political, and economic specificity."[24] These moral processes are found in the daily living and discussion of ordinary people as they encounter conflicts, make decisions, and pass judgments on those in their own communities. Kleinman points out these discussions and judgments are also affected by "large-scale changes in political economy, politics, and culture."[25]

An ethnographic approach to morality, therefore, must begin in what Kleinman calls a "local world . . . the ethnographer's village, neighborhood, networks, family, and other institutions," and uncover what is important in this local context, even while understanding that this can vary over time.[26] As such, an investigation of moral ideas in everyday life is necessarily ethnographic. Ordinary people discuss morality "not just by speaking words," states Richard Madsen in his study of a Mao-era village, "but by performing dramatic gestures; they summarize their arguments not in essays, but in aphorisms; they usually argue not by giving lectures, but by uttering invectives; they evaluate each other's arguments not in polite colloquia, but in gossipy table talk, noisy altercations, and sometimes nowadays in raucous public meetings."[27]

To understand moral concepts through ordinary discourse, therefore, there is no substitute for the old-fashioned anthropological method of participant observation—living with people over an extended period of time and slowly observing and learning what issues are important to them in the context of their lives.

In my own case, extended stays during two different decades gave me a particularly useful vantage point from which to observe both changes and continuities. The higher standard of living of the reform period, which we have already noted, has also been accompanied by feelings of insecurity. An unexpected accident or sickness is now a family's responsibility, which can suddenly land it in debt. Education is not free beyond middle school. Yet this occurs at a time when young people feel the pressure to study longer in order to secure higher-paying jobs.

In this environment, many long-lived concepts such as reciprocity *(bao)* and making use of one's social network *(guanxi)* have been reinvigorated. In the Mao era, village leaders often needed to use their connections to procure resources for the village and to push past bureaucratic obstructions. Now, ordinary villagers try to utilize contacts and connections most frequently in the struggle to keep their own families ahead—for instance, finding a job opening or admission to a training program for a child or securing a permit to build a house in a particular location. They often say that you need both contacts and money to get anything accomplished. Most residents of Moonshadow Pond complain, however, that they are neither wealthy nor well connected enough to be taken seriously. "We're just peasants" is a frequent refrain.

Red envelopes, which are traditionally used to enclose cash gifts at weddings and at other festive occasions, are now also used much more directly to "buy the road" *(mai lu)* so as to gain access to benefits, privileges, or jobs. The brother of a neighbor told me, "Nowadays, officials want a lot of money; they won't just take a few hundred. And they won't even look at your red envelope if you don't have any connection with them first."

This phenomenon, in which both rural and urban Chinese have utilized social networks to gain access to goods and services in contemporary China, has often been observed by journalists and even visitors and it has been exhaustively studied by scholars. Practices range from those considered to be utilitarian and even unethical in Chinese eyes to ongoing social relations based on mutual help that are considered to be highly moral.[28]

When I first arrived in Moonshadow Pond, I had not yet decided to investigate local moral concepts. Rather, I had hoped to investigate the use of a specific set of Chinese terms that are related to this manipulation of social networks and which are often translated into English as "face." The first of these terms is *mianzi,* and it is often taken to refer to worldly status, the distinction one creates and accumulates from owning an expensive car, inviting hundreds of guests to a banquet, or living in an elaborate house. Someone with a big *mianzi* is likely to have a large web of connections that can be used to advantage in a continuously widening circle of contacts. The word *lian,* which is also translated as "face," has more disparate meanings. Some anthropologists have reported that it is used interchangeably with the word *mianzi.*[29] However, the word can also refer to basic morality and character as opposed to material possessions or social achievements. To lose *lian* in this sense can mean to have engaged in a shameful act, to have committed a moral indiscretion.[30] In Moonshadow Pond, I often heard residents use another expression to refer to loss of face in terms of moral deficiency. They might literally point at their face while using the words "does not know shame" (*buzhi xiuchi* [Mandarin]; *m di xiu* [Hakka]) to describe a person in terms of a moral lapse.

As I lived on in the village, I began to see that the use of the terms I originally wanted to investigate often had a moral dimension. As such, my focus began to shift from an investigation of cultural categories such as *mianzi* and *lian* that I had chosen in advance to a more broadly defined investigation of local moral discourse.

But what kind of everyday discourse qualifies as that which is concerned with the moral? Certainly one important element involves ideas about obligations. In his examination of morality and culture in the Nepalese city of Bhaktapur, anthropologist Stephen Parish defines the "moral" in everyday life and in a given cultural context as simply that which is felt as "overriding obligations."[31] Says Parish, " 'The moral' identifies the core commitments that define who we are and what we must do, overriding other considerations, at least in our rhetoric of the ideal."[32] These core commitments can be understood only in particular cultural contexts. Thus, "witchcraft, marriage, patriotism, religion, defending civil liberties and so on, are also cultural practices and not free-floating meaning systems. . . . The 'must' and 'should' meanings attached to them do not attach themselves . . . people do."[33]

But some might question whether the idea of "overriding obligation" is a sufficient definition of morality in a given cultural context. As the moral philosopher Bernard Gert has pointed out, many actions might be considered moral in certain contexts—such as helping people in need—that are not necessarily obligatory.[34] Perhaps a more fitting guideline with which to begin an ethnographic investigation of moral discourse comes from the anthropologist Caroline Humphrey, who states rather succinctly that morality in a given cultural context is, "the evaluation of conduct in relation to esteemed or despised human qualities."[35]

As subsequent chapters will illustrate, in the specific context of rural

Meixian, obligation *is* a major component of people's ideas about morality. Nonetheless, using Humphrey's definition, which is concerned with the evaluation of conduct in a broader sense, leaves room for the possibility that people's ideas about morality in a given context may extend beyond ideas about obligation.

Additionally, when people make moral judgments about others or themselves, they are also evaluating choices. As the anthropologist James Laidlaw points out, even when morality is understood as a matter of fulfilling one's obligations, there is still the matter of choosing to do so or not.[36] In this sense, moral discourse is a running commentary on the choices people make. It should come as no surprise, therefore, that the commentary people often put forth in everyday situations is concerned more with moral breaches than with praising actions considered good. Moral knowledge, says the anthropologist John Barker, who studied moral culture in Melanesia, is often "tacit" and "moral orthodoxy" is often "confirmed not so much in positive statements as in criticisms" of those who transgress norms.[37]

Moral discourse, therefore, is frequently about expectations. Some of these may be fulfilled, but often such discourse centers on cases where expectations are disappointed or dashed. As explained above, my interest was in understanding these expectations in context, listening to people talk about actual situations as they carried out their lives. I should also note that there is already an extensive literature in both anthropology and psychology which engages subjects in terms of hypothetical moral conflicts. This literature is based not so much on fieldwork, but on extensive interviews of people cross-culturally. Interviewers may pose hypothetical moral dilemmas to subjects, and try to ascertain if there are differences in concepts of morality employed by respondents of different cultures. Do some cultures employ a "rights based" approach to morality, trying to utilize the same standards no matter what the context? In other cultures, do ideas about morality take context into greater account? Do people distinguish between custom and morality, or social duty versus moral duty?

As subsequent chapters will reveal, these questions will come up in the course of my investigation of moral discourse in Moonshadow Pond (specifically questions of context versus universality in chapter 2 and custom versus morality in chapter 4). However, I would emphasize that as an ethnographer in one setting, I will address these issues as they arise in the course of actual social life. My approach here is unabashedly ethnographic. Hence, how people might respond to an imagined case is less important for the purposes of this study than how they use concepts in their actual lives.[38]

WHAT COUNTS AS A QUESTION OF MORALITY?

Honor, Status, and Morality across Cultures

Even if we begin with a guiding framework—that moral discourse is about the "evaluation of . . . esteemed or despised human qualities," and that furthermore it often concentrates on an evaluation of whether people have met their obligations—it is still not always easy to delineate the "moral" component out of a specific judgment. In particular, in many cultures, moral concepts are interconnected but certainly not equivalent to ideas about status, just as in the example above of different uses of the concept of "face" *(lian* and *mianzi),* some of which refer to status in the world, while others refer to basic moral character.

If we define status broadly as encompassing notions of rank, esteem, respect, or honor, we can quickly see that notions of status and morality, though connected, are never precisely equivalent. One can certainly garner status by acting in moral ways, and lose it by engaging in immoral acts. But there are plenty of examples where the two diverge as well.

For instance, as an example, we can look at a society such as that of the United States, where many would argue that wealth is equivalent to status. Taking a cue from the sociologist Pierre Bourdieu, we might expand on this and add that status can also be garnered through social connections, cultural knowledge, or elaborate ritualistic displays, or what he calls "social capital," "cultural capital," or "symbolic capital."[39] And yet, we all know of situations where people of great wealth, power, fame, connections, or cultural appeal are convicted of corruption or even violent crimes. In these cases, they lose their status because of their morally objectionable acts. In contrast, we also know that a wealthy or powerful person's indiscretions may sometimes be ignored, while a poor person who lives by what she believes are high moral standards may feel that society does not esteem her.

To further complicate matters, people often hold contradictory notions about what is moral as well as what attributes actually create status, or in Bourdieu's words "social" and "cultural" capital. Hegemonic or dominant ideologies may coexist with alternative ideologies—we may simultaneously esteem and mistrust the rich entrepreneur, and praise and then ignore the social-service worker who lives on a near minimum wage.[40] (And we are very ambivalent about the role of a person's educational level in all these judgments.)

Some analysts have tried to talk about these issues by distinguishing between "inner" and "outer" honor, or the difference between a good reputation and an honorable character.[41] Others have pointed out that while social status and virtue, as conceived in a particular culture, may not always coincide or coexist in one person, power itself can transform evaluations of virtue. As Julian Pitt-Rivers stated in a classic essay on honor in Andalusia, "The plebeian adulterer desecrates his family by taking a mistress, the *señorito* demonstrates his superior masculinity by doing so."[42]

Class and caste systems, as well as ideas about gender, all come into play when discussing the cultural constructions of morality and status. In many cultures, women may "embody" male honor, and a woman's sexual indiscretions can dishonor her brother or husband more than his own actions.[43] In caste and racially segregated societies, women are viewed as embodying the "purity" of their entire race or caste groups, and for that reason their activities are highly controlled so as to prevent "contamination" of their group through sexual relations with men from "lower" caste and racial categories.[44] Yet even in the most rigidly hierarchical societies, it is not clear that everyone subscribes to the same ideas about morality or status. Some scholarship on India, for instance, questions whether lower castes actually accept the assumptions through which higher castes claim their status. And even members of high castes may critique or be ambivalent about their own system of status and the values that bolster it, just as some members of racially segregated or class stratified societies may question the moral justifications articulated in defense of these systems.[45]

Morality in Different Spheres

We have seen that it is not always easy to extricate judgments about status from moral judgments. Further, as the anthropologist Alan Fiske points out, societies don't necessarily judge all social relationships by the same standards of morality. When people judge the morality of an action, they often do so on the basis of the particular relationships being assessed. Hence, a culture's ideas about moral obligations inherent in market-based exchange relationships may be different from those that they would apply to internal familial relations. And obligations seen as applying to hierarchical or authority relations might not be the same as those applied to relationships amongst equals. This means, says Fiske, that in most cultures people are actually moral relativists. As he says, "In the same domain at the same time you can't have true kindness, and fairness, and respect for status and rank, and freedom of opportunity. . . . Applying different models to the same action yields different moral judgments about that action."[46] Just a small example of how the notion of different spheres might work out in evaluations of morality can be applied by thinking about borrowing money. Few Americans would think it immoral for a bank to charge interest for the money it lends (presuming this interest is not exorbitant)! But if one's sibling lends money and then asks for interest upon the return, many would judge this action differently.

Cultures may also differ in the way they categorize specific types of action. Thus, says Fiske, Americans view the allocation of labor as belonging primarily to the domain of market-based exchange relations. But in some other cultures this same activity might be placed within the domain of familial relations. Naturally, moral judgments regarding the obligations inherent in market exchange may differ from those regarding family relations. Hence, cultures may evaluate what superficially looks like the same kind of action—labor allocation—in different ways.

Contending Schemas

Evaluating moral ideas in any society is therefore a complicated proposition. One has to consider how to separate moral judgments from other judgments (such as ideas about status), and one has to think about what domain of action the judgments are being applied to—since moral evaluations may not be the same in different realms.

As I became more familiar with the situation on the ground in rural Meixian, I realized that understanding notions of morality there would be as complicated as peeling and eating a pomelo, a citrus fruit commonly grown there with a thick outer layer. Once you have peeled this layer off, you still can't eat the fruit, because each wedge of fruit is encased in another layer of skin. Similarly, in Moonshadow Pond, there were many layers of daily life that I would need to understand in order to even begin to get a sense of how people made moral judgments in different domains of action.

To begin with, there were several layers of ideology available for villagers to use or ignore in making moral judgments. First, there was a layer of official discourse. The state, after all, promulgated its own set of ideas about almost every area of cultural and social life—from gender roles to religious ritual to economic exchange and social class. However, looking at its impact on local life is complicated by the fact that during various decades since Liberation, the state has pursued very different paths. There have been a number of contrasting and often contradictory official ideologies espoused. For instance, as we have noted previously, a radical rhetoric of class struggle promoted by Mao Zedong during the Cultural Revolution resulted in the stigmatization and persecution of many from the "wrong" classes or ideological orientations. The subsequent discourse initiated by Deng Xiaoping downplayed class struggle and eliminated class labels as a basis of inherited status. Citizens were encouraged to invest their energies in economically profitable activities as long as they did not challenge the political hegemony of the Communist Party.

But changing official discourse hardly exhausts the possibilities by which Moonshadow Pond residents might understand their lives. Liberation did not mean the end of preexisting models of social relations and expectations, and the reform era did not end modes of thinking that had developed during the collective era. Rather, old and new ways of looking at the world and making moral judgments were combined and digested in a variety of ways by individuals to suit the changing context, as well as to make sense of their own particular experiences and identities.[47]

That Moonshadow Pond villagers drew ideas about morality from several different eras should come as no surprise. One might expect that periods of change would be characterized by greater moral anxiety, and less self-confidence in any one moral code. But one must also keep in mind that even in societies that have not undergone the rapid transformations of China, one can expect a degree of moral ambivalence. To a certain degree, moral ambivalence is a feature of all moral systems. As anthropologist Bradd Shore points out, many societies have alternative or even contradictory ethical norms that pull people in conflicting directions. He gives as one example the American idea of equality that contradicts the just as strongly held belief that individuals are entitled to the fruits of their labor.[48] Another example he provides is from Samoan culture's emphasis on harmony and community and its similarly strong emphasis on personal heroism and loyalty to one's group. Adherence to the highly valued code of personal heroism and group loyalty can destroy equally valued community harmony by creating internal divisions.[49] As such, Shore points out that in most societies "ethical situations are highly charged" because they involve not "choices between right and wrong," but "dilemmas of competing virtues or evils."[50] In the course of actual social life, individuals ultimately have to "legitimize one course and depreciate an alternative, even though both possibilities exist as ethical alternatives."[51] Shore concludes that in all cultures individuals are often faced with "conflicting virtues," and maintains that anxiety and ambivalence are inherent in all ethical systems.[52] He surmises that perhaps this ambivalence isn't all bad, because though it can paralyze, it can also serve to hold people back from extreme behavior and reactions.[53]

Therefore, contradictions in people's ideas about how the world does work or should work are characteristic of all cultures. As I explained above, the imperatives of all moral systems inevitably create ambiguities and contradictions. In addition, as literary and cultural theorists have long pointed out, contradictions in the surrounding context are inevitably mirrored in people's opinions and outlooks. Several people, or even one person, may hold conflicting ideas in even one cultural context.[54]

Some anthropologists refer to such ideas, whether conflicting or consistent, as cultural models or "schemas." According to the anthropologists Claudia Strauss and Naomi Quinn, "Cognitive scientists have traditionally used the term 'schema' to refer to generic knowledge of any sort . . . a great many schemas are cultural schemas . . . you share them with people who have had some experiences like yours, but not with everybody."[55] Elaborating on this idea of schemas, Patricia Ewick and Susan Silbey state, "Society furnishes images . . . how the world works, what is possible and what is not."[56] These schemas include "cultural codes, vocabularies of motives, logics, hierarchies of value, and conventions, as well as the binary oppositions that make up . . . a society's fundamental tools of thought."[57]

As such, schemas can include everything from moral codes to what to expect when you go to a restaurant. Strauss and Quinn use a very ordinary example to describe schemas. As they explain, a simple schema might be "Guests should be offered a drink." In such a case, if you determine that a person is a guest, you go ahead and offer a drink. But, of course, it is never that simple. In actual social life, there are multiple connections and links between schemas, making even small decisions rather complex. For instance, as Strauss and Quinn point out, even a guest can be wanted or unwanted, someone you hope will leave soon or someone you hope will stay. They can show up in the morning or the evening, and the drink you offer (if you do) may be hot or cold, alcoholic or nonalcoholic, sweet or bland.[58]

In societies such as China's, which have undergone revolutionary transformations, the ordinary trials and tribulations of life also become testing grounds for previously held schemas. Some will be found wanting, but people may hold on tenaciously to older concepts because they still make sense to them and seem applicable to some aspect of the situation. As we shall see in subsequent chapters, when residents of Moonshadow Pond judge each other and come to different conclusions, they are in part using schemas from different historical eras about what constitutes moral obligation. But, as stated above, we also need to keep in mind that moral systems by their very nature often contain contradictory imperatives, even in societies that have not experienced dramatic social changes such as contemporary China.

Ultimately, it is in the daily conversations of ordinary people, as they judge those around them, that we can see how they use the moral schemas they have inherited to make sense of their own lives.

LIVING WITH TEAM 2

Fortunately for me, the residents of Moonshadow Pond were hardly shy, retiring, or reluctant to say what was on their minds. Differences of opinion between people and even ambivalence on the part of any one person were often openly aired. Rural Hakka culture is hardly uptight. Gossip and talk pervade daily life. People speak directly and loudly and often proclaim their points of view while sitting in or on benches in front of local shops, or simply in the course of the day, walking in and out of each other's houses after breakfast, during the midday break, or in the hours between dinner and bedtime. Shyness about stating one's opinion is not encouraged, and it is not uncommon for everyone to be talking at once as a discussion becomes particularly animated. Women certainly do not defer to men in this regard, and as women age and their children grow up, they gain even more confidence.

My introduction to my neighborhood began on my very first evening in Moonshadow Pond in 1995. Ruolan had brought me to the village and was going to stay with me for a few days until I got my room set up in Baoli and Songling's house. That evening we sat in their living room in a typical daily activity—drinking tea after dinner. Baoli poured boiling water from a thermos into a small teapot from which he dispensed endless tiny cups of tea while neighbors poured in to meet me and greet Ruolan. These neighbors included Uncle Wei, the former party secretary of the production brigade, and his wife, Aihua, who had been a production team leader (more on team and brigade organization later in this section). Uncle Wei and Aihua were a handsome couple in their late sixties who had played a decisive role in many of the events of the collective era, in whose achievements they took much pride. They had two grown sons who remained in the village raising pigs, cultivating fishponds, and selling pork.

Also drinking tea that night was Skinny Hong, a village intellectual in his late fifties who had embroiled Uncle Wei in some political scandals during the collective era, which we will learn about later in the book. Skinny, like Baoli, was one of the few people of his generation to have completed a high school education. Physically tiny and constantly chain smoking, he eventually succumbed to lung cancer in 2005. His wife, five adult sons, and one daughter remained in the village or the surrounding area. The village doctor, Jiawen, and his wife, Guizhen, who was a midwife, were also there that night. Jiawen, who was sent to study medicine during the collective era, now ran a prosperous medical practice in Moonshadow Pond and he had some of the most far-flung social connections in the area.

Finally, two other individuals came for tea on my first evening in Moonshadow Pond. These were Miaoli and Wentong, who were close relatives of Baoli in their mid-forties. Muscular and deeply tanned, Miaoli and Wentong were known for their hard work in farming and also in home construction. They had no particular connections and had never served in any official capacity, but were simply seen as industrious and honest, a trait for which they were both respected. Miaoli was also known, however, for the difficulties she had in getting along with her mother-in-law, something about which village opinion was much more divided as we shall see in chapter 3.

On that night I was showered with questions about my own purposes in coming to the village as well as about my life in the United States. This loquacious group of people, from whom I ended up learning so much, was also very curious to learn about my own society, especially in my first few months in the village when I was still something of a novelty. Over time, they and their neighbors became an inexhaustible source of help to me in my research. But I should also add that my early and easy entry to the village was certainly explained by the fact that I was introduced by Ruolan, a person who had already implicated herself into village networks of give and take through her years of living in the village and subsequent relationships.

As I stayed on in the village, I first pursued my fieldwork by visiting with a different family every afternoon while spending mornings teaching English to fourth graders in the local village school. When visiting, I

rarely went on my own, but was usually introduced to a family by someone else who knew them well. In that way, I slowly became acquainted
with a large number of families. Over time, I participated in an array of
life-cycle events and yearly rituals, frequently photographing or videotaping them, so that I could ask questions about what was going on in
these events after viewing them. In both 1997 and 2007, I collected basic information on the size and composition of every family in the village (see chapter 3). Through my visits with individual families and by
spending time in the village, I gradually became more familiar with the
histories and situations of about fifty families, or a quarter of the total.
As my visits to the village spanned two different decades, I was also able
to track changes over time. For instance, the fourth graders whom I had
taught in the mid-1990s were young men and women when I returned
in 2006 and 2007. Some had found jobs in the local area, others had migrated to work in larger cities, and a few were in college. Many now had
access to the Internet, providing me with an easy way to continue com-
municating from afar, something that had not been possible ten years
earlier.

Notwithstanding surveys, visits, and even the ultimate addition of the
Internet, it was from my daily contact with the small number of families
amongst whom I lived that I learned the most. These families were
Songling and Baoli's neighbors, some of whom were the individuals who
came in to ask me questions on my first night in the village. During the
collective era these individuals had all been members of one production
team known as Team 2. Team 2 was composed of approximately thirty
families (the exact number varied over time due to the normal processes
of family formation and dissolution resulting from marriage) and was
one of six production teams in Moonshadow Pond. There were nine more
production teams in the neighboring village (which I call Riverbend Village), and together they composed one production brigade. This brigade
was one of twenty-two brigades that formed a local commune (which I
call West Town commune). Together, these composed an administrative
area with a population of thirty-seven thousand[59] that was redesignated
as a township in 1987 (see figure 4).[60]

During the Great Leap Forward, communes of such size were the basic units of agricultural production and consumption. As mentioned earlier, these communes proved to be far too large as units to motivate and
organize workers, and the disastrous economic consequences of the Great
Leap lead to the creation of smaller collective groups to manage labor
and divide income. By the early 1960s, communes were broken down

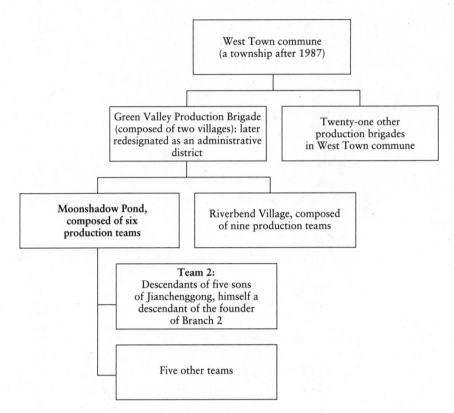

FIGURE 4. Moonshadow Pond and Team 2.

into production brigades and teams. The brigades and communes continued as administrative and political units, but the teams actually organized day-to-day work.

As the basic units of labor management and accounting within each brigade, every team would choose its own leader and accountant. The leader had the responsibility of allocating jobs to his or her team members each day and the proceeds of their work were then handed over to the brigade. In return, the brigade compensated team members with a basic grain ration plus additional cash and grain based on the number of work points each individual accumulated. While the criteria for allocating work points fluctuated in part according to national policy—for instance, during the Cultural Revolution one's degree of revolutionary fervor was taken into account in deciding a person's pay—the team leader usually had some room for maneuver. As Aihua, the former leader of Team 2, told me, she could often get people to do difficult jobs by telling them that they would receive more work points for these chores. Further, if the team as a whole produced more for the brigade, they would receive more back from the brigade at the end of the year. So, even in this collective system there was some room for individual motivation, and the various teams definitely developed a sense of identity over time. For instance, even in the 1990s I heard members of Team 2 boast about their output during the collective era, saying that it far exceeded the output of Moonshadow Pond's other five production teams.

Hence, during the collective era these production teams became the most significant groups outside a person's immediate family affecting the organization of daily life. But since production teams were based on physical proximity, most members were closely related anyway. Team 2 members were neighbors and relatives who would have interacted with each other frequently, with or without the collective structure into which they were incorporated. Before the spate of new house building that began in the early 1980s, many of them lived crammed into five old houses. Each of these five houses had originally been built by one of five sons of Jiancheng-gong, a founder of one of several subbranches of Branch 2 (see figure 3).

Ironically, one of the last collectively organized activities of Team 2 was allocating land to individual families on which to build new houses and to farm for themselves. When communal land was broken up in 1981, everyone in the team was allocated land, including children. Team members were then free to use the land as they pleased, as long as they paid an annual tax (which has since been abolished). However, high-grade rice-paddy land was not supposed to be wasted on things like house construction, so team members drew lots on dry land that was on the outskirts of the village and ultimately all but three families from Team 2 built their new houses there.

The result was that most of the neighbors who originally comprised Team 2 relocated to another part of the village where they remain neighbors. Their shared identity as descendants of Jianchenggong is now celebrated once a year with a New Year's banquet. But their crowded old houses, built of non-fired mud-brick and wood, with sloping tile roofs and courtyards shared by several different families, have been replaced by more spacious flat roofed new houses constructed of brick and cement. Each is the property of an individual family and is a work in progress. As families earn money they add additional floors or tile facades. Built outside the old village boundaries guarded by Gongwang and other gods, Team 2's new houses are located between the two ridges of hills on either side of the village. Some face in less auspicious directions than the old houses, and since they don't nestle into the hillside, they are actually colder in winters and hotter in summers. They are certainly less aesthetically appealing to the outside observer than the traditional designs of the old houses, but nonetheless nearly three-quarters of all Moonshadow Pond residents have opted to build such new homes, eager to move out of their old, crowded dwellings.

The members of Team 2 therefore became the individuals with whom I interacted most frequently. I lived with Songling and Baoli during each of my stays in the village. During my last visit in the spring of 2007 I came with my husband, and Songling and Baoli's own family situation had also changed. Their son was now married, and their household now included a daughter-in-law and young grandson. They had added an addition to the second floor of their house which my husband and I occupied while there. Nonetheless, during all my visits the basic pattern of interaction between villagers did not change. There were frequent comings and goings between members of different households, and this provided me with a constant source of news about local events.

TWO LIVES, MANY POINTS OF VIEW

Over time, I began not only to focus on the attitudes and opinions of the people I lived with, but on their complex and ongoing relations with one another. Fortunately for my research, two of the women with whom I spoke on a daily basis often had divergent opinions and interpretations of past events.

Songling, my landlady, was the daughter of the only individual given the class label of "capitalist" at the time of Liberation. Her father operated a tannery in the village and later went into business trading in finished leather. As Songling was just a small child at the time of Liberation, she had no memories of the old society, but many of the most disastrous events of the early collective years were intertwined with her memories of childhood, adolescence, and the early years of her marriage. Because her family, had a "bad" class label—that of capitalist—her childhood memories were not without bitterness, as she and her siblings remembered being taunted by classmates on account of their class identity. Nonetheless, Songling studied through high school, which was quite unusual for village women at the time. She was a wonderful source of local knowledge, in part because her marriage to Baoli was a love marriage that kept her within the same village in which she grew up. She therefore knew the histories of almost every family in the village.

Although physically slight, Songling was clearly the commanding presence in the family. Her husband, Baoli, as mentioned previously, was also well educated for a villager of his age, and unlike Songling he had a "good" class status as a poor peasant (marred only by the fact that one brother had fought with the Nationalist Army and fled to Taiwan at the time of Liberation). Nonetheless, despite his good standing in the village and high level of education, he had avoided promotion to any post in the village beyond that of Team 2 accountant. This decision may well have saved him a great deal of trouble over the course of his life, since by taking on few public responsibilities, he did not have to worry much about becoming the target of the political struggles of the 1950s and 1960s. Indeed, long after these political struggles were over, Baoli's characteristic response to any issue was to smile and avoid conflict, and he was reticent to offer public or even private criticism of anyone in the village. Songling, in contrast, was not loathe to articulate her ideas, whether it was stating an opinion to a fellow villager or telling a family member what she thought they needed to do.

Unlike Songling, our neighbor Aihua grew up in a poor peasant family. Over a decade older than Songling, she was already a teenager at the time of Liberation. Barely educated at the time, her only schooling came in a few years of night school after Liberation. Liberation brought tangible benefits for Aihua. She was an active participant in the Land Reform movement of the early 1950s, and she joined the Communist Party in 1955. Tall, striking, and also physically strong, she was chosen as the team leader of Team 2 and served in that capacity for most of the 1960s and

1970s. Her husband, Uncle Wei, served as party secretary of the production brigade during the late 1960s and much of the 1970s as well, and both of them took great pride in the achievements of that era and their role in building the infrastructure of the village. They were still quite vigorous during my visits to the village in the 1990s, but during my last visit in 2007 they had not only aged physically but were noticeably more careworn. The achievements of the collective era in which they had participated were now long past, and their new struggles had less to do with building public infrastructure than with the trials and tribulations of old age in the village (more on this in chapter 3).

Aihua's and Songling's class labels indelibly influenced their interpretations of past events and experiences in small and large ways. For instance, Songling might remember an individual in terms of her harshness, and assume that the demands she made upon Songling or another family member to work hard were based on her family's bad class status. Aihua, in contrast, might remember the same individual with admiration, recalling her great energy and ability to "eat bitterness" (chi ku), a frequently used expression that denotes a person's great capacity to work and endure hardships.

Songling remembered her family's past in terms of constricted opportunities—a younger brother who was smart, for instance, but who could not be recommended for higher education because he was a capitalist's son. Aihua also talked about constricted opportunities, but for different reasons. Her husband, as the party secretary of the production brigade from 1966 to 1976, was unable to recommend their own sons for any kinds of educational or job opportunities because it would have looked like nepotism.

Growing up in different age cohorts was likely another significant element to Songling's and Aihua's outlooks.[61] Since Songling was not much older than the revolution, her memories were about growing up under Communist rule. Because of her father's class status, the family was often at a disadvantage. During the Cultural Revolution her father was the object of ridicule at "struggle meetings." He was marched through the streets in a dunce cap and was finally jailed for two months, where he had to write a confession every day. Aihua's experience of the revolution was quite different. Since she was a teenager at the time of Liberation, she did have memories of the old society. Going from the experience of an uneducated daughter constantly working in her family to that of production team leader was a huge change in her public status. She vividly remembered the homespun dramatic performances put on in the village at the time of Liberation, which ridiculed male dominance and other "feudal" customs. When I walked around the village in the 1990s with Aihua, she would proudly point out the accomplishments of collectivization: the leveling of the fields, the digging of irrigation canals, and the construction of two reservoirs.

"They had it easy before Liberation," she told me one day, speaking of Songling's family, "because they didn't have to work the land themselves. Naturally, they were not as satisfied after Liberation."

Nonetheless, although Songling's family did not have to work the land before Liberation, and she inherited a disadvantageous "capitalist" class label from her father, she still identified herself very forthrightly as a peasant *(nongren)*, and in this way saw herself as sharing the same fate with the other residents of Moonshadow Pond. She was a source of constant proverbs about the difficulties and ironies of being a peasant, such as "for every grain of rice there are three grains of sweat," and "those who till the fields produce food for those who sit at wide desks."

In their married lives, Aihua and Songling had also found themselves in very different situations. Aihua's family looked like a Chinese ideal. She had two sons, and each of these two sons had two sons. But, in fact, it was this very ideal that encapsulated them within a closed structure. Without daughters, a family loses an important source of connections— which they can activate for assistance—through the families into which their daughters marry. To further compound their relative insularity, Aihua's family had no overseas relatives. This was an asset during the collective period, when overseas connections were bad for one's class status, but in the present it meant that the family lacked another potential source of financial assistance.

Songling's family, in contrast, was mainly structured around networks on her side of the family. Her husband's only surviving brother was overseas and his parents deceased, so almost all their connections went through Songling—especially her ties to a younger brother, and the ties activated to the families into which her two daughters had married. Baoli's connections, though fewer, were also critical for the family. His surviving brother in Taiwan sent occasional financial help.

Of course, Aihua's and Songling's responses were not always predictable reflections of their class status or age cohort. Songling, after all, had grown up with the revolution, and she used the discursive structures it had supplied very freely. When Songling and Aihua spoke at different times about scolding their adult sons in regard to matters which displeased them, they both described this as "thought work" *(sixiang gongzuo)*. Thought work was a phrase initially used during the collective period to describe the methods by which cadres would try to change the attitudes of workers or peasants in their units through the formation of small study groups.[62] Even today the term is often used in official discourse along with the word "propaganda" *(xuanchuan)* to refer to more diffuse efforts to retain cultural and ideological control throughout society.[63] The term, however, has also been appropriated freely by Moonshadow Pond residents, particularly older and middle-aged women, who use it to refer to their efforts to change the behavior of wayward family members.

Furthermore, Aihua—the good Communist—was as likely to use ideas and categories from the old society as Songling was likely to draw from collective-era discourse. For instance, in the midst of the Cultural Revolution, when customary religious practices were attacked as feudal and suppressed, Aihua burned paper money and made offerings to the ancestors. She asked them to forgive her young son who had defiled some funeral urns containing the bones of these deceased ancestors.

While these two women might have seemed an odd couple, Aihua was often in Songling's house. The relations between the two families, though not extremely close, were friendly and cordial. As we have already discussed and will examine in greater detail in the next chapter, nothing in Moonshadow Pond could ever be viewed in the mere present tense. Songling's father had employed both Aihua's husband and his mother in the old society. After Liberation, Aihua's mother-in-law had been asked to publicly denounce Songling's family for exploiting them. For whatever reason she chose not to, saying merely that the family had given them employment when they needed it. Since then, the two families have had good relations. These good relations were not an accident in Aihua's view. Instead, she thought they flowed from earlier actions—specifically her mother-in-law's earlier decisions not to denounce Songling's family. By contrast, if Aihua and Songling had not gotten along well, and if Aihua had ever felt slighted by Songling, she most certainly would have raised the issue of her mother-in-law's help toward Songling's family at a critical time in the past.

In such cases, the first insult that is often thrown is to accuse a person of having no *liangxin*. The word *liangxin* can be roughly translated as "conscience," and it can be used to refer to someone who is thoughtless and who forgets or ignores past help. *Liangxin* is a great leveler. No matter how wealthy or well connected an individual is, it is possible to flatten his or her reputation, at least momentarily, by charging that this person has no conscience.

Thus, to say a person has no *liangxin,* as we shall see in the next chapter, is to accuse him or her of having no moral compass. But of course, as we have explained in this chapter, separating the moral element out of the evaluation of an action is not always easy. Some actions may be viewed as having no moral implications, while others may be viewed only partially with a moral lens. For instance, as we shall see in a later chapter, death ritual and ancestral worship in Moonshadow Pond provide powerful arenas for the enhancement of social status through opportunities to spend exorbitant sums of money, invite people to feasts, and organize elaborate rituals. Nonetheless, while some features of a funeral may be viewed as required by custom, but not moral duty, a funeral is also an act of filial remembrance, and, as an act of memory and conscience, has an important moral dimension that goes beyond merely enhancing one's social capital and following convention (see chapter 4).

ENCOMPASSMENT AND CONTRADICTION

While certain key concepts, such as the notion of "conscience," were employed by all residents of Moonshadow Pond, this obviously does not mean that everyone came to the same conclusions when judging any specific act. People such as Songling and Aihua, with their own sets of problems, social relationships, and life histories, can hardly be expected to approach every problem with an identical and formulaic response. Generational cohorts, class position, gender, age, family situation, life experiences, and individual personalities can all have an influence on how an individual applies the idea of moral obligation in a given situation, or even if they view a situation in moral terms at all.

Furthermore, as with all anthropologists, my own particular identity in the field gave me better access to some areas of life than others, and to some people more than others. For instance, in looking at contending ideas about family obligation, I was able to get a much more nuanced picture of women's ideas than men's, since women were more forthcoming with me than men about family matters. Nonetheless, by examining moral ideas in more than one domain, I was ultimately able to include perspectives from a varied group of village residents.

My examination of moral discourse in different domains will certainly probe what its contradictions can tell us about ongoing changes in rural China. But, we can also look beyond these changes for continuity in a "deep structure." The French anthropologist Louis Dumont spoke of cultures as containing certain "encompassing" sets of values.[64] While he has acknowledged that cultures contain contradictory values and motives, he also pointed out that certain cultural values may contain and encompass their opposites. For instance, in a Marxist schema, production and consumption are opposites at one level, but ultimately "production" encompasses consumption because even consumption must be "produced," by generating desire for consumer goods through advertising and other media. Likewise, in speaking about the economy we often differentiate between goods and services. Yet, services are ultimately a form of goods. In both of these examples, one value is opposed to but also encompasses the other.[65]

In the next chapter, I take a closer look at one such important and encompassing category in the study of moral life in rural China by examining the concept of "conscience" or *liangxin* in greater detail. In subsequent chapters, we will be able to see the different contexts in which it is used, intentions with which it is articulated, circumstances in which it is an unspoken assumption, as well as situations in which it is deemed irrelevant.

In the contemporary popular press there has been a tendency to economize China and to see the country as one vast economic machine. But while people are working and certainly trying to prosper, economic actions are themselves constantly subject to other kinds of scrutiny. It is my hope that in the chapters that follow I can provide a more nuanced picture of how residents of at least one village in rural China think about their own obligations and those of others in a variety of social domains.

CHAPTER 2

Liangxin

For the residents of Moonshadow Pond, *liangxin* ("conscience") is a core concept. To say that someone has no conscience is to say that he or she is not a moral person. Yet curiously, in the study of both traditional and contemporary China, the analysis of the concept *liangxin* is undeveloped as compared to the extensive study of concepts such as *guanxi, mianzi,* and *bao,* which were introduced in chapter 1 and can be translated roughly as "connections," "face," and "reciprocity."

Because *liangxin* is so central to understanding moral discourse in Moonshadow Pond, we will examine its meanings and uses in this chapter. Our analysis will look at its relationship to other Chinese moral concepts, as well as its particular uses in Moonshadow Pond.

In recent studies some scholars have asked if there is a moral system at all in rural China, or if the demise of Maoism with its clear-cut ideology coupled with China's incorporation into the world of global capitalism has left a moral vacuum. Examination of how *liangxin* is used can certainly help address this question. It can also help us think about the nature of the self implied by the use of this concept. How does it comport with different forms of inequality or hierarchy? Can we characterize it as "modern" or "traditional," oriented toward the present, future, or past? Or does the use of this concept demonstrate the difficulties of categorizing people and their outlooks as "modern" or "traditional" and instead provide us with a window on the continuities in Chinese moral ideologies across time? Finally, our investigation of the concept of *liangxin* must ask how widely the net is cast. Is the concept of *liangxin* applied primarily in one's local world or can it be used to evaluate people with whom one does not have a direct personal connection?

As we shall see, *liangxin* embodies ideas about individual moral responsibility and the importance of memory, for to accuse someone of lacking conscience is to say that she has forgotten her obligations. But in a society that is changing rapidly, people are unlikely to agree on the nature of these obligations. Examining the ways in which the concept of *liangxin* is utilized in Moonshadow Pond can serve as a starting point for thinking about those areas of social and cultural life that are now most open to moral contention.

I should caution at the outset that while *liangxin* is translated as "conscience," its connotations are not exactly the same as the English word. As with many culturally embedded concepts, a literal translation cannot explain the contexts in which a term is used or the expectations it embodies. Only an ethnographic examination can uncover its meanings in context.

THE ETHNOGRAPHY OF MORAL DISCOURSE IN CHINA

How have ethnographers approached the study of moral systems in rural China? This question is naturally complicated by the rapid succession of changes in contemporary Chinese history, which were discussed in the last chapter. Despite local variations, an abbreviated summary of traditional Chinese moral precepts, at least those that were operative in day to day rural life, would likely agree on certain basic points. According to Xiaotong Fei, peasants understood morality as best attained through superordinate control of subordinates: "Parents, therefore, must correct the mistakes of their children; lineages of their kinsmen; village elders of their fellow villagers; merchants of their fellow merchants; and officials of their fellow officials."[1] In this moral system, good behavior was also supposed to radiate outward from the self to the family, the state, and then the empire,[2] and ethical concepts were embedded in particular relationships such as those between parents and children, rulers and subjects.[3] Fei proposed, therefore, that moral concepts were relative to one's station or place in the rural universe and to the particular relationship being considered. Fei's description of rural moral systems involved both hierarchy and maintenance of moral order by example. One's specific obligations in this moral universe were constrained by one's particular role.

To this general outline of a hierarchically modeled moral universe, one might also add the notion of reciprocity to the mix of elements in the Chinese peasant's moral world. The Chinese word *bao,* most often translated as "reciprocity," has many dimensions because it can connote everything from "revenge" to "repayment," but it certainly has a moral element. Indeed, in almost all cultures, ideas of reciprocity are articulated in at least partially moral terms, since they promote notions of obligation.

Many specific moral obligations in traditional rural China can therefore be understood through the lens of one or more of these three general principles of reciprocity, hierarchy, and moral modeling. For instance, the notion of filial piety *(xiao)* contains aspects of all these three elements. Children are indebted to their parents for the gift of birth and for raising them, and must repay them not only through support in old age, but through death ritual and ancestral worship. Filial piety also exemplifies a hierarchical relationship and is a behavior that needs to be modeled for others.

Another example is *renqing,* a word that is often translated as "human feelings." *Renqing* refers both to one's natural feelings as well as to the obligations that flow from social interaction.[4] As Mayfair Yang points out, while *guanxi* or connections have "ethical, instrumental, and aesthetic" values, "*renqing* discourse" emphasizes "obligation and indebtedness."[5] Hence, Yunxiang Yan tells us that not to act according to *renqing* is considered "an immoral act."[6] *Renqing* need not necessarily involve hierarchy, but it does entail both reciprocity and modeling.

While filial piety is perhaps the most important moral virtue when it comes to intrafamilial relations, *renqing* is both a virtue that characterizes individuals and an asset that is exchanged amongst those who have a "mixed tie."[7] That is, it is most relevant in relationships amongst people who, although not family members, have a relationship that goes beyond an impersonal one.[8]

It is fair to say that "traditional" notions of morality often differentiated among dissimilar relationships within a hierarchy. Mao-era morality, in contrast, has been characterized by what Richard Madsen describes as the imperative to "serve the people . . . without any thought of the self."[9] All people in China except "class enemies" were included in this injunction, and the morality was therefore meant to be universally applied and not dependent on particular relations, such as those between elders and their descendants.[10] Indeed, putting your own kin's needs above those of the collective would have been a breach of a pure Mao-era moral code. Madsen emphasizes that this discourse was imported into villages from the outside, and in his study of Chen Village, he shows that it was eventually modified as more utilitarian reformers came into power in the village. This modified paradigm, which actually predated the advent of the reform era, accepted that people could not renounce all their specific family and kin obligations, and that a certain amount of self-interest or at least family interest was inherent in people's actions.[11]

Of course, the prerevolutionary, Maoist, and reform periods are not only marked by chasms but also by continuities with respect to the way people utilize moral ideas. People did not throw away all earlier moral frameworks in either the Mao or reform periods, and sometimes old frameworks were simply inserted into new contexts. Nonetheless, in thinking first about what is *different* between prerevolutionary and Maoist moral systems, I have found Charles Taylor's work useful. Discussing variable ideas of moral orders, he points out that ideas of moral order can be "ultimate, like the community of saints, or for the here and now, and if the latter, it can either be hermeneutic or prescriptive."[12] By hermeneutic, Taylor means that certain ideas of morality are meant to justify the existing order—that is, what exists is what *should* be and should be upheld. Prescriptive ideas, in contrast, advocate change.[13]

In thinking of traditional Chinese notions of morality, the "hermeneutic" notion seems generally more applicable. Society and polity were seen as a cosmically ordained hierarchy. One's behavior within this society was supposed to reinforce this hierarchy, whether it was to uphold hierarchical superiority of ruler to subject, father to son, or husband to wife. Of course, the hierarchical superiors in each of these relationships also had responsibilities; parents had to raise their children to adulthood before they could expect filial support, and the emperor had responsibilities to his subjects. Hence the "mandate of heaven" also justified revolt against an emperor if he did not fulfill his responsibilities by guaranteeing the livelihood of the people. Nonetheless, such a revolt would be understood as restoring the old order and not creating a new one.

In the modern era, Taylor says, the notion of a cosmically ordained hierarchy, whose members exist for the purpose of upholding it, has been altered. Modern notions of moral order turn the table, so that the entire idea of a moral order is that it is supposed to serve the needs of the people in it. It is not its own justification.[14] Therefore, Maoist morality, with its emphasis on overturning traditional class hierarchies (though it instituted new ones), and on the collective as a form of organization that served the people's needs, was both "prescriptive" and "modern" according to Taylor's definitions.

However, even in this revolutionary context where preexisting social relations were being questioned and overturned, many traditional frameworks were still employed. A particularly interesting, though chilling, example is provided by Richard Madsen in an essay on Cultural Revolution violence. During the Cultural Revolution, violence between local gangs, each claiming to be the true revolutionaries, broke out in many areas. Frequently, there were few or no ideological differences between the opposing groups. Instead, these gangs were often comprised of those with common clan loyalties or other preexisting social bonds, such as common production team membership. Sometimes, in attacking each other they brought up incidents from the past that incriminated leaders of rival gangs, playing upon collective memories of past injuries to fuel the conflict.

As Madsen points out, traditional ideas of obligation to one's moral community were employed here. These were coupled with the idea of *bao*. *Bao* entails the expectation that for all actions there is a return or response, and this entails a response not only to favors but also to injuries.[15] Hence, revenge can be conceptualized as a kind of repayment for past injuries, and therefore as a form of "moral reciprocity." As Madsen states, "revenge is not a means, but an end in itself."[16] It was undertaken to honor commitments to one's own social group, commitments that constituted a person's own social identity. In this sense, of course, revenge morality undercut the revolutionary universalism of "serving the people" that was supposed to be part of the new Maoist morality. Often the violence between gangs seemed self-defeating—because every attack could provoke a counterattack that could result in one's own destruction. But as Madsen reminds us, "In a certain kind of moral tradition, revenge can be something one must seek even at the expense of one's own concern for one's own well-being."[17]

Thus, while a certain amount of violence during the Cultural Revolution was indeed "pragmatic" in that people used the rhetoric of revolution simply to dethrone old foes from power, Madsen shows us that other actions have to be viewed through the lens of the traditional morality of repayment. People were motivated by their own understanding of moral obligation. Hence, in the case of revenge taking, Madsen is explaining a phenomenon that occurred in Maoist China in terms of traditional moral frameworks applied to a new context.

Turning next to work on reform-era rural China, there is still little consensus about the shape and parameters of the contemporary moral system. Some ethnographers have pointed out that a contemporary version of "traditional" morality has been reconstituted through kin- and village-based rituals.[18] Other scholars, however, have asserted that rural residents have little to hold onto in making moral decisions—since neither Confucian nor Maoist ideas about how to order one's life are pertinent anymore. Describing China as a whole (as opposed to rural residents in particular), Xiaoying Wang suggests that the new "post-Communist personality" is someone "without a sense of proportion or limit . . . an unorganized assemblage of desires."[19] She goes on to state that this new personality reflects "hedonism without individualism" since individualism would imply that one had the "ability to subject one's desires to the direction of one's own will . . . under a new constellation of values."[20] Wang explains that individualism implies a "conception of the rights and responsibilities of individuals."[21] However, in the moral universe of the "post-Communist personality," asserts Wang, such a concept of social responsibility is lacking. For instance, resentment against corruption in this moral universe just leads to socially disruptive acts or to emulation of the corrupt agents one rails against in order to get a piece of something for oneself.[22]

In a similar vein, Jiwei Ci tracks the movement from utopianism to hedonism in modern China. He points out that Maoist morality was based on "the subordination, one might even say reduction, of virtue to belief along with the total politicization of belief."[23] As such, he says, when the belief system collapsed, "the whole moral order collapsed with it."[24] Since almost any act could be "moral" in the Maoist system if it furthered the Maoist political program, the demise of that political program and ideology left people with no moral system at all. The political repression that followed the democracy movement, Ci contends, further sublimated people's aims and goals into "material and sensual gratification"[25] and turned the possibility for the emergence of "idealistic individualism" into "crude hedonism."[26]

Writing from a more ethnographically based standpoint, Yunxiang Yan nevertheless comes to some similar conclusions. In his study of the emergence of private life in rural China, he states, "With neither traditional values nor socialist morality, villagers faced a moral and ideological vacuum in the postcollective era."[27] Yan attributes this phenomenon to many things, but one cause is the shift in family life from a "social institution to a private haven for individuals."[28] This change in the family from a social to private institution in the northern village Yan studied was accentuated by the fact that, unlike in contemporary southeast China, many family and community rituals, including ancestral worship and visits to ancestral tombs, were not revived in the reform era.[29] Further causes cited by Yan for the moral vacuum he found were the "decline in public life, the new absence of community power, the increasingly predatory local government, and the accelerating pressure of competition in a market oriented economy."[30] Yan observes, "excluded from political participation and public life, villagers were forced to retreat to their private homes and have grown increasingly cynical about any moral discourse. As a result, their sense of duty and obligation to the community and to other individuals continues to shrink in both the public and private spheres."[31]

One more example of the notion of moral vacuum comes from the work of Xin Liu.[32] Describing a north China village, Liu states, "There was no consistent 'moral' order to guide and determine social action or cultural meaning. . . . Arguments about rules of the game have become the game itself, as the players constantly challenged and contested how this game should be played."[33] Liu goes on to explain that with neither a gentry class nor a class of authoritative revolutionaries, no one can create a local framework within which meanings and morality can be evaluated.[34] One might add here that what Liu really seems to be saying is that there is a lack of moral modeling in the new order, since there are no longer any authoritative local hierarchies.

Such pictures of moral nihilism might be moderated if analysts also looked at the use of the concept of *liangxin* in contemporary rural China. For, if residents of Moonshadow Pond do not agree on what obligates them, they do seem to agree on the concept of obligation itself, and on the ultimate responsibility of individuals in fulfilling their moral debts.[35] Before examining the ethnographic evidence in this regard, I will discuss *liangxin* as a general cultural category. I will then consider how it is used in the particular "local world" of Moonshadow Pond.

LIANGXIN IN THE UNIVERSE
OF CHINESE MORAL CONSTRUCTS

To take *liangxin* apart as a concept, one can begin by deconstructing the word into its two elements. *Liang* can mean "good" or "virtuous." The second part of the word, *xin,* however, is a bit more complicated. In English *xin* is often translated as "heart," but in Chinese it actually connotes both "heart" and "mind." Many philosophers and Sinologists translate *xin* as "mind/heart."[36] As Sarah Allen points out, the conventional Western distinction between emotion and reason, and between heart and mind, is not mirrored in this Chinese term, which refers to both thought and emotion.[37] "The term *xin*," David Hall and Roger Ames tell us, "refers indifferently to activities we would classify as thinking, judging, and feeling."[38] And, they add, no translation of *xin* that reflects mind/body dualism is accurate. Building on this idea, Lung-Ku Sun analyzes the Chinese notion of a person as constituted by a "body" *(shen)* with a "heart/mind" *(xin)*.[39] This "body" is only made whole by the exchange of *xin* with others. Thus, if one asks, "How is your health?" (*Ni shenti hao ma?*, or literally, "Is your body okay?"), then the appropriate response is "You have a heart/mind" *(Ni you xin)*.[40] In essence, to say someone has a "heart/mind" is to say that they have thought about you—an act that is both an act of "feeling" and "mind."

Xin is also the location of "moral goodness."[41] Hence, the word for "conscience" *(liangxin)* is literally someone with a "virtuous heart/mind." While a person with conscience reciprocates other people's "good feelings," a person without conscience is someone who "fails to reciprocate."[42] This concept recognizes that it is ultimately the individual who is morally accountable, a theme with a long history in Chinese thought. As Ambrose King points out, "Confucianism attaches a good deal of autonomy to the individual. The expression *wei ren you ji* testifies that the highest virtue *(ren)* is in the final analysis, in the hands of *ji* (self)."[43]

The idea of moral debt is certainly a key one in Chinese culture, and it is described in various ways by ethnographers. Lung-Ku Sun notes that one is indebted to parents from the moment of birth, and that this debt to parents becomes the "prototype for all reciprocal transactions of society."[44] Yunxiang Yan analyzes this in terms of the idea of *renqing* ethics. This ethical system relies amongst other things, on the concept of reciprocity *(bao)* and is enforced by "rational calculation, moral obligation and emotional attachment."[45] A person who violates this system risks social censure. Yan also notes that certain acts of extreme kindness or *enqing* can never be fully repaid. What is important is that they never be forgotten.[46]

Liangxin is therefore a quality of those individuals who *remember* their moral obligations and try to act on them. A person without a conscience is a person who either does not remember moral debt or at least acts as if this is the case. In this sense, the word *liangxin* has a different connotation than the English word "conscience." In English, we might speak of someone who commits a bad deed, but who is bothered about it later, as a person with "a troubled conscience." But in Chinese, words other than *liangxin* would be used to describe this type of situation.[47] Simply put, a person lacks *liangxin* if he violates his moral obligations, even if he is troubled about it later. Both the English word "conscience" and the

Chinese word *liangxin* imply an inner voice.[48] But *liangxin* contains within it both that inner voice and the actions that it should prompt.

A particularly stark example of this comes from an account of an incident in a Guangdong village from the book *Chen Village*. The authors Chan, Madsen, and Unger relate the story of a man they call Stocky Wang. He had been imprisoned in the village "cowshed" during the Cultural Revolution for political infractions. When he was finally released he was a "political pariah," but despite his status, another man named Four Eyes Wu housed and fed him. A few years later, Wu was himself a target in a political campaign, and Stocky Wang succumbed to pressure to testify against him. This act cost him the respect of most of the people in the village, who saw him as betraying a friend who had helped him in time of need. He became such an outcast in the village that he finally fled to Hong Kong, where he was unable to sleep at night because of the terrible memories of his betrayal.[49]

While Stocky could not sleep at night after he betrayed his friend, it would not be correct to say that he had *liangxin*. The reason is that although one might translate *liangxin* as "conscience," *liangxin* means more than thinking about what you should do, must do, or could have done. It implies an attempt to act accordingly, even if complete repayment of previous help is impossible.

How, then, are these ideas utilized in the day-to-day life of Moonshadow Pond residents? In chapter 1, I laid out an initial argument that remembrance and reciprocation of moral debt is indeed a key way in which Moonshadow Pond residents evaluate each other. The "moral vacuum," as described by Liu and others, doesn't apply to this case. Indeed, the idea of *liangxin* is used in many contexts in ordinary conversation in Moonshadow Pond, and it is applied to a diversity of situations from ritual behavior and remembrance of ancestors to supporting parents, reciprocating good works, remembering friends and family, and returning to one's native village to visit after residence in other parts of China or abroad. I will consider some preliminary examples and their implications shortly. The chapters that follow will investigate conflicts over the nature of obligations in more detail.

Day-to-Day Interaction

A frequent form of praise about even relatively "small" things in Moonshadow Pond is to say that a person never forgets. "Auntie Mei never forgets," said a young woman about an older neighbor in 1995. "My father helps address letters for her, and she always remembers by giving us some coffee during New Year."[50] But just as remembering small things greases the wheel of ordinary interactions, those who forget past help are often branded as "without *liangxin*" and feelings are soured. This past help can be something that happened a year ago or decades ago, and the time that has elapsed is not significant.

Chapter 1 introduced the story of Songling's mother, who employed Aihua's mother-in-law before Liberation. After Liberation, Aihua's mother-in-law had been asked to publicly denounce Songling's family for exploiting them, but she chose not to. Present relationships between them therefore must take into account this past history. Were Songling to slight Aihua, then she could accuse Songling of lacking memory and therefore *liangxin*. Instead, Aihua told me that one of the reasons she and Songling had good relations was that Songling remembered this previous help.

Indeed, in many interpersonal disputes that occurred in Moonshadow Pond, it was not the immediate disagreement that roused the most ire. Rather, it was an accusation by one party against the other that this infraction showed a lack of mindfulness about the past and hence no *liangxin*.

One example came from a dispute between Aihua and Skinny Hong, another member of Team 2. When Aihua's husband served as party secretary of the production brigade from the late 1960s to the late 1970s, he used his influence to help Skinny Hong take a job supervising some village men in construction projects in neighboring Jiangxi Province. But some of the workers on Skinny Hong's projects returned to Moonshadow Pond and complained that he was exploiting them, not giving them enough remuneration for the projects, pocketing the funds for himself, and cutting corners on the work. Skinny Hong was arrested and sent to a labor camp, but Aihua's husband intervened and Skinny Hong was freed. Later he helped Skinny Hong once more to get permission to work outside the village.

Years afterward, Aihua said that her husband helped Skinny Hong because he understood that as a father of six children, Skinny Hong needed extra income to support his family. Aihua denied vociferously that her husband had ever accepted any gifts from Skinny Hong in return for this help. Nonetheless, he had to step down as party secretary in the late 1970s, and many said that suspicions he had taken bribes from Skinny Hong were one reason for this.

Although these events occurred in the 1960s and 1970s, they continuously played into the relationships between Aihua and Skinny Hong's family in the mid- to late 1990s. Every time Skinny Hong failed to take Aihua's side in a contemporary village dispute, she would hurl the insult that "he had no conscience." Didn't Skinny Hong remember how her husband had to step down because he had gone out on a limb for Skinny Hong? The contemporary disputes were not over life-shattering issues, but often over small grievances. Nonetheless, past memories were often brought into play. For instance, in the 1990s Uncle Wei, as Aihua's husband was now referred to because of his advancing age, started to work part time as a cook at village banquets. This enabled him to earn extra money and not be completely reliant on his two grown sons. One day Aihua heard that Skinny Hong had gone to a wealthy overseas Chinese returnee and convinced him not to hire Uncle Wei, but to hire someone else for an upcoming banquet. Whether this actually occurred is immaterial to Aihua's response. What is significant here is how she characterized the situation. Describing how much her husband had sacrificed several decades earlier in order to help Skinny Hong, she quoted from an old proverb about a person who saves someone else's dog, only to have its owner send it back to bite them!

Songling's husband, Baoli, also complained about Skinny Hong in similar terms. Baoli had a rice-threshing business across the path from Skinny Hong's store, and Skinny Hong complained that it was too noisy. Baoli grumbled, "He forgets that when he was in the hospital I visited him every day!" This kind of forgetfulness is exactly the kind of action that was frequently labeled as "without *liangxin*" by Moonshadow Pond villagers.

If bad relationships were characterized by lack of memory, good relationships were characterized by memory. For instance, Songling often spoke about Ruolan's situation when she lived in the village in the early 1970s. Ruolan's husband held Hong Kong residency and she had all the requirements to leave the country. But every time she went to apply, they told her that her number was not up, and she could not leave. Baoli helped her every night with the paperwork, and finally she was able to leave. "After that," Songling said, "Ruolan always used to bring clothes for all the kids when she came to visit, since at that time our life was very hard here. So, she helped us, but she remembers all the help we gave her as well." Songling went on to emphasize that Ruolan was not a rich person, and had a hard time making ends meet herself once she moved to Hong Kong. The gift of old clothes was especially welcome at the time, not only because they could use the clothes, but also because the gift indicated that Ruolan *remembered* past help.

As *liangxin* is a *virtuous* heart/mind, simply having *xin* at all is an important ingredient of everyday social relations. For instance, a conventionally polite expression of greeting for visitors is either to say that they have "so much *xin*" *(hen you xin)* or simply to say that they "have *xin*" *(ni you xin)*. These expressions mean that a person took the time and trouble to visit. In essence, as discussed previously, someone with *xin* acts with consideration and thoughtfulness about others. Of course, stating that a person has a good supply of *xin* is basically a formulaic politeness, while stating that a person does or does not have *liangxin* is a serious moral judgment. Nonetheless, both a "virtuous" heart/mind and a good supply of same connote the capacity to remember.

Another ordinary use of the word *xin* occurs during gift giving. In the case of small gifts such as food items that are exchanged during holidays, when visiting, or as ways of showing appreciation for favors, a person can say that the gift is a small token of one's regard, or *xinyi*. This word combines the character for *xin* with the character for *yi*, which refers to meanings, thoughts, and sentiments. One might literally translate *xinyi* as "heart/mind, thoughts and sentiments." In other words, when giving a gift in such cases, one is demonstrating that thoughts about the recipient remain in one's heart and mind, or simply that one has remembered the recipient.

As such, the capacity to remember is a critical component of morality in Chinese contexts—whether it is remembrance of ancestors, parents, or good deeds bestowed on one in the past. In Moonshadow Pond, commonly quoted aphorisms make reference to the connection between memory and morality. For instance, "when you drink water, remember the source" refers to the necessity of remembering who is responsible for assistance you may have received. Another common expression, "when a person leaves, the tea becomes cold," acknowledges that people *do* forget their obligations when they physically leave a place. But, it also suggests that this forgetfulness is wrong and should be avoided.

Emigrants and Returnees

In China, return visits of family members are often ritualized and celebrated events. As Charles Stafford points out in his fascinating study of separation and reunion in China, "narratives and rituals of separation and reunion" are highly elaborated in Chinese society.[51] These include reunion rituals and banquets at New Year's time when family members from all over China and even further away return to their natal homes.[52]

Certainly, in Moonshadow Pond return visits are an integral part of family life for almost all families. At the very least, married daughters traditionally return to visit their natal families on important holidays (and actually more often now). Additionally, about 24 percent of Moonshadow Pond households have family members who labor or are in business beyond the immediate area, and 11 percent of households have a relative who lives overseas or in Hong Kong.

Being physically distant from the village does not release one from moral obligation or close the book on memory. The story of Old Man Guosheng, who returned to Moonshadow Pond after many decades, is an interesting example of how obligations that may have accrued decades earlier can be remembered. Guosheng was a former member of the Nationalist Air Force. When the Communists were victorious in 1949, Songling's father helped Guosheng and his family flee by providing them with the cash they needed to get to Hong Kong, and ultimately to Taiwan. "My father was his lifesaver" *(jiuming enren)*, Songling told me one day. If one were to translate her words literally they would be "lifesaving kindness bestowing person." The use of the word *en* ("kindness") in this phrase is very important since, as discussed previously, while certain forms of extreme kindness can never be fully repaid, they must at least be remembered. In this case, *en* is used with the word "lifesaver," which makes the connotations of impossibility to repay even stronger.

In the 1990s, as it became easier for Taiwan residents to go to China as tourists, investors, or to visit family, Guosheng returned to Moonshadow Pond to build a house where he could spend a few months each year. While the house was under construction, he stayed with Songling and her family. However, he made everyone miserable with his bad temper. Being such an unpleasant guest in normal circumstances is bad enough, since an unpleasant guest is by definition failing to reciprocate kindness. But to be an ungrateful guest when a family member of your host saved your life decades earlier is certainly an extreme act of moral forgetfulness! This can only be explained by a deficit of *liangxin*.

Of course, there are other general expectations of returnees from overseas that are less freighted down with moral weight. If the relationship is with the village as a whole, for instance, and not with specific individuals, the expectations about memory and repayment do not apply. For instance, overseas returnees often contribute funds to roads, ancestral halls, bridges, and other village-wide projects. These gifts are highly appreciated and even sought after through specific requests for donations (a topic we consider in more detail in chapter 5). But no one would describe an overseas relation who did not contribute to one of these projects as somehow lacking in *liangxin*. In contrast, an overseas relative who had means and did not help his own family would be seen as shirking his "responsibilities" *(zeren)* and lacking *liangxin*. For instance, another Nationalist soldier had fled to and remarried in Taiwan. He was not blamed for remarrying, because villagers said he thought he would never be able to return. After Taiwan-China relations relaxed, this former soldier sent considerable remittances to his wife in the village and her adult children. Villagers did not judge him harshly because through the remittances he showed that he remembered his family and helped fulfill his responsibilities to them.

Liangxin *in Family Relations*

It goes without saying that moral debt is intrinsic to the relationship between parents and children and ancestors and descendants in the Chinese context. Charles Stafford describes these relationships as part of the "cycle of *yang*" or the "system of mutual obligations between parents and children which centrally entails the transfer of money and the sharing of food."[53] As Stafford points out, this cycle of *yang* is also extended to ancestors, "who similarly receive food and money from their (heavily obligated) descendants."[54] By definition, any descendant who forgets his or her obligations to parents or ancestors is lacking in *liangxin*.

But what about people who are not as obviously implicated in this cycle of *yang* as parents, children, and ancestors? As Stafford points out, "*Yang* may produce its own return" and someone may care for you who is neither an ascendant nor a descendant.[55] In these cases obligations still remain, and the concept of *liangxin* is also used to speak about remembering such debts.

In Moonshadow Pond, relations between segments of a family created by married brothers are characterized by both harmony and discord. The problem of relationships between brothers has been well documented in the literature on China. Sooner or later, brothers usually divide their own families from the extended family, and they begin to eat separately and account for their own finances.[56] As we shall see in chapter 3, joint families characterized by more than one married brother living together are not common in Moonshadow Pond. But mutual help can occur between married brothers living in separate households as well as between married brothers and their married sisters. Nowadays, medical expenses, educational expenses, and contacts for jobs are just a few of the areas where siblings might turn to each other for help.

One day in the summer of 1997, Aihua entered the house and began to recite a litany of complaints about her husband's younger brother and his family. Her complaints were triggered by an event that happened earlier that day. Apparently five men had come to her nephew's house and demanded money they had lent him because of his gambling debts. (This nephew was nicknamed Ironpot Number Two, because he was the second son in his family and was known while growing up for eating rice directly out of the cooking pot that his mother asked him to watch.) Aihua reiterated how sickly this nephew had been as a child, how she took care of him, and how she gave him food whenever she could.

"He doesn't remember this," she exclaimed, "and he doesn't help his parents out now." (The situation persisted ten years later when I returned.) But then, Aihua turned the topic of conversation over to her nephew's father, her husband's younger brother. "He never helped take care of his own mother either," she exclaimed. "I took care of her. And my husband has no feelings for this younger brother now. Most people at least send a bottle of liquor at New Year, but he doesn't even do that, even though he got a great job because of my husband's help." Aihua then detailed how Uncle Wei, her husband, was the party secretary of the production brigade in the late 1960s when a job at the local petrol company opened up. Uncle Wei furnished his younger brother's name, saying he had already served in the army and would be a good fit. The job had a good monthly wage and ultimately provided a pension, a highly coveted benefit which few rural people receive even now.

In Aihua's series of complaints, the issue was not the expectation of any major material reciprocation for the help provided to her nephew's family. Rather, what she was looking for was a demonstration that they remembered the previous help her family had given them.

When relations among family members go sour, the concept of *liangxin* is often used in speaking about the situation. For instance, two widows in Moonshadow Pond told me how they had helped the families of their husbands' brothers in the past. Years afterward, when both needed assistance from these brothers-in-law, they received none. In the first case, the widow claimed her husband had paid her nephews' school tuition. Later on, when her husband died and she needed some help, her husband's brother did nothing. In the second case, a widow claimed that she did most of the work for her brother-in-law's family because his own wife was too sickly and unable to work. The segments of the family finally divided. Since then, this brother-in-law has been very unfriendly—so much so that they cannot plan for an important postmortuary ritual for his mother.

In both these cases, the brothers-in-law were characterized as lacking *liangxin,* not so much because they were related through marriage, but because they acted as if they had forgotten past help. Of course, in some cases, each side of a family may claim it shouldered a disproportionate burden caring for the other and that this was conveniently forgotten. In such circumstances, *each* side accuses the other of lacking conscience. For instance, in the second of the cases cited above, the brother-in-law claimed that far from receiving his sister-in-law's help, he had actually supported her after her husband died. When years later she received money from relatives abroad and did not give him any, he used this to claim that she had no conscience.

In these cases, the concept of *liangxin* can be employed in a negative way to describe the behavior of any family member who does not remember obligations. One woman in Moonshadow Pond, for instance, used it to describe her former daughter-in-law who abandoned her husband. In the mother's account, her son helped his wife find a job in town, yet she still ran off "without conscience" and later took half of his savings in the divorce settlement.

In chapter 1, I discussed the idea that moral discourse is often focused on those who breach moral norms, rather than on those who reach or exceed them. This is understandable, since as pointed out in that chapter, moral norms are often tacit and taken for granted until they are broken. However, *liangxin* is not always used in a negative way in describing family relations. It can also be used as a concept in praise of proper family behavior. In one case, a woman who worked as a servant before Liberation was married after her childbearing years to a man whose wife had died. She cared for all her stepchildren, but they treated her poorly when she was old. Villagers said that the stepson she lived with (known in the village as "Slippery Cheng") was particularly ungrateful, feeding her nothing but watery congee while his own family dined on nourishing foods. Of all the stepchildren, only one remembered her, and although this stepdaughter lived away from the village in Guangzhou, she sent money that helped keep the old woman afloat. "She is the only one with *liangxin,*" one villager told me.

Liangxin can also be used to turn the tables on obligation. Whereas obligation in family relations is usually framed as a debt from the younger to the elder generation (after adulthood), the idea of *liangxin* is also used to describe obligations between generations in less traditional ways. For instance, Songling's younger daughter, Fengying, had worked in the city of Dongguan for several years before she married. During that time she remitted a large part of her earnings home, and this helped Songling and her husband, Baoli, to build their new house in the village. Songling often said that she always listened to Fengying and took her opinions seriously, because she had sent such substantial remittances back.

Liangxin *and Death Ritual*

In Moonshadow Pond, death ritual involves a complex interplay of moral obligation and status emulation. A large funeral service is certainly a template for a display of material wealth and social connections. Nonetheless, the role of moral obligation and at least the appearance, if not the reality, of *liangxin* is still extremely important. This stress on moral obligation need not be tied to the traditional belief that the soul travels to the underworld and journeys through bureaucratic purgatory to be judged according to its deeds in the present life. Many men in Moonshadow Pond voice doubt about the existence of any spirit world, but they still express the opinion that commemoration of the dead is important. Furthermore, while expensive funerals with many guests and Buddhist monks are the preferred form of a status-enhancing funeral in Moonshadow Pond, such elaborate funerals are not viewed as the only way to fulfill one's obligations. Villagers' reactions to a woman who deviated from this pattern demonstrate that moral obligation to the dead is still viewed as more important than the mere show of an expensive funeral. Bright Ling, a young and unmarried thirty-year-old woman who was a devout Buddhist, refused to undertake the standard village funeral when her father died. Instead of inviting monks, providing a large feast for mourners, and having funeral services that extended throughout the night, she insisted on calmly reciting sutras by her father's coffin. When I queried villagers about Bright Ling's means of mourning her father, many expressed the view that as long as she had still commemorated him that was acceptable, at least in terms of their judgments about her motives.

As with moral obligation in other settings, its expression in death ritual is not limited by family boundaries. An elderly woman in Moonshadow Pond told me how she had donned funeral garb and cried at the funeral of a childless widow who had helped take care of her own children. By mourning and crying at the widow's funeral, she felt she was expressing gratitude for the help that she received from the widow and possibly helping the widow's soul in her underworld journey. (Chapter 4 examines funerals in more detail.)

A word closely related to *liangxin* that is used in connection with the commemoration of ancestors is *xiuxin*. As mentioned in chapter 1, it can be translated as a "cultivated or renovated heart/mind," and it is often employed in conversation to refer not only to acting charitably, but also to accepting one's ritual responsibilities. Those who do not honor their ancestors are said to lack *xiuxin*, and if they have subsequent misfortunes then these may be blamed on their deficit of *xiuxin*. This deficit can be exhibited by not going to ancestors' graves during the Lunar New Year holiday, or in the case of overseas relatives, not visiting the ancestral hall to make offerings on a return visit to the village.

Memory, Morality, and Exchange

"Memories are not simply stored images drawn out of the brain at appropriate intervals, but are very much formed as an interaction between the past and the present."[57] So states David Sutton in his work on memory and food in a Greek village. Memories, he continues, "can be publicly memorialized in writing and other official sources," or they can also constitute what is "left out of official histories." From the examples provided in this chapter, we can conclude that memory is also a resource which can be exchanged, whether in a small private way such as in a gift that constitutes a token of one's regard, or in a larger more public way as in a death ritual.

The work of the anthropologist Jun Jing on the idea of "sacrifice" *(xisheng)* in China can also throw some light on this. Jing reminds us that in the customary rituals of Chinese popular religion, the sacrificial offerings entitled one to a god's protection as reciprocation. Similarly, in the rhetoric of revolutionary China, sacrificing oneself for the cause was also to be reciprocated, in this case by the everlasting memory of one's sacrifice. In Mao's famous eulogy about the Canadian physician Norman Bethune, for instance, "revolutionary fighters were repeatedly promised and assured by the Communist Party that if they died for the revolution they would be forever remembered."[58]

Hence, in Moonshadow Pond the condemnation of a person for lacking *liangxin* was particularly harsh when the sacrifice they chose to ignore or had forgotten was a particularly painful one. One example was the case of Meirong, the woman whose husband had been beaten to death by an angry mob during the Cultural Revolution. After this horrible event, she raised two sons, each of whom went on to marry and prosper. By 2007, however, she was making her own meals and eating alone. This time her fate was not the result of politics, but rather a much more mundane and common situation—she did not get along with her daughters-in-law.

One villager said to me, "Her story is the most bitter one. She married in the late 1940s, but then the revolution came and they lost everything. She had to climb the hills to harvest rice in the farthest place. Well, maybe that wasn't so bad for the family to live like everyone else. But then during the Cultural Revolution what happened to them was truly horrible. Now, after all that, neither of her adult sons pays attention to her. Probably her sons would not be that way, but it is the fault of her two daughters-in-law. They are the ones with the least *liangxin*, to do this to her after all she has been through!"

The fact that Meirong's current problems were blamed on her daughters-in-law is an issue explored in more detail in the next chapter. What is important here is that her family members were judged especially harshly because they seem to have forgotten what she had suffered through in the past and how much she had endured in order to raise them.

Despite this emphasis on memory, the discourse of *liangxin* not only allows for, but actually commends one kind of intentional oversight. This is when one purposely ignores a past injury in order to repair or reconstitute a relationship. Much of this purposeful "forgetting" necessarily occurred in China after the events of the Cultural Revolution, which as mentioned before, often pit family or lineage members against one another. Songling provided me with a particularly interesting example one day in 2007. My husband and I were preparing to go on a trip to Beijing, and Songling gave us several Hakka specialties to bring to her uncle who lived there.

Songling's uncle, her father's cousin, had made his way all the way from the village to Beijing to study and then become a professor of economics in the 1950s.[59] It was certainly an incredible accomplishment at a time when college entry was a rare feat in China, and even rarer for peasants. As Songling gave us the Hakka food items to pass on to her uncle in Beijing, she told us how her father had helped him financially so he could go to Beijing for his higher education. Nonetheless, she said, during the Cultural Revolution, this uncle came back to the village from Beijing to denounce her father as a former Nationalist (a charge that he denied in any event).[60]

As Songling thought about what happened, she said that this uncle had truly been "without *liangxin.*" But then she added that many years later this uncle visited Moonshadow Pond and went to see her father again. Her father just brushed off the past by saying that past events were "over with." Ultimately, when Songling's father was dying in the late 1990s, this same uncle sent some money down to help the family care for him.

In this story the act of consciously putting aside the past repaired the relationship between Songling's father and his cousin. Of course, one might say that the cousin's trip to see Songling's father was the first step, since he demonstrated he had *xin*. Her father's agreement to put aside the past at that point might be interpreted as a positive response to this first gesture. It also restored the cycle of mutual help as well as the ordinary gift giving in which we were implicated on our trip.

LIANGXIN AND THE DEBATE ABOUT POST-MAO MORALITY

This introduction to the role of *liangxin* in Moonshadow Pond can help provide some preliminary answers to questions asked at the beginning of this chapter about moral systems in reform-era China. First, we can begin with the "moral vacuum" issue. As indicated above, some contemporary ethnographers of rural China have noted the lack of a clearly defined moral standard or system in reform-era China for people to make use of in their daily lives.

However, a focus on *liangxin* would seem to indicate that while we can certainly debate whether there is a consensus about specific obligations and moral standards, the idea of moral obligation itself and individual moral accountability for these obligations is still strongly felt and used in evaluating others. At least this is the case in Moonshadow Pond.

Second, as we have seen, some theorists who write primarily about urban China have suggested that the contemporary self in China is "now" oriented, as opposed to the future orientation of the Communist self and the ancestral orientation of the traditional self.[61] But the idea of a "hedonistic" and "now"-oriented modern self is antithetical to a self that is focused on memory and conscience.[62] By definition, a "now" orientation cannot describe a system in which the past never becomes irrelevant and in which one's morality depends upon remembering and acting upon past obligations, no matter how long ago they were accrued.

And how does *liangxin* comport with other forms of evaluation, such as the status that comes with wealth? When I posed direct questions to villagers about the relative status of different individuals, they usually insisted that those with the most *mianzi* ("face") or status were those with the most money. But when individuals are not asked this question directly, but simply converse with and about one another, it is clear that evaluations of each other are much more complicated than a simple accounting of status based on wealth. For instance, a disunited wealthy family that also was not generous to community helpers during the funeral rites for their father was disapproved by community members. In contrast, many community members attended the funeral of a poorer family with good personal relationships. In the course of conducting the funeral rites, this family exhibited exemplary social relations adding further to their esteem.

Clearly, social status is a complex topic of its own. But the point here is that moral evaluations are not correlated in an easy relationship with wealth in Moonshadow Pond. Moral evaluations can be harsh, and money cannot necessarily buy one out of social obligations or buy one the license to forget. Chapter 6 explores many such instances, but for the time being an interesting example from a popular expression will suffice. Those who try to benefit themselves without regard to their obligations are often called *shili gui,* a label one might translate as "opportunistic ghost." This term is freely applied to people who are seen as using others or opportunities merely to benefit themselves, and wealth certainly does not protect one from such an appellation.

To fully consider the role of *liangxin* in post-Mao morality, we must also think about the discourse of *liangxin* in terms of ongoing debates about "modernity" in China. Is the idea of *liangxin* unchanged from its meaning in "traditional" culture but simply applied in new contexts, or does the meaning behind it reflect a "modern" sensibility? Of course, to ask this question one is assuming a clear distinction between "traditional" and "modern" sensibilities. Nonetheless, defining the elements of such a distinction for purposes of analysis, while conceding that these are just ideal types that don't exist in pure form in actual social life, may help us get a better grasp of the ways the concept of *liangxin* is used within the specific context of Moonshadow Pond.

Anthony Giddens's analysis of the differences between premodern systems of trust and those of the modern world is useful in this regard. Giddens points to a distinction between modernity's "trust in abstract systems," versus the premodern necessity of putting trust in persons.[63] For instance, he contrasts actions such as getting on an airplane or taking money out of a cash dispenser, which depend on our trust in systems of expertise and technology, with actions that depend on trust in particular people.[64] Security in premodern societies, asserts Giddens, was gained by putting one's trust in the institutions of kinship, place, religion, and traditional customs.[65] When it came to non-kin relationships such as friendship, "codes of honour were in effect, public guarantees of sincerity."[66]

Seen in this light, a code of morality that stresses memory and moral debt is a "traditional" code, one that emphasizes the long-term dependability of people and their internalized sense of obligation. Further, Giddens points out that in the "modern" world many interpersonal relationships have to be worked out from scratch, and "trust in persons is not focused by personalized connections within the local community and kinship networks."[67] Hence, moderns have great interest in "relationship" discourse because relationships are so fluid and not bound by local communities and social ties. In contrast to this, it is fair to say that my discussion of *liangxin* has emphasized its use in a context firmly defined by long lasting local community ties.

In contrast, before declaring a focus on *liangxin* in Moonshadow Pond as a simple holdover from pre-Maoist China, we need also to think about the contexts of its use as a term. First, moral obligation in a traditional sense often involved hierarchy such as in the obligation of children to parents, or offspring to ancestors. However, in Moonshadow Pond, *liangxin* is used to evaluate a person's sense of moral responsibility in many areas that are not defined by hierarchical social relationships. As discussed above, some examples actually involve a turning of the tables—for instance, Songling's sense that she was obligated to take her younger daughter's advice as a way of acknowledging this daughter's previous financial help. In addition, as explained earlier, there are many instances in which charges against a person for lacking *liangxin* are levied against an equal. This was true of Aihua's harsh evaluation of Skinny Hong, a fellow team member, because of his apparent forgetfulness about the way her husband helped him during the collective era. Hence, it is also fair to conclude that Moonshadow Pond residents apply their expectations of memory and moral obligation not only to hierarchical relations but to egalitarian ones, and not only to traditional forms of relationships but to newly evolving ones as well, as seen in a mother's feeling of debt to her adult daughter.

A final question is whether expectations about *liangxin* can be extended beyond the village community. As mentioned above, my material applies primarily to those who have longlasting relationships because they share ties of kinship and place. Would Moonshadow Pond residents talk about someone's "conscience" in regard to interactions with strangers? Or, by definition does it include only those who come into a person's life through interaction, and hence is the concept confined naturally to those with kin and community ties?

Because of the particular focus of my research, I primarily encountered the concept when it was used to speak about people with whom one had relationships, and not when it was applied to "humanity" in general terms. However, it is important to remember that Moonshadow Pond residents, like rural dwellers throughout China, were integrated long before the twentieth century into a polity and economy that extended well beyond their village borders.[68] To the extent that villagers have always had relationships with those beyond these borders, both sides incurred debts and obligations—whether as general as the obligation of the traditional emperor to fulfill his "mandate of heaven" and see to the prosperity of the people, or the obligation of the Communist Party to make good on their promises for the future.[69]

The anthropologist Hok Bun Ku has looked at the concept of moral obligation in another Hakka village in terms of the idea of responsibility *(zeren)*, and he points out, "The villagers applied the principles of *zeren* to define *guanxi* between villagers and ancestors, villagers and gods, villagers and nature, and villagers and the state."[70] Ku goes on to say that the "connotation of *zeren* is not fixed. . . . It is defined and redefined by the villagers in everyday practice."[71]

As such, it is fair to say that the potential circle within which individuals are expected to act in accordance with their memory of moral debt is conceivably quite wide and might be extended to evaluate relationships with people beyond the village community, such as government officials or those involved in economic transactions. Even strangers might potentially be included in the circle of people for whom the concept of *liangxin* is utilized. This is due to the mechanism through which strangers become nonstrangers once an interaction has taken place and hence become involved in relationships that entail memory and obligation.

For instance, chapter 5 describes how residents of Moonshadow Pond like to talk about the Hakka people as good hosts *(hen hao ke)*, and how they take pride in the attention they pay to guests. Once a person (such as a visiting anthropologist!) has accepted hospitality, however, she is no longer a stranger, and hence becomes embroiled in a web of mutual obligations. Similarly, subsequent chapters (particularly chapter 5) will also illustrate the way the Buddhist concept of *gongde* ("charitable deeds" or "meritorious works," used to build up karmic merit) is employed as a justification for charitable giving to strangers. But as Marcel Mauss has reminded us, the act of giving inevitably creates some relationship between giver and receiver. Hence, even donations made to initial strangers can ultimately create new moral debts.

Since some minimal notion of obligation is also entailed in market transactions, the concept of *liangxin* could conceivably be used here as well. In the recent food and medicine scandals in China, the words "without *liangxin*" have been applied in the wider society to those who sell fraudulent medicines or adulterated foods. Similarly, though I did not hear it in Moonshadow Pond, the use of the term to refer to relationships with the government has been noted in other Chinese contexts. One particular example comes from Richard Gordon and Carma Hinton's documentary about the 1989 Tiananmen Square political protests. In that film, a student protester refers to the soldiers who ultimately entered the square and fired on the protesters as being without *liangxin*. The context here is that the student was describing the army as a people's army. Hence, turning on the demonstrators was an act of forgetting what was supposed to be the army's prior relationship of solidarity with the people.[72]

As such, *liangxin* is certainly a concept that *can* be applied to relationships beyond the village community. Nonetheless, the fact that the concept can be used in references to the wider world doesn't mean it is always employed in this manner. For instance, as described in the chapters that follow, many Moonshadow Pond residents, like other rural Chinese, complain vociferously about official corruption. But one should be careful in analyzing the language used to decry such behavior. While a corrupt official is clearly someone who has violated the public trust, other categories may be more important to Moonshadow Pond residents in evaluating their actions than the notion of memory and obligation.

For example, while I lived in Moonshadow Pond in 1996, the Grain Department from a nearby prefecture asked farmers to invest savings and promised them high interest rates. The farmers lost all the money and rumors spread that the money had been used to invest in real estate deals that had gone bad. When the farmers learned they could not get their money back, hundreds of them went to the department to protest. But they never received their money.

When Moonshadow Pond residents talked about this incident, they used words like "corruption" *(fubai, tanwu)* and condemned the officials involved in the harshest terms. However, they did not evaluate them in language that connoted a violation of moral debt or failure to remember and repay past help. (One could conceivably describe the situation this way, since the farmers provided "help" in the form of financial investments, and the officials failed to remember and repay by presumably absconding with or mismanaging the funds.)

In some situations, such as family favoritism, even the word *corruption* is used with caution or not at all. Jieguo and Weiguo were two brothers from Moonshadow Pond who secured excellent jobs with good salaries and retirement benefits because of help from a half-brother in another village. Weiguo became a guard in the cigarette factory run by the county government—ironically the most luxurious workplace in all of Meixian—and Jieguo became a police officer. People in Moonshadow Pond knew that their brother used his connections to help them. But this was sometimes seen in the positive light of helping family and sometimes seen in the negative light of taking advantage of his position. Still others would not make any moral judgment because they said it was good to have access to local people, such as Jieguo and Weiguo, who had good connections. As such, there were few people who talked about their situation in black-and-white moral terms, since it was an ambiguous situation in many of their eyes.[73]

Further, while many of the examples in this chapter are about disappointment in people who do *not* have *liangxin*, this should not be taken to mean that the principles it signifies are unimportant in Moonshadow Pond. After all, there would be no need at all for concepts of right and wrong if everybody agreed all the time on what was the right thing to do and acted accordingly. Breach of an important moral principle and disappointment that it is not followed doesn't point to its lack of importance in a culture. As stated earlier, moral discourse very frequently focuses on the breach of moral principles, simply because following moral principles in daily life (as opposed to when undertaking extraordinary or heroic measures) may not excite comment.

A popular aphorism in Moonshadow Pond states, "One hundred different kinds of people were all nourished by the same kind of rice." It is expected that people will differ, and that a community will contain many types. Nonetheless, this does not necessarily suggest that a state of moral cynicism exists.

However, while moral obligation is an important idea for the people of Moonshadow Pond, the question of who is obligated and what kind of obligations they have is clearly a matter of interpretation. Residents of

Moonshadow Pond expect kin, friends, and village mates to have long memories, and to demonstrate this through their actions. But as we will see in subsequent chapters, the nature of obligations in different domains of life has changed over time, and this in itself can lead to disputes. While in Moonshadow Pond a person without conscience is most certainly a person without morality, this does not in itself ensure agreement on just what needs to be remembered. The following chapters will consider moral quandaries, contradictions, and dilemmas in greater detail.

PART TWO

Moral Discourse in Social Life

CHAPTER 3

Weighty Expectations

Women and Family Virtue

One day I was speaking with a middle-aged widow in the village across the road. She told me of her daughter's impending marriage. As I started to congratulate her, I was a bit surprised at her response.

"Oh, it's good all right," she said, "but who is going to support me if my daughter marries? I'll need a daughter-in-law now to help me out."

When I queried her more, she responded, "It's easy to marry off your daughter, but it's not so easy to get a daughter-in-law. For that you need to spend a lot of money. If she [the potential daughter-in-law] comes and sees that you don't have a new house, you don't even stand a chance!"

If one's debt to one's parents and ancestors is a prototype for moral debt, then it goes without saying that the family is a central domain of moral life. But this certainly does not mean that everyone agrees on the nature of family obligation. This chapter examines contending ideas about family obligation in Moonshadow Pond. In particular, we will explore the evolving and sometimes contradictory expectations surrounding the roles of daughter and daughter-in-law. Women face conflicting demands in these roles, but these demands are themselves changing and evolving as reform-era rural families find their way in a rapidly changing economic system. In this context, moral discourse is a way that individuals articulate ideas, often contradictory ones, about what obligation means in the family.

In Moonshadow Pond, such issues are not merely theoretical. Ideas about family obligations are typically expressed not in times of quiet reflection, but in the course of actual family disputes and problems. As people explain their actions, they draw from a number of different family moralities. These ideas sometimes ratify traditional "Confucian" hierarchies of age, gender, and generation. Other ideas from the Maoist and reform eras challenge these formulations. But when it comes to family dynamics, people are rarely unwavering "conservatives" or "liberals." In a fluid situation, where there are several cultural models to draw from, even the same person may speak in different voices about family obligations, depending on his or her structural position, or the situation he or she faces. Hence, a woman speaking as a mother of a son may praise a compliant son and daughter-in-law who do not put their own interests as a couple above supporting his parents. But speaking as a mother of a daughter, she may hope her own daughter marries into a family that makes few demands on her.

While there is already a vast scholarly and popular literature on changing family and gender roles in China, the aim of this chapter is not merely to add to an already existing literature about family transformation. Rather, this chapter is concerned with the moral discourse surrounding these changes. As explained in chapter 1, each chapter in part II will conclude by focusing on a key individual or situation that illustrates the tensions in moral discourse explored in that chapter. In keeping with this plan, the end of this chapter focuses on Songling's particular responses to issues within her own family—ideas she articulates not in the abstract, but in the course of confronting different situations in her roles as mother, mother-in-law, and daughter.

RURAL FAMILIES AND CULTURAL SCHEMAS

The traditional family system in China assumed a multigenerational household in which sons remained after marriage, sharing expenses and supporting their parents. In a perfect world, these households would extend to five generations, and authority was allocated to the senior generation over the younger generation, to husbands over wives, and to older males within each sibling cohort. A woman had little initial power in this system, as she married into her husband's family (patrilocality) and into a different village. The arranged marriage system also meant that her husband and his family were strangers to her. But over time, the daughter-in-law gained informal influence within the family. As she herself became a member of the senior generation, she utilized her emotional bonds with her adult sons and her authority over her own daughters-in-law to exercise informal power. This informal power base within the family is what the anthropologist Margery Wolf has called the "uterine family."[1]

The joint family in China could take several possible forms. For instance, members of the family might disperse geographically but still retain economic ties, operating as a single economic unit and pooling their resources. Or family members might actually reside in one household. But in either case, the cultural ideal of five generations under one roof, or even five generations simply operating as a single economic entity, was rarely achieved in practice. As mentioned in the previous chapter, at some point in the life of a joint family, married brothers usually separated their segments of the family in order to create their own families. Nonetheless, patrilocal residence was widespread in China, and certainly in Meixian, as was the normative ideal of multigenerational living, even if actual five-generation households were rare.[2]

Legal, social, and economic changes in the collective and reform periods, however, have had an impact on rural families over time. Recent studies of contemporary rural families in other areas of China have pointed to several trends: a shift in power from the older to the younger generation, smaller households with less generational depth, and a growing equality and intimacy between husband and wife. Yet these trends themselves open up spaces for conflict, or at least contending motives within families. If households have less generational depth, what does this imply for the rural elderly, most of whom have no pensions and must rely on their grown children to support them? In particular, if the conjugal bond is more important than before, and families smaller, how can rural elders ensure the loyalty of their adult sons? And, if relations with daughters-in-law are more equitable, and the younger generation has more power, how can mothers-in-law count on their daughters-in-law to relieve them of burdensome household work as they age?

Chapter 1 introduced the idea of cultural schemas as assumed scripts or models about the social world. In Moonshadow Pond, the schemas about how families do and should work are multiple. In particular, the roles of daughter and daughter-in-law are understood with just such a combination of old and new mental models. As the "stranger" who married into her husband's house, the daughter-in-law was always a boundary crossing figure who embodied contradictions.[3] She was difficult to integrate as an outsider, but necessary if the family itself was going to continue. As we shall see, economic and cultural changes have complicated the daughter-in-law's role. While in some respects they come into families with greater power than before, the pressure on them to exhibit the traditional virtues of uncomplaining service to their husband's families is still strong, especially from elders who feel increasingly insecure in the new economy.

Daughters, on the other hand, were once viewed as impermanent family members whose fate it was to leave their natal families. However, contemporary birth planning programs, changes in the upbringing and education of girls, their subsequent employment experiences, and the economic anxieties of aging parents have all combined to create a changed relationship between daughters and their natal families over time. Married daughters may now play significant roles in the lives of their natal families, including providing some economic support. The hope of securing such help may also create a reversal of roles, in which parents take on extra burdens not only for their adult sons, but also for their adult daughters, in the hope that when they are truly frail all their children will help care for them.

To understand the context of ideas about family obligation in Moonshadow Pond, I first needed to know how households were actually organized. I surveyed all households in the village in both 1997 and 2007. I additionally collected more detailed family histories of over fifty households, and was also able to observe for myself changes over time. The information I collected from my surveys enabled me to answer at least a few basic questions. What kinds of marriages were prevalent in what generation and how had these changed? How many people married for "love" as opposed to arrangement? Did people still live in multigenerational households?

This kind of information allowed me to compare Moonshadow Pond's families with those I read about in other recent studies of rural China. But in order for me to see how village residents themselves understood family life, I had to draw information from a much smaller number of people whom I knew more intimately. These were the people who walked in and out of Songling and Baoli's household on a daily basis. If there was a family dispute going on in the village, they would not refrain from tossing their own opinions about it into the open. If a son, daughter-in-law, mother-in-law, husband, wife, or brother was thought to be out of line, I would hear a vigorous explanation of why they had neglected their obligations.

Below, I begin with an overview of current knowledge about rural Chinese families in the reform era. I next ask how Moonshadow Pond fits into this larger picture. Having established both a national and local context, I will then examine the contrasting claims about family obligation advanced by the residents of Moonshadow Pond—claims put forward as they confront daily family dilemmas.

Approaches to Reform-Era Rural Families

Studies of reform-era rural families in China have noted a number of different trends. In his magisterial study of family life in a north China village, Yunxiang Yan details the rise of courtship and romance, changing youth employment patterns and more independent incomes, the spread of popular culture available through the mass media, birth limitation policies, and expanding consumerism as elements in new family relationships that privilege conjugal families over complex ones and the growing power of the junior generation as opposed to their elders.[4] Yan notes that these changes actually began during the Maoist era, when collectives undermined the authority of lineage leaders and when "the authority of elder kinsmen was undermined by revolutionary youth."[5] Another result of the transformations noted by Yan is the creation of zones of privacy. This is physically manifested in changing architectural patterns that construct bedrooms as private space for couples rather than shared family space, an indication of a greater emphasis on the conjugal relationship as opposed to the joint family.[6]

Many other studies have also pointed to the rise in conjugality, although not everyone agrees on how far back one should look in seeking causes.[7] For instance, Sara Friedman notes that in the area she studied in southeast China, collectivization failed to fundamentally diminish the importance of extended patrilineal kin groups. However, post-Mao market reforms have created a consumer culture. Coupled with birth limitation policies raising the allowed age for marriage, this has created a new desire and ability of village youth to seek matches that stem from emotional compatibility.[8] Tracing changes further back, the historian Neil Diamant has used archival evidence to assess the influence of the Marriage Law of 1950. In Diamant's view, this law "put forth a decidedly modernist version of 'proper' family structure, based largely on the ideals of individualism, monogamy, and 'free' choice in selecting marriage partners." And, Diamant contends, it actually had immediate and continuing influence throughout the collective period.[9] During the marriage law campaign, he explains, older women were frequently targets of daughters-in-law during "speak bitterness" sessions.[10] Younger women seeking divorce also used the new law assertively and did not hesitate to appeal beyond the village authorities if they felt they were being obstructed.[11]

Certainly one element in the emergence of greater conjugality is the change in the legal basis of marriage. Traditionally, marriage was "a contractual relationship between families" where "the marriage and the bride 'belonged' to the groom's family."[12] In contrast, the view of marriage promulgated by the Marriage Law of 1950, and all subsequent revisions, is of a legal bond between two individuals rather than between families.

Analysts concur that declining support for elders has been one result of greater conjugality in rural Chinese families. Diamant documents significant incidences of "abuse and neglect of elders" dating as far back as the late 1950s and elder neglect is also noted in more recent studies.[13] Pang, deBrauw, and Rozelle's analysis of a nationally representative sample of rural elders shows that population policies limiting family size have reduced the number of children elders can rely on to support them. Coupled with rural emigration by young workers[14] and decreasing numbers of elders living in extended families, this has led to the phenomenon of "working until you drop."[15] Most rural elders remain in the formal workforce until their seventies and may continue to work informally to help their adult children, even those in different households.[16] This help is provided partially in the hope that these adult children will reciprocate their elders when sickness or extreme physical disability leaves them physically unable to continue working.[17]

Other recent studies point to additional changes in the situation of the elderly, some of which arise from greater conjugality. These include reliance on married daughters to supplement support given to parents by sons, and meal rotation for the elder generation among the households of several married sons.[18] In one village in Hubei Province, the anthropologist Hong Zhang discovered that middle-aged parents who have fewer children than their own parents also invest greater resources and time in each child, thus hoping to establish a "reliable reciprocal relationship" that they can use to their advantage when they become elderly.[19]

However, some scholars point out that while birth-planning policies have certainly lead to similarities in household *size* throughout rural China,[20] this has not necessarily led to similar household *structures* during the reform era.[21] For instance, differences in economic possibilities from area to area, or even within one village, can have different implications on family power dynamics. Ellen Judd gives one example. A married son may actually have less independence now than during the collective era if his father runs a nonagricultural household enterprise through which the son earns his own living.[22] In this case, the son is directly dependent for his income on his father, rather than on the production team, as he would have been during the collective era.

Hence, the rise of conjugality does not necessarily mean that the younger generation always wields greater power in any given situation. It also opens up the possibility that the new exercise of power may be contested. As Wu Fei points out in a study of suicide patterns in rural areas, the elders in a family can no longer "rely on a hierarchical order to maintain a power balance. Instead family members have to play a series of games of power to strike a balance, which has made the situation more complex. . . . People have to adjust their familial relationships carefully."[23]

But how do people explain such fine-tuned negotiations of power? Where there is no longer a clear-cut hierarchical order, there also may no longer be one clear-cut family ideology that people draw upon in explaining or justifying their own positions. Hence, ideas about how people should act within families, or in other words what is moral, are pulled from different and even contradictory family ideologies.

The Changing Family System in Moonshadow Pond

How do Moonshadow Pond families fit in with the general trends discussed above? In assessing the families of Moonshadow Pond, we first need to clarify just how families are defined there. When married brothers separated to form new families prior to 1949, they actually signed separation contracts to ratify their family division and to allocate property and wealth. However, after Liberation this practice was dropped. During the collective era there was little property to divide, so family separation was usually indicated by nothing more than establishing separate stoves for each family segment. Joint families, those in which several married brothers lived together and ate together, were and are relatively rare. But the senior generation was rarely alone, since elders would usually live with one of their married sons, even if his other brothers had established separate family units.

Despite the transformations in rural China, this general pattern still characterizes Moonshadow Pond families today. Few elders live alone and many families still remain multigenerational. Yet these multigenerational families are more likely to be "stem" families, those in which the senior generation resides with one married son, rather than "joint" families, in which several married brothers remain together. The rise of migration to cities for employment also means that in some families mem-

TABLE I   FAMILY TYPES IN MOONSHADOW POND, 1997 AND 2007 *(including nonresident family members)*

Family Type	Number of Families in 1997	% in 1997	Number of Families in 2007	% in 2007
Single person	5	2.7	3	2
Conjugal family (two generations)	84	45.6	82	41
Stem family (three generations, one married son)	79	43.0	90	45
Joint family (three or more generations, two or more married sons)	16	8.7	23	12
Total	184	100.0	198	100

bership is dispersed. Between 1997 and 2007, the proportion of Moonshadow Pond families where at least one member had migrated to the city rose from 11 percent to 24 percent.

This change raises the question of whether to count migrants at all when categorizing Moonshadow Pond families. In considering this issue it is important to point out that including migrants to the cities as part of Moonshadow Pond families reflects both official and local views of what constitutes a "family." In the official census, the numbers reported reflect registration. So, if a family member lives in a city but has a rural registration, they are recorded as part of the rural family.[24] Local villagers may also define migrants as part of the rural family, not so much because of their rural registration, but because for villagers the "family" *(jia)* is defined as those who share economic obligations; and those who share economic obligations are those who reunite in the village over the Lunar New Year holiday. So if a couple has migrated to a city for work, but returns to eat and live with the husband's parents during the Lunar New Year, then Moonshadow Pond villagers characterize them as being members of one family. It is not uncommon in such cases for a couple's children to stay with their grandparents in the village while their parents earn money in the city.

Indeed, when I asked young migrants who had returned home for the Lunar New Year where they would eventually like to live, most of them said Meixian. Though none of them saw a future in agriculture, they expressed the hope that they would find other work that would allow them to return home eventually. The factory workforce in China is overwhelmingly young, and the conditions of urban work for migrants are often

TABLE 2   FAMILY SIZE IN MOONSHADOW POND, 2007 *(including only resident family members)*

Persons in Household	Number of Households	% of Total
1	3	1.5
2	24	12.0
3	36	18.0
4	43	22.0
5	49	25.0
6	19	10.0
7	9	4.5
8	9	4.5
9	4	2.0
10	0	0.0
11	1	0.5

too exhausting for even middle-aged people, so one can understand that the concept of home for these young workers is still very much located in Meixian, rather than the large metropolises in which they work.[25]

Nonetheless, the desire to return home does not negate the fact that at present many households have family members employed away from home. As such, it is also crucial to get a sense of what "households" as opposed to "families" look like. If an elderly couple are supported by children who have migrated to the city, but live alone on a daily basis, this certainly seems like an important fact to consider. Therefore, my description of the family system in Moonshadow Pond attempts to take account of "families," as defined in both official and local views, as well as "households," as they are constituted on a daily basis.

What, then, do Moonshadow Pond families and households look like today? As indicated earlier, a majority of families in both 1997 and 2007 were comprised of more than two generations (see table 1). Still, it is important to point out that while the number of families composed of only one or two people was small, it was not insignificant. In 2007, fewer than 10 percent of families consisted of only one or two people, at least when families were defined as including migrants who returned at New Year and who provided support for family members back in Moonshadow Pond. However, when looking at village "households," and only counting as household members those who resided in the village for the entire year, the proportion of one- or two-person households rose to 13.5 percent (see table 2).

These statistics are an important backdrop to our discussion because they give us a sense of the family landscape that Moonshadow Pond residents see when they consider possibilities for themselves. On the one hand, we can see that despite the social and economic transformations in rural China, there are still few elders in Moonshadow Pond who have to fend entirely for themselves. Most elderly are part of larger households. Even the relatively few who live for a good part of the year on their own are still part of a geographically dispersed but economically interdependent family unit. Nonetheless, the fear still exists of being isolated in old age, and there are a few existing examples that give credence to it.

This fear of abandonment has considerable impact on how Moonshadow Pond elderly view family relations. As we shall see later in this chapter, contradictory images of the "daughter-in-law," as either an elder's savior or abuser, often provide a focal point for the expression of these fears. These are traditional images, but the sea change in the rural economic system has actually reinforced them. On the other hand, as we shall see, this same fear of abandonment has also strengthened connections between married daughters and their natal families.

FROM ADOPTED DAUGHTER-IN-LAW
TO MARRIAGE BY CHOICE

Understanding ideas about both daughters and daughters-in-law in Moonshadow Pond first entails a look at the changing nature of marriage. An older woman in Moonshadow Pond who could remember family and marriage before 1949 would certainly portray a system that succeeding generations would have a hard time recognizing. In Meixian, many young women in the first half of the twentieth century were adopted daughters-in-law. They were given away as infants to their future husband's families. Then, on the eve of the Lunar New Year before their eighteenth birthday they would summarily be left to spend the night with their adoptive "brothers." Having grown up as virtual siblings, such couples would feel little sexual attraction. But they had no choice, and for the girl, this was often the only family she had ever known.[26]

The scholarship on the institution of adopted daughters-in-law has emphasized the psychological aspects of the practice, noting that by incorporating the future daughter-in-law into the family as an infant, she would become habituated to the family's way of doing things and thus family harmony would be sustained.[27] Since she and her husband would not have a strong sexual attraction to one another, having grown up as siblings, the mother could be assured of her son's continued loyalty and support.[28] Many older residents of Moonshadow Pond, however, characterized the practice as a response to poverty. They point to the fact that wealthy families married their daughters only after they came of age, and that infant girls were given away to avoid the expense of raising them, a conclusion that the analysts of the *Mei County Gazetteer* also agree with.[29] But there is no doubt that whether intended or not, relationships between an adopted daughter-in-law and her husband were seldom emotionally close. At the same time, her attachments to her husband's family as a whole were strengthened, while her connections with her natal family were minimized.

While the literature on adoptive daughters-in-law often recounts tales of abuse, many of the elderly women with whom I spoke recounted warm feelings toward their adoptive mothers, sometimes heightened by cold relations with their husbands and bitter feelings about their natal families, whom they saw as abandoning them. For instance, Songling's mother, who grew up as an adopted daughter-in-law, felt doubly rejected when in the 1940s her husband, who ran a successful leather business and was one of the richest men in the village, took a second wife in a neighboring county. Many years later she asserted that only her adoptive mother's love and affection supported her in difficult times. "When my mother [adoptive mother] was dying, I wanted to go with her," she told me, "but she reminded me I already had small children to take care of." Another elderly woman told me that she too had very affectionate feelings for her adoptive mother. This woman had at best a negligible relationship with her husband. He migrated to India and came back only twice, during which times they conceived two children. After he returned to India a second time, she never heard from him again.

Prior to Liberation, Moonshadow Pond families with means, as in many other areas of southeast China, preferred to wait for their daughters to reach maturity before arranging a marriage. Such "major marriages" granted families higher status, and were marked by wedding banquets and the fanfare of the bride coming into her husband's household with dowry and other wedding gifts. Families were also able to expand their social network through ties of marriage. But even in the case of major marriage, the new bride and her husband still had little choice in selecting their partner, and by their wedding day, they would barely have had opportunity to lay eyes upon each other. Conjugal intimacy was certainly not a goal.

The marriage law implemented shortly after Liberation stipulated that marriage was to be the choice of the partners involved, and outlawed practices such as infant betrothal.[30] But young people did not all begin choosing their own partners just because there was a new law. Sexual mores and even the idea of young men and women spending time together without inviting scandal took some time to change. Nonetheless, such change did occur over several decades.

By the 1990s, Moonshadow Pond residents categorized marriage arrangements into two basic types, "falling in love" *(lianai)* and "introduction" *(jieshao)*.[31] "Introduction" was the catch-all category used to refer to all those matches where the couple did not meet and fall in love on their own. It included any match that did not get initiated by the couple themselves, whether the match was suggested by parents, other family members, or friends. However, such "introduction" marriages by no means implied the same thing as arranged marriages in traditional society, when the couple might not even see each other until the wedding. By the reform period, plenty of opportunities existed for engaged couples to spend time together, no matter how they had met in the first place. Even premarital sex was not viewed as transgressing any social mores. I attended one rather grand wedding banquet in 1996, for the village doctor's son. The date was advanced because his fiancée was pregnant, and indeed she had been spending most days and nights with his family. When Guizhen, the future mother-in-law, spoke about the reasons for the date change, she did so with a chuckle. "Her stomach is getting big, so it's time for the banquet," she laughed. There was little sense that this was embarrassing or shameful.

Into the 1990s, while the number of "love" marriages in Moonshadow Pond increased among younger cohorts, the real change occurred in the nature of "introduction" marriages and the intimacy of the relationship that was allowed to develop between the engaged partners (see table 3).

When I returned to Moonshadow Pond in 2007, however, I discovered that the expectation of intimacy and choice in mate selection had finally risen to the point where the categories of "introduction" and "love" had collapsed altogether and were no longer used. I was preparing to update my information on families and decided I would categorize the marriages that had taken place since my last stay in the village in 1997. When I started to use the terms "introduction" and "love," people told me it was impossible to distinguish anymore. "Even if you introduce two people," one villager told me, "they have to decide to get to know each other and then fall in love."

The change was dramatically illustrated for me one night in 2007 when

TABLE 3 TYPES OF MATCHES IN MOONSHADOW POND, 1997

Cohort Age	Love	Introduction	Adopted Daughter-in-Law	Unknown	Total
19–30	10 (24%)	31 (76%)	—	—	41
31–45	19 (17%)	93 (83%)	—	—	112
46–65	13 (18%)	59 (82%)	—	—	72
65+	≠3 (4%)	41 (58%)	18 (25%)	9 (13%)	71
Total	45 (15%)	224 (76%)	18 (6%)	9 (3%)	296

Songling and Baoli's neighbor Miaoli came over to the house and started to complain that her son still didn't have a girlfriend. "I cursed him out last night," Miaoli complained, "because he is thirty years old and not interested in getting to know any of the women that people want to introduce him to, and he also doesn't have a girlfriend. He is getting too old, and soon no one will want him, and I'm getting too old, and soon I won't be able to take care of his kids!"

Songling and Baoli laughed behind her back, saying that Miaoli should understand that nowadays children had to "do it themselves" when it came to finding a mate. "Introduction" was now understood as nothing more than helping people meet possible mates. But the people who were introduced had to decide on their own whether to pursue a relationship. Indeed, I found Songling's reactions to Miaoli quite striking, because as we shall see below, she herself had arranged her younger daughter's marriage in the early 1990s. Yet now she was indicating that this was not the way things were done anymore.

Similarly, when I asked my former fourth grade students, now young men and women in their early twenties, about their expectations about marriage, they indicated to me that almost all their classmates already had girlfriends and boyfriends. The idea that someone else would arrange any of this was foreign to them.

Migration for work has also meant that potential mates are not only freely chosen, but may also come from much further away than in the past. In fact, when in 2007 I surveyed Moonshadow Pond families and looked at marriages that had occurred since 1997, I found an increase in marriages with "outsiders" (people who were not from the Meizhou area). Almost one-quarter of the recent marriages were with individuals who were not Hakka and who came from other areas of Guangdong Province or even other provinces. Prior to 1996, this number had been very low.[32]

In the wake of these changes, questions about the conception of family obligations arise again. Is the household still conceived as a multi-generational unit, where obligations to the senior generation are paramount? Or, as discussed above, does the stronger emotional bond between husband and wife inevitably de-emphasize the importance of such obligations? As we shall see below, many of these ideas are sorted out in the discourse about daughters-in-law.

Speaking about Daughters-in-Law

Despite dramatic changes in mating practices, rural parents still have a large stake in who their children marry. Married daughters, a topic we will address in more detail later, no longer play an insignificant role in their natal families. But sons and daughters-in-law are still viewed as the primary sources of long- and short-term financial support and labor assistance in families. The dismantling of the collective system and the new reliance on wage labor has added to feelings of insecurity amongst rural elders. As these feelings intensify, the figure of the daughter-in-law has loomed prominently in parental discourse about their own situations. She may be praised as a wonderful caregiver and hard worker or maligned as the chief culprit in the mistreatment of a helpless older family member.

As a result, the work abilities and personality of a proposed daughter-in-law are still of tremendous importance to parents in Moonshadow Pond, and daughters-in-law are even now viewed as important economic assets to the family. Among middle-aged and older people marriage is still referred to in colloquial speech as "bringing in a daughter-in-law" (*t'au sim k'iu* in Hakka, *qu xifu* in Mandarin). A daughter-in-law is often viewed as the single most significant factor in lightening the workload of a mother-in-law. As Ellen Judd has remarked regarding her research in rural north China, "The arrival of the woman's first daughter-in-law may provide her first substantial relief from a double burden carried through the course of many years, including years of much more difficult economic circumstances."[33]

Indeed, it is not unusual in Moonshadow Pond for families to refer to their present good fortune as springing directly from the diligence and hard work of a daughter-in-law. I remember my first visit to Aihua's house in 1995. As we sat down and Aihua and her husband offered me tea, her husband exclaimed, "See my new house, we wouldn't have it without my second daughter-in-law." Aihua's two sons both worked extremely hard. Guofei, the younger son, was a butcher. Each day, he would rise in the

PHOTOGRAPH 6. "Bringing in a daughter-in-law." Bride, groom, and mother-in-law welcome guests to a wedding, 1996.

middle of the night to slaughter a pig. By early morning he would be selling the meat. His brother Guobin tended fishponds. Yet Aihua's husband, Uncle Wei, considered his second daughter-in-law's unceasing work tending the family's agricultural plots, helping her husband with his business, and literally laying the bricks of their house to be critical factors in enabling the family to prosper.

Contrastingly, bad fortune may also be blamed on a daughter-in-law. Aihua often lamented the economic difficulties of her first son. "He can do anything," she once told me. But, she would add, his wife was not as capable or hardworking as her second son's wife, and worse still she was an inveterate gambler. This was clearly the reason, according to Aihua, that her eldest son had not prospered. When I returned to Moonshadow Pond ten years later, the situation had only worsened, and Aihua's disappointment with her eldest daughter-in-law had only intensified. By that time, her eldest son was one of the few members of Team 2 who still had not built a new house, although he had procured land on the highway to do so. Although this son had expanded his operations from fish farming to include pig raising as well, she asserted that it was impossible for him to prosper without the help of his wife and that all his earnings were just gambled away.

Another frequently cited example of a daughter-in-law who helped bring her family good fortune was the doctor's wife, Guizhen. This family had other sources of income as well—through her husband's work as village doctor and their business selling medicines. Guizhen learned midwifery from her own mother-in-law and was viewed as partly responsible for their exalted economic status in the village, since she brought much extra income into the family.

Middle-aged women in Moonshadow Pond yearn for a daughter-in-law even if they themselves did not have to shoulder these burdens when they were younger. For instance, Songling had avoided the fate of being a daughter-in-law in her own Maoist era marriage. Nor was her own marriage an arranged one, but a love match. She was stirred by Baoli's determination to marry her despite her bad class status. When they married in 1964, they set up a household of their own, without an elder generation to serve or support. (Baoli's father had recently died, and his mother was living in Burma with Baoli's eldest brother.)

Songling and Baoli's marriage really did pivot around the relationship of husband and wife, the kind of conjugal union envisioned by the new marriage law of 1950. While some villagers caustically commented that Baoli was too compliant to Songling's wishes, the fact was that their relationship was not unique in Moonshadow Pond. This did not prevent Songling, in the mid-1990s, from looking ahead to the day she would have her own daughter-in-law to relieve her of some of the burden of housework and agricultural work (her son finally did marry in 1998).

At the same time, while mothers-in-law (or expectant mothers-in-law) still desire the help of their sons' wives, they recognize that they cannot assert their power over them in the "feudal" ways of the "old society." Daughters-in-law now openly articulate their own demands—what they expect in return for the important help they provide for their husband's families. Many daughters-in-law expect that childcare will be the primary responsibility of the grandparents, and, indeed, this is frequently the case in Moonshadow Pond. While parents go out to work, for wages or in the fields, one usually sees young children with grandparents, male and female.

Songling's own case is a good example. Though she spent much of the 1990s yearning for a daughter-in-law, in the end her workload remained heavy even after her son finally did marry. Songling's daughter-in-law, Lianfang, traveled to the county capital daily for her factory job, so Songling took care of her grandson before he was old enough to go to school. Later, after he started school, she began taking care of her younger daughter's baby, since this daughter was also busy from dawn to dusk running her business in town. Likewise, Weiguo, the villager who had prospered with his cigarette factory job and who was now retired, told me one day in 2007, "My new job now is taking care of my grandson." He could be seen every day with the young boy while his son and daughter-in-law went out to work for pay.

Young women can now watch out for their own interests in ascertaining information about potential in-laws. The older generation is not unaware of this and as such, bringing a daughter-in-law into the household is an event now laden with a great deal of contradictory emotional freight. There are the age-old concerns about integrating a new person into the family and about competition between the mother-in-law and the daughter-in-law for the son's affections. But there is also a new awareness about the expectations of daughters-in-law themselves.[34]

For instance, Songling once said to me, "Nowadays young people are different from before. They don't want to marry into a household with in-laws who can't work. They'll ask, 'Does this house have a lot of *feipin* [literally "scraps, waste, or rejects"] around?' If it does, they won't even dream of marrying into that household."

Since few rural people are like Weiguo and his brother Jieguo, both of whom retired from waged jobs with pensions, elders perceive their dependence on their adult children for support as a lack of power. Of course, in the collective period this was also true. But at that time, the collective provided all its members with at least a basic grain ration. Now, elders express the idea that they are at the mercy of the younger generation. Songling often talked about a pension as the most desirable thing one could ever attain in life, because then you could be independent. And Aihua frequently lamented the precariousness of her own situation. Her younger son was burdened with school fees for his two sons, and her elder son was poor. She often had to listen to her younger son make veiled remarks about his older brother, who was unable to contribute to the support of their parents. In the eighth decade of her life, this once vibrant and physically active former team leader often had a look of dejection about her.

Aihua even grumbled about her younger and more favored daughter-in-law, despite all the work she did for the family, including growing and harvesting all their rice and vegetables. "My daughter-in-law gripes if I don't swab down the floors of the house every day," she would say. "She'll say that other mothers-in-laws are better than me because they help out more. Both of my daughters-in-law forget that I raised all four of their children!"

A frequent complaint of elders is to say that you have to work constantly for your children in the hopes that they will take care of you later on. The most envied seniors in the village were the few who did have pensions. Songling once said to me, "If you have a pension you have power, otherwise [the younger generation will think that] you are useless!"

In truth, it sometimes seemed to me that the workload for all to complete was simply very high and it inevitably lead to each party feeling they were being used by the other. In the case of Aihua's family, for instance, her son would rise at three in the morning to slaughter a pig every day. By 5:30 AM, he and his wife had to have the cuts of pork ready to sell for villagers. During this time, Aihua was often expected to help out by getting breakfast and by going to the river to do the laundry. Even though she was less energetic and clearly suffering from arthritis when I returned to the village in 2007, this morning ritual remained the same. Likewise, Songling would often complain that her daughter-in-law was not helping enough. From an outsider's perspective, it was hard to see how she could do more, given that she worked full time in a factory.

Men's shifting roles, a topic we deal with below, also exacerbate tensions between mothers and daughters-in-law, since many domestic and agricultural chores still fall primarily to women. When there is a family squabble, however, outside observers in the village are still more likely to blame the daughter-in-law. Everyone knows at least one story of an older person, such as Meirong, who was discussed in the last chapter, who eats alone or is not supported by a son or sons. There are also stories of older people who leave their son's homes due to discord with a daughter-in-law and who come to live with an adult daughter's family—an arrangement that is still not considered ideal. Such was the situation with Baoli's nephew, whose wife's mother was living with them.

Stories of severe discord between mother and daughter-in-law are therefore still common. While I was in the village in the winter of 2007, a story circulated about a family in the village where tensions apparently broke into violence, as one of the daughters-in-law actually beat her mother-in-law. Finally, several village officials came to mediate and help settle matters, but not before the mother-in-law had been seriously bruised. Such stories were hardly representative of a statistical norm, but they expressed the fears of many elderly people about what might be possible and about their feelings of helplessness at the hands of the younger generation.

Even in cases where people recognize that the daughter-in-law is not always the party at fault in a family dispute, they may still voice disapproval if she complains about her in-laws too publicly. For instance, Miaoli (who was introduced in chapter 1) was an energetic middle-aged woman who had a close kin connection to Songling and Baoli. She was hardworking (qinlao), a quality highly prized in Hakka women, and so most villagers liked her, though they also considered her to be both intentionally and unintentionally comic at times. Villagers also said that Miaoli and her husband had "good feelings" for each other. Her husband had a mild temperament, and they both helped each other in their work. In fact, they had built many of the new houses in the village. It was not unusual to pass Miaoli laying bricks as she built an addition to someone's home, or to see her harvesting rice or planting vegetables. She was typically in constant motion.

"If you want to interview someone, interview me!" she said to me one day in 1995. She was all too eager to spill out her tale of woe regarding her relations with her mother-in-law. "She always beats me and curses me. Sometimes she tells my husband that he can get another wife."

I asked her if she really meant beatings.

"Yes," she asserted, "she'll beat me, or take food away from me while I'm eating, or come and pull my hair."

Miaoli added that her father-in-law had not treated her well either. However, she said, when Baoli's brother came to visit from Taiwan, he urged Miaoli's father-in-law to treat Miaoli better, and the father-in-law reformed himself. "But my mother-in-law has *not* changed. When she returns home at night, she bangs the door loudly."

I asked Miaoli about her husband's younger brother's divorce. She replied that her sister-in-law used to quarrel with her parents-in-law, especially about money for her children's studies. Tensions rose in the house and soon she and her husband started to quarrel.

"One day, his parents drove her away. They said, 'In the morning he has this wife, in the afternoon he can marry another wife.' But it's already been three years and no one wants to marry him. No one wants to marry him because he is a gambling devil and also because *no one would want in-laws like that.*"

I asked how the divorced wife gets by.[35]

"She is fine because her eldest daughter works in Guangzhou and supports herself working in a garment factory. She has only to support herself and also works in a factory."

"But don't people look down on your sister-in-law now?" I queried.

"Of course they look down on her! If your household is constantly arguing and you're not prosperous either, then people will look down on you. But it wasn't her fault. She had a bad mother-in-law and father-in-law. If everyone in your house gets along and you are doing well, people will look up to you."

Miaoli continued, "Some people are lucky! Guizhen has a good mother-in-law. She taught her how to deliver babies. Guizhen delivered my daughter. Aihua is also a good mother-in-law, and her daughters-in-law are fortunate. These people must have done something really good in a past life, because they have such good mothers-in-law! I do everything, I harvest the rice, I build houses, but they don't appreciate it."

Miaoli's tale of mother-in-law woe was the exception in Moonshadow Pond, noted precisely because her relations with her mother-in-law were particularly bad, and not because they were considered in any way typical. Nonetheless, despite the changes in power relations between generations, there is still a sense that it is wrong to complain publicly about one's in-laws, as Miaoli did to me. Indeed, as she delivered her story, her friend Yuping listened in. At the end of the story, Yuping pointed to her own face. She told Miaoli that it was not good to speak that way, even if one's mother-in-law was truly bad.

"They are still *ziji ren*," she said. (The use of the term *ziji ren* is interesting here. In Moonshadow Pond, as in many other Chinese villages, this term refers to people related through patrilineal descent. But women usually marry out of their lineage into another one. So when a woman who has married into her husband's village speaks of *ziji ren*, which literally means "one's own people," she is actually speaking of her husband's lineage.)

Yuping continued, "It's not good to talk about your mother-in-law this way. You will not have *mianzi*."

Yuping then spoke about her relationship with her own mother-in-law. She said she was also not treated well by her. But, said Yuping, she didn't talk back, even when her mother-in-law was in the wrong, and when her mother-in-law lay on her deathbed, she finally said some very good things to her.

Yuping was articulating a very old attitude here, symbolized in many proverbs such as "Endure a small amount of humiliation and avoid one hundred days of worry" *(rende yishi zhi qi, miande baitian zhi you)* and "If you can endure humiliation, you will prosper" *(ren qi liu cai, shou qi de fu)*. Needless to say, these are attitudes that upheld hierarchical gender and class orders, and Yuping's use of them was not singular. While the younger generation might speak of elders who did not help them as "waste," these ideas coexist with an older discourse about endurance and submission of younger to older.[36]

The exact balance of these ideas is subtle and situational. For instance, on one occasion I went with Songling to meet with her friend Qiaomei, a resident of Moonshadow Pond who was not in Team 2. Songling told me how Qiaomei had fallen in love with a man who was seven years younger than she. After they married, her mother-in-law would criticize her, and when Qiaomei did things in the house that the mother-in-law did not like, she would insult Qiaomei by saying she was too old. "She cried in private and wiped her tears and didn't talk back," Songling recounted. Eventually, she said, Qiaomei's mother-in-law had a change of heart.

In accounts such as these, it is the ability to withstand criticism without complaint that ultimately is seen as creating power for the daughter-in-law. She gains respect and thus power through her virtuous qualities of patience and forbearing. An interesting example of the persistence of this way of understanding daughter-in-law virtue occurred in 2007, when a friend of Songling and Baoli came by to invite them to her son's wedding. The couple had already legally registered their marriage and were living together in the extended family. Now the wedding banquet would finally take place. (This delay between legally registering a marriage and celebrating it in a wedding banquet is discussed later in the chapter, and is now common because of the cost of wedding celebrations.)

On the day Songling's friend came to the house with the invitation, I asked her about her new daughter-in-law. Her vivid account of her daughter-in-law's natal family made it clear that she thought the daughter-in-law was marrying "up."

"All they do is gamble all day," she said of her daughter-in-law's natal family. "They come from a very poor area of Guangdong, and they will even sell one egg just to get more money to gamble!" Expanding further on just how uncultured the family was, she also asserted that her daughter-in-law's father had two wives, and that her daughter-in-law was very happy to be moving in with a new family because her own family was so poor.

As I heard this explanation, I was reminded of a traditional pattern of marriage in China in which women characteristically married into a higher-status family (hypergamy). The bride's lower status vis-à-vis her husband's family reinforced her less powerful position in his family.

When I asked Songling's friend how she liked her new daughter-in-law, she answered without embarrassment and with the forceful delivery and direct style of many middle-aged Hakka women. "Oh, she is somewhat shy," she said, "but if you curse her out, she doesn't mind. Her personality is good!"

Examples such as these demonstrate that despite the fact that a couple might make their own choice about whom to marry and be intimate with each other long before the wedding date, they are often still marrying into a larger family where the virtue of the daughter-in-law will be evaluated by her ability to demur politely to the senior generation.

However, this was not the way all daughter-in-law situations were understood or interpreted. For instance, Guizhen, who was mentioned earlier and much admired as a midwife and hard worker, was no longer "diplomatic" with her mother-in-law. One day in 1996 she came by the house and said, "The old Guizhen would endure others' bullying [shou ren de qi], but the new Guizhen won't do that any longer!"

After she left, I queried others about this. How was Guizhen viewed? Songling and Aihua immediately chimed in, saying that Guizhen could assert herself because she had her own income (as a midwife). Also, people generally felt Guizhen's mother-in-law was not always easy to live with or reasonable. Their lack of criticism of Guizhen contrasted with Yuping's advice to Miaoli to silently endure her mother-in-law and earn respect the old way.

In looking for an explanation for the difference between the two approaches to Miaoli and Guizhen, I could find only two possibilities. First, Guizhen was a more highly respected person in the village at large. All women in the village talked about her as the person who had delivered their babies. Second, the different attitude toward Guizhen may also have been because women thought that Guizhen had already paid her dues as a respectful daughter-in-law. Many villagers said that Guizhen's mother-in-law had always looked down on Guizhen's natal family because they were very poor. Villagers said that when Guizhen initially married, her mother-in-law would lock up any nice clothes she had, and if she wanted to go out, she would have to ask her mother-in-law for the clothes. Still, Guizhen would not talk back to her mother-in-law. Quite to the contrary, said one village woman, she would respond to complaints by asking, "Would you like some eggs?" (In those days eggs were expensive and a special treat.) Whether these stories were true or not, they portrayed Guizhen as a very respectful daughter-in-law who did not let her mother-in-law's difficult demands frazzle her.

As such, there were a number of different formulations available in talking about how to be a daughter-in-law. Villagers chose the more traditional formulation in giving advice to Miaoli, but were more charitable in their evaluation of Guizhen. Ironically, though Miaoli had a history of trouble as a daughter-in-law, by 2007 her most ardent wish was for her own son to marry, in part so that she could have some help with her own work and some security in old age.

Considering Daughters

The contradictory discourse about roles and responsibilities of daughters-in-law emphasizes many old themes about the virtues of respectful submission. Ironically, these themes may have been fortified by dramatic changes in daughters' relations with their natal families during both the Maoist and reform periods.

Traditionally, when a daughter left her natal family for marriage, her responsibilities shifted to her husband's family. Infant betrothal, of course, minimized a daughter's relationship with her natal family even more. In Meixian it was colloquially referred to as "borrowing breast milk" *(jie ru wei)* since it implied that a mother would breastfeed someone else's daughter after giving away her own. Not surprisingly, daughters sent off in this fashion usually had minimal and unsatisfactory relations with their natal families. Songling's mother, for instance, would still return to her natal family each year for a New Year's meal, even though she had been sent off as an infant bride to her husband's family. But she spoke of being extremely resentful of (*hen si*, or literally "hating to death") her birth mother for giving her away.

Before the 1940s, even if a girl in Moonshadow Pond did not become an infant bride, she was unlikely to grow up in her natal family. Some girls were originally brought into families as adopted daughters-in-law, but for some reason relations between them and their future husband were poor. These girls (called *huadun mei*) labored hard within their adoptive families and were ultimately married off by them. Much worse was the fate of *binü*, young girls brought into families as indentured servants. In the Hong Kong region, they might eventually be married off. But in Meixian, it was more common for them to remain unmarried. Sometimes they adopted a child after being released by their masters.[37]

None of these girls received any education. "If you wanted to learn to read," Aihua told me, "then you had to be given up to a monastery to become a nun. I always envied them, because they were the only girls who were sent to school." Uncle Li, a former schoolteacher, remembers teaching in the village elementary school in the early 1930s. "There were over one hundred students in the school," he said, "but only one or two girls."

Even before Liberation, the 1940s marked the beginning of gradual changes as more girls began to attend school in the village, and infant betrothal waned. Nonetheless, as previously indicated, Liberation brought an abrupt end to many practices. Not only was infant betrothal outlawed, but also familial servitude. Girls who were living with families as *huadun mei* or *binü* became overnight "sisters." Songling had one "sister" who had been brought into her family as a *binü*. As far as I could tell, as an adult she was included in family affairs and rituals equally with other adult siblings, including the work of mourning family members at funerals.

But changes in daughters' roles did not end in the first few years after Liberation. During the collective era, for instance, both girls and boys in Moonshadow Pond were sent to primary school in equal numbers, and both helped in collective agriculture outside of school. Still, during the collective era girls and their mothers always spent extra time provisioning for their families outside of their work for the collective. Skinny Hong's daughter Ailing said to me one day, "I had five brothers, so I had a lot of work to do. I had to go several times a day to the stream to get water, and I had to go up the hills to get kindling for cooking." She went on to recount how her brothers did not work equally as hard because they did fewer household chores.

Nevertheless, economic, technological, and ultimately cultural changes during the collective era slowly began to alter the childhood experiences of girls. For instance, the necessity of gathering kindling ended in the mid-seventies, when village families began to purchase blocks of coal for cooking. And the first wells were dug in the late 1980s, reducing the need for water carrying. After the reform era, girls rarely engaged in physical labor around the village for their natal families.

The changing birth control policy in rural Guangdong must also be taken into account in evaluating daughter's roles. During the 1990s, rural families were allowed to have two children, but after 2000 the policy was changed. Now, if the first child is a boy, the family is not allowed to have any more children, while if the first child is a girl, a second child is allowed. The present policy privileges the idea that in rural Guangdong, sons are still more likely to reside with their parents after marriage, and are therefore necessary for old age security. Nonetheless, we should not lose sight of the other obvious fact—with one or at most two children, parents must look to all of them for future security. As we explain below, married daughters are playing a greater role in helping their natal families than in the past. I never heard villagers articulate the traditional idea that educating or investing in a daughter is wasteful because she will leave the family at marriage. A successful daughter, even after marriage, can now be a great boon to a family.

Both boys and girls in Moonshadow Pond now study at least through lower middle school since the first nine years of education are compulsory in China. But if a child has not tested well, the cost of continuing to study beyond this is exorbitant. In these cases, families are often asked to give extra money to insure admission, a cost which is impossible for many rural families to shoulder.[38] A family may decide that if their child is not interested in studying anyway, it is not worthwhile to continue educating him or her. But if a child shows promise and does well enough on exams to pay the lower admission fee, then the sex of the child is irrelevant.[39]

Options for boys and girls are not nearly as different as those that existed even a few decades ago. Academically successful children of both sexes are encouraged to study. Others, whether they are boys or girls, will usually start working after completing lower middle school. The experiences of students from my 1996 fourth-grade primary-school class are illustrative. When I returned to Moonshadow Pond in 2007, I found that ten of them were already working, while two of them (one young man and one young woman) were in college. Four of the students remained in Meixian, and were able to find local jobs, while the rest had migrated to larger cities. The young men's jobs included working as cooks specializing in Hakka food, as drivers, and as guards at banks. The young women worked as hostesses in restaurants, in clothing factories, in stores, or in one case at a day-care center.

It was hard to see that the parents of these young adults had invested any more or less in their daughters or their sons. Further, the experience of working for a wage has given daughters both more voice in their natal families, as well as more independence from them if they choose. Ailing is an example of the latter trend. She already had teenage children in 2007. But during the 1980s, she was amongst the first group of female labor migrants from the village. What motivated her to leave the village in the first instance was her dissatisfaction with her role as daughter at home. As we mentioned above, she had grown up in the collective era and shouldered more work domestically than her five brothers. Escaping from this situation and earning money for oneself was an attractive, new and somewhat dramatic possibility at that time.

Indeed, the practice of migrating to urban areas was so new at that time that Ailing's parents did not actually want her to leave home. Ailing ran away from home in the middle of the night and didn't write to her family for a long time. In her view, her escape to Shenzhen allowed her to earn good money in a factory making wigs, a skill she had learned from a teacher and of which she was quite proud. Later, Ailing fell in love with another young man from Moonshadow Pond who would take trips down to Shenzhen in his work as a driver. They finally returned home to the village and married there. Ailing took satisfaction in the fact that she paid for her wedding clothes and many other items in the wedding by herself, and since her marriage she has continued to work as a teacher's aide in a nearby village school.

While Ailing's work experience gave her more independence from her natal family, daughters' new work roles can also enhance their influence in their natal families, strengthening their connections after marriage. For instance, as mentioned in the last chapter, Songling's daughter Fengying had worked in a sneaker factory for many years before her marriage and she had used her money to help Songling and Baoli build their new house. They acknowledged her help openly and talked about it as a factor in continuing to take her advice on family issues.

On one occasion in 1996, I witnessed an incident in Songling's family that underscored the way married daughters can now weigh in heavily on a family matter. Their brother Yanhong had migrated to Guangzhou for a job as a cook during my stay in Moonshadow Pond. The pay was somewhat better than he received for his work in the county capital. But the conditions were grueling—he had to prepare meals for forty workers and twelve managers each day. Twenty workers shared one bathroom and there were long waits at night in order to bathe. After a few days, Yanhong could bear it no longer. He packed his bags and returned to the village. Both his sisters, Fengying and Meiying, swept down on the family when they heard the news.

"My brother needs to learn how to put up with hardship," Fengying asserted. "I've had experience working, I've had to go out and labor, I know what it is like!" Indeed, by the next day, Yanhong had gathered his belongings and was back on the bus to Guangzhou. Interestingly, this incident occurred before Fengying had really established herself as a successful businesswoman. As the years went on, she was able to help her natal family more, but in turn they were also more obligated to her (a topic we will later explore in more detail).

It should be stated that even in traditional society, married daughters' connections with their natal families were never completely negligible.[40] They returned for visits during New Year and provided their natal families with new alliances. Such links through married daughters were always viewed as assets. Families without daughters still may see themselves as relatively more circumscribed. As Aihua said to me one day, "We don't have any daughters, so the only contacts we can use are through our daughters-in-law."

Songling's family, in contrast, was a good example of one in which contacts through married daughters played a dominant role. Unlike the traditional model, interaction between Songling and her married daughters was constant and not limited to the return for Lunar New Year. The families into which Songling's daughters married contained many layers of pre-existing relationships with their natal family. Younger daughter Fengying married a relative who shared a great grandfather with her (since he was on the maternal side, they were not in the same lineage). This was an "introduction" marriage from the early 1990s that Songling had arranged. She thought that Fengying would receive good treatment in her new home if she married into a family that had a connection with her. Songling also liked the idea that the new in-laws were a merchant family, thus ensuring that her daughter would not have a life in agriculture.

By contrast, the marriage of Songling and Baoli's older daughter, Meiying, was a love marriage. But her husband's father was Big Gao, a man who was Baoli's closest friend in the village, and their families therefore shared many connections long before Meiying's marriage. For instance, Baoli was the "dry son" of Big Gao's own mother-in-law, a ritualized relationship that entailed no material responsibilities on Baoli's part, but required him to mourn this adoptive mother as a son at her funeral.[41] Further, one of Big Gao's daughters, Small Gao, ran a rice-threshing business with Baoli.

In both cases, there has been ongoing contact between Songling and her married daughters. Songling has helped care for all her daughters' children, and at other times her daughters have come by to help their mother. I particularly remember a flood in the summer of 1997. The houses in Moonshadow Pond were inundated by water as high as two to three feet on the first floors. As soon as the water had begun to recede, both daughters arrived at the house to help clean up.

While the great variety of connections between Songling, Baoli, and their affines may be unusual in their scope, their continuing relationship with their married daughters is not unusual in Moonshadow Pond. Stories of married daughters who help their parents range from daughters who have purchased automobiles for their parents or helped them gather money to build a new house to married daughters who took in a parent after alleged abuse by a son or daughter-in-law. It is not surprising, therefore, that comments like "Nowadays, a daughter is as good as a son, and may help you more," are not uncommon. One villager said to me, "Daughters are as likely to help you as sons now, and they cost less to marry" (since the major wedding expenses are shouldered by the groom's side).

The closer connections with married daughters and the help they provide their parents, however, can also create additional sets of obligations for these parents. We have already discussed how Songling cared for both her son and daughters' young children. By 2007, Songling was in her early sixties, and the physical exhaustion of taking care of toddlers was starting to show. She would not infrequently complain about her younger daughter's own mother-in-law, who did not help with this task because she was herself busy caring for her ailing husband. Nonetheless, after spending a particularly tiring day with her boundlessly energetic two-year-old granddaughter, Songling would wistfully say that it was impossible to turn down her daughters' requests for help. After all, she said, she and Baoli had no pension and they knew they would need to rely on all their grown children as they aged.

Despite these important links between married daughters and their parents, however, patrilocal residence in the majority of cases means that ultimately there are still time and financial limits to the assistance daughters give their parents. There *are* a few cases in the village of married daughters and their husbands actually living with the daughter's parents. These usually occur when all the sons have migrated and there is no one to take care of the parents. Nonetheless, when parents reside with married daughters, these arrangements are understood as ad hoc and temporary. Further, the number of marriages in which a man not only moves into his wife's household, but also takes her surname, is still very low. I knew only of one such family in Moonshadow Pond. In this case, there were seven daughters and no sons in the family. (They were all born before the onset of the birth control policies of the reform era.) One of these daughters remained at home, her husband married "in," and the children took the mother's surname. Older villagers were dismissive when they spoke about this marriage, pointing out that whenever the mother-in-law was dissatisfied with the son-in-law she would put him down by saying he changed his name.

Such uxorilocal marriages in Meixian were traditionally characterized in negative ways. Colloquially, they were compared to wrapping an egg in a blade of grass. The idea here is that the egg will quickly fall out of the blade of grass and break. This precariousness was viewed as natural precisely because no one thought a man would submit to in-laws in the way a woman was expected to submit as a daughter-in-law. Another customary way of characterizing these marriages was to say that a woman who remained in her natal family after marriage did not know shame. A slang expression still used to categorize the daughter who stays in her natal home after marriage, rather than marrying into her husband's family, is to call her a "woman who moves in the wrong direction" *(daotou ma)*.

Hence, the changing role of daughters has not diminished the idea that "bringing in a daughter-in-law" is still the most respectable course of action in a family's life history. Daughters-in-law are still looked to by middle-aged women as a way to address a shortage of household labor. And the changed role of unmarried daughters has actually accentuated this felt need, since, as mentioned earlier, daughters no longer contribute to domestic work. After all, if parents hope their daughters will be in a position to help their natal families, even after marriage, then burdening them with household work in their childhood will only impede this long-range goal—since a daughter who spends her childhood laboring inside the house is unlikely to develop the skills she will need to succeed economically in the future. Hence, it is not surprising that in this context, middle-aged women begin to imagine a daughter-in-law as a great boon to their own workload at home.

One day in 1997 Songling took me to meet her friend Lijia. "You really need a daughter-in-law," Lijia said to her. Then she added humorously, "Once you have a daughter-in-law you won't have to work so hard anymore and you can have a life like mine, playing cards and mahjong!"

On the way home, Songling said to me, "Lijia's own son is already married and he has three children and Yanhong is still not married."[42]

In fact, Yanhong's marriage in 1998 did not result in the imagined life of card playing and mahjong for Songling. As we have seen, Songling instead raised all her grandchildren as they came along, and was still raising the youngest of these in 2007. Her own daughter-in-law helped when she was home, but she worked full-time in a clothing factory in the county capital, and was gone from morning until early evening every day.

In the end, the overwhelming importance of marriage in village life has not been diminished, nor has the idea of the daughter-in-law as a long awaited helper for an overworked middle-aged woman. But the reality is becoming more complicated.

Men Retreat from Agriculture

What are the men doing while middle-aged women dream of daughters-in-law who will help them at home? First, it would be wrong to portray men as not contributing to household labor at all. Childcare for young children is not performed only by grandmothers, but by grandfathers as well. One sees elderly men in Moonshadow Pond with small toddlers, even if not as frequently as one sees women in this role. Men now also help with cooking, and some village men are excellent cooks. In a survey of the food practices of thirty-five village families that I conducted in 2007, I found that men cooked at least some meals in one-third of the families.

Nonetheless, middle-aged women are still responsible for the bulk of domestic chores, as well as agricultural tasks that relate to subsistence—tending to rice fields and vegetable plots. Those men who continue in agriculture do so as a business—contracting fishponds and orchards to sell the produce, or charging for the use of specialized machinery for seasonal tasks such as plowing and threshing. Other men seek wage employment outside the village or run small businesses within it. Village women, too, may engage in some of these activities, such as raising fruit trees. However, while a village woman cultivating tangerines would also likely be responsible for washing her family's laundry, one never sees a man washing clothes.

Indeed, a major shift in the sexual division of labor has occurred since the beginning of the reform era. During the collective era, men labored for work points in agriculture just as women did. But this participation in intensive agricultural work was the odd pattern—sandwiched between very different sexual divisions of labor in the pre-Communist and the post-Mao era. Many villagers said that in the old society, Hakka men were reluctant to take part in everyday agricultural tasks. They might help plant and plow, but the daily maintenance of crops was done by women. Many local men migrated overseas to Southeast Asia or India, leaving the women to take charge of agricultural production. People liked to quote an old Hakka rhyme, "Father earns the cash flow while Mother plants and hoes" *(Nanba zhuanqian, mama gengtian)*.

Only during the collective era did most Moonshadow Pond men work full-time in the fields. But many women still remember men as less than perfect farmers. Of the six production teams in Moonshadow Pond, three of them were headed by women. Aihua had been the head of Team 2. She frequently joked about the days when she had to get everyone out to work.

"The men would limp along and I'd have to shout, 'This doesn't even resemble work!' just to get them moving," she reminisced one day. And, she added, the small private plots retained for each household during most of the collective years were also cultivated mainly by women.

The breakup of the collectives spelled the end of most men's participation in subsistence agriculture. Meiying's husband, Shaowen, explained his family's thinking with regard to rice cultivation in this way: "If you earn a good wage, it is almost as cheap to buy rice as to cultivate it, because the inputs for rice cultivation are so expensive. However, since my mother doesn't work for a wage, it is worth it for her to cultivate rice." So, while other family members work for wages, Shaowen's mother cultivates each and every family member's parcel of land to grow rice for the entire family.

Scholars who have examined economic reform in China have found diverse effects on family structure. The dismantling of the collective system of agriculture has resulted in different outcomes.[43] In one town, women may return entirely to the domestic sphere, while in another, women have started a variety of rural enterprises.[44] In other areas, agricultural work may become increasingly feminized, and in more highly industrialized rural settings other patterns may prevail, such as the hiring of migrant labor.[45]

However, in Moonshadow Pond, both domestic work and subsistence agriculture have fallen mainly into the hands of middle-aged married women. It is not surprising that these same women hope they will be assisted in this work by their daughters-in-law.

The "Price" of Daughters-in-Law

The rising "price" of marriage for the groom's side has been noted in many areas of rural China.[46] It has led to something called "spatial hypergamy" by the demographer William Lavely, the phenomenon in which the men from the poorest, most remote villages are at the bottom of the marriage totem pole and have a very difficult time finding brides to marry.[47] Earlier, I gave examples of hypergamy, showing how it contributes to a daughter-in-law's initial lack of power upon marriage into her new family, since she comes from a relatively lower-status family. But there is another side to this, because it also means that families have to create conditions where a young woman will view her move to their family as an advantageous one and truly a "step up."

From the point of view of senior generations, this translates into a very

PHOTOGRAPH 7. Bride and groom joke with friends at 2007 wedding. A traditional part of the wedding is friends' teasing of the bride and groom. Note that the second story of this house has been almost completed in time for the wedding.

simple idea—acquiring a daughter-in-law is an expensive proposition (a predicament alluded to in the exchange that begins this chapter). While young people may marry for "love," the implication here is that a young woman may be quickly turned off and fall out of love if she discovers she might be marrying into a home without good conditions. Of course, Moonshadow Pond is neither a poor nor a remote village, as it is located in a valley and near the county capital. Nonetheless, the cost of marriage is still rising as each family has to make the best case possible for their future daughter-in-law. Indeed, when the bricks for a second or third floor start to be added to a house, it is often a good indicator that a marriage is soon to take place.

"During the collective era everyone just worked for work points," Aihua once told me. "You didn't have to wait long to get married since everyone was doing the same thing."

By the time a young man during the collective era was twenty-five, there was little doubt about his future. But now, Aihua pointed out, life-long employment was no longer a certainty, so people had to establish themselves economically before they could contemplate marriage. Hence, in the postreform era, there were still several men in the village who had reached the ripe old age of thirty, or even older, who remained unmarried. Most of these men had shifted from job to job, had gambled excessively, or had gotten into trouble borrowing money they could not pay back. They were looked upon by villagers as lazy, unsuccessful, and therefore unmarriageable.

Still, one might ask, if young women do not want to work in agriculture, and if they have more control over their own lives, why do they want to return to village life to get married at all? One answer to this question is that being married is still the most acceptable way to be integrated into the community as an adult. (In chapter 4, I discuss one exception, the devout Buddhist Bright Ling. But she stands out precisely as an exception.) Furthermore, having children is considered a necessity for both economic reasons (support in old age) and cosmological ones (support in the afterlife). And though one could conceivably meet these requirements as a single parent, no one views this as a desirable alternative to marriage. Even if one marries "up" and away from agriculture, marriage itself is still viewed as a given. Nonetheless, even if marriage is still viewed as the only ultimate option for adulthood, young women earning their own income can still afford to wait and decide what conditions would be best. Hence, "competition" for brides can also be seen as another factor in the inflation behind the cost of marriage for the groom's side.

Aside from a bride's rising expectations about living conditions, such as a new house provided by the groom, several other expenses are shouldered by the groom's family during the course of a marriage. Traditionally, the groom's side would send food items and the three sacrificial offerings of chicken, pork, and fish to the bride's family. In addition, the groom's family sent money to the bride's side (sometimes called "bride price"). These funds were understood as a "thank you" to the bride's family for raising her, but in Hakka culture they were used by the bride's side to invite guests to a banquet the day before the wedding. If the bride's family was very well off, they also would send the bride away to join her husband's family with gifts, cash, and jewelry.

By 2007, however, the sacrificial offerings and food from the groom's side had been dispensed with altogether, but the cash payment to the bride's side had risen dramatically. Songling remembered that when her eldest daughter married in the late 1980s, her family received 299 *yuan*. (One *yuan* [or Chinese dollar] is always held back in the belief that a full payment might be inauspicious and prevent the bride from actually leaving her natal family.) By 2006, one Moonshadow Pond family received 9,999 *yuan* when their daughter was to be married. The bride's family was very well connected to the township government and the groom's family also very wealthy, so this was much more than family's of ordinary means could afford. Nonetheless, these figures give a sense of the inflationary pressures on "bride price." For the groom's family and the bride's family, this expense is another status enhancing element of the wedding. The ability to pay and to receive a higher "price" enhances the status of both sides.

Finally, wedding festivities themselves have assumed a more elaborate character with each passing year. In the past, grand spectacles were out of reach for most peasants in Moonshadow Pond, and many marriages had no banquets or display at all, since they were based on infant betrothal. In the first few years after 1949, extravagant spending on weddings was criticized as a remnant of the old society, and in the early 1950s, shortened rituals followed by small banquets were common. Aihua remembers her wedding of 1956, which was followed by a banquet of four tables. (Moonshadow Pond tables are square and seat eight people each). By the Great Leap Forward even simple banquets were dispensed with. But banqueting on a small scale reemerged in Moonshadow Pond by the mid-1960s, although these usually comprised just a few tables.

Then in the reform period, a great escalation of banqueting occurred, partly as a result of increased prosperity and also due to the generally looser attitude toward traditional customs. Ironically, this marks the first time in history that a cultural ideal practiced by those at the top of the rural class structure—large wedding banquets—has become a widespread status marker for all.

While I was in Moonshadow Pond, I attended a number of weddings and also watched videos of several others. In January of 1996 I observed two weddings. The larger banquet was for Weiguo's son. Weiguo, as we mentioned in the last chapter, had a good paying job as a guard in the cigarette factory at the county capital. His son's wedding banquet consisted of thirty-eight tables. Because the banquet was held at noon in the village, however, another five tables were invited for the evening, because Weiguo's city coworkers were unable to come in the daytime. Weiguo had many contacts outside of Moonshadow Pond from his work world, and so this was a larger wedding. In contrast, Lanfang and her husband cultivated fruit trees for a living and did not have extensive contacts in the working world. Nonetheless, the more modest wedding of Lanfang's son in the same month still comprised seventeen tables.

As mentioned earlier, two events mark marriage in rural China today—one an imposition of the state, the other based on custom. Registry marriage is the legal registration that a couple goes through for recognition by the state, but most couples in Moonshadow Pond today also want a *jiuxi,* or wedding banquet, as well as its associated rituals.[48] This distinction between registry marriage and banqueting in China has also created an interesting social space, because now it is possible for a couple to wed "twice." Most villagers agree that a registry marriage alone is not ideal. The *jiuxi* symbolizes and strengthens a family's social relationships within the community. Time and time again I was told, "If you just get a registry marriage, you won't have any *mianzi.*" Yet this need for status creates difficulties for families who don't have the money in hand for an expensive banquet. So in Moonshadow Pond, more than one couple has undertaken a registry marriage and started living together, although they have not yet had a *jiuxi.* Then, after the groom's family has gathered enough money, they invite guests to a banquet.

This space between marriage registration and a wedding banquet is not new to the reform era, but the sequencing is now reversed. The sociologists Parish and Whyte note in their work on rural Guangdong Province in the 1970s that couples might have a banquet first and then only register the marriage later, when they reached the legal marriage age.[49] However, given the rising "price" of marriage and the ability of young working women to defer it, there is now little chance that a couple in Moonshadow Pond will marry when under the legal age (minimum age for men is now twenty-two and for women, twenty) as in collective-era Guangdong. If one form of marriage is to come first, it is likely to be the marriage registration, postponing the banquet until the family can put together enough funds for the status-enhancing event.

In-Laws and Out-Laws

The end of infant betrothal, the rising "price" of marriage, and the increasing need for connections in the liberalized reform economy have underscored an old theme in family relations and given it new prominence—the critical connections created by the in-marrying bride. These affinal connections were always highly valued and strategically useful in China, but not all classes could take advantage of them.

Traditionally affines provided more than connections. They provided, in the words of the historian Patricia Ebrey, "gifts of respect."[50] The hypergamous nature of marriage not only ensured deference from the new bride, but was also a symbolic affirmation of status of the groom's family.[51] But in the past, it was mainly wealthy families who took greatest advantage of affinal connections since they were more likely to undertake a major marriage. The wealthy used marriages (in China, as elsewhere) to widen their circle of relationships and to reinforce their privileges.[52]

The importance of affinal relations is articulated symbolically in the Hakka wedding ceremony. During the ceremony, two small children, a boy and a girl, accompany the wedding couple. These two children are dressed up as miniature bride and groom and are supposed to represent the sister and brother of the bride—that is, the maternal aunt and uncle of the newlywed's future children. Thus, the bride enters her new home with her symbolic or actual siblings, representing the importance of the relationship that will develop in the future between her natal family and her husband's family. After the banquet, the significance of this connection is again reiterated as the bride and groom must first offer tea to the bride's relatives.[53]

Interestingly, the miniature bride and groom escort the actual bride and groom through the front door *(da men)* of the groom's house. This door is a highly charged location, extremely permeable to *fengshui* influences. Protective amulets and phrases usually adorn it, and as the newly married couple walk across the threshold, fireworks explode to ward off bad spirits.

Such affinal connections, like so many other features of rural life, were once possessed primarily by the wealthy. But as with major marriage itself, or elaborate funeral rituals and wedding banquets, the revolution and subsequent economic reforms have universalized in practice an ideal widely held but previously difficult to attain.[54] Affinal connections are now important for all rural residents in order to widen their circle. We have already talked about connections between married daughters and their natal families from the standpoint of their natal families. But from the husband's side, these connections are important as well. Several families in Team 2, for instance, received loans for small businesses from the natal families of their daughters-in-law.

While the need to widen contacts is more nebulous and harder to articulate than a mother-in-law's immediate need for help at home, it is not less important. The nature of the connections between in-laws remains a critical element of Moonshadow Pond kinship relations, and at least one marriage in Moonshadow Pond actually broke down in part because relations between the proposed affines deteriorated greatly in the buildup to marriage.

In that case, the proposed mother-in-law and her married daughters all advocated strenuously against the marriage. The registry marriage did take place, but the banquet was never held, and the couple eventually divorced under the strain of bad relations between both sides.

After the divorce was finalized, the mother of the groom summarized the situation succinctly: "Being enemies like that, how could we be *qinqi* [relatives]?"

Songling: Feminist or Traditionalist?

These many developments have yielded complex and what outsiders might understand as "contradictory" ideas about family obligations. Songling's views on family life illustrate this well. She sometimes spoke from a "universal" point of view—not as a mother-in-law, or even as a mother or daughter, but in a voice that identified with women in general. "In the old days women were very pitiful," she once told me. "You even had to hang women's clothes out to dry on the bottom rung! But now things have changed."

When Songling spoke in this voice, she was a "feminist," critical of male power and prestige, and welcoming any social changes that enlarged women's opportunities and status. Songling had personally experienced the hardships created by male privilege in the old society as she witnessed her father take a second wife and her mother powerless to stop him.

"We forgive him now," she once told me, "because that was the old society. But the life of women like my mother was very bitter."

Most often, however, Songling's statements about women's roles were relational rather than abstract or universal. Her point of view often varied depending on who she was speaking about, and from what particular vantage point—as a mother-in-law, a mother of daughters, a wife, or a daughter. Speaking from these particular positions, she articulated a variety of contending conceptions of gender and kinship. At times, she articulated a "familial" concept of marriage in which the role of the individual was to serve the family. At other moments, she expressed notions very much in keeping with the idea of marriage as a bond between two individuals.

One of the people Songling admired most was her sworn sister, Xue-

lan. She admired Xuelan and her husband, Sicong, because they had tran-
scended their peasant identities and their middle-school educations to
rise in the ranks and acquire good jobs in the government. Xuelan was
an accountant in a public health department and Sicong wrote title
deeds for new houses. After 2000 they both retired and received generous pensions.

In addition to their successful careers and financial stability, Xuelan
and Sicong had a close and mutually helpful relationship. In fact, when
Sicong married Xuelan he agreed to move in with *her* family, since Xuelan had no brothers and at the time her parents were old and in poor
health. Although their children took Sicong's last name and remained in
his lineage, Songling saw Sicong's willingness to move in with his wife's
family as further proof of the couple's ability to work together. In describing this kind of relationship, Songling referred to a customary Hakka
proverb: "The balancing beam is useless without the weight, but the
weight is useless without the beam." This proverb envisions marriage as
a scale, and implies that mutual help is its most important element.

While Songling admired the mutual helpfulness of Sicong and Xuelan's marriage, she also praised their family in terms of a more traditional
attribute—harmony between the older and younger generation. Of course,
this harmony was purchased, as it were, by the fact that Sicong and Xuelan had generous pensions and their two sons had good jobs. Wrangling
over who would support the senior generation was irrelevant when their
generous pensions meant they could support themselves.

Songling's emphasis on the importance of family harmony was echoed
by many other comments I heard in Moonshadow Pond. A peaceful
household is a key element of maintaining *mianzi* in the village, as we
saw in Miaoli's earlier discussion of the discord in her own household.
A focus on this element of families emphasizes the idea that the family is
a whole whose sum is much greater than its individual parts—a notion
of the family as a collective unit rather than an assemblage of individuals
with separate interests and rights.

Yet when Songling thought about her own family, her ideas also varied
according to the vantage point from which she was seeing a particular
situation. As mentioned, she had acted strategically to make sure her
youngest daughter, Fengying, would marry into a family in which she
would not have to engage in agricultural work. She also worked to make
sure that this same daughter, who did not have a boyfriend of her own,
would have in-laws who were not strangers, but who knew her well and
would therefore not restrict her.

Indeed, by the time I returned to the village in 2007, Fengying and her husband had separated their business from the business of her husband's father and brother, primarily because Fengying was so commercially successful that the inequalities between the branches of the family were unsustainable. Fengying was clearly the force in her family—expanding from one to two stores, buying another building in town, and working constantly to widen their circle of customers (and this success also enabled her to help her parents, as we saw earlier in this chapter).

It is hardly surprising that given her own daughter's success, Songling also frequently criticized the idea that sons were more essential than daughters. In addition to the example of her own family, like other villagers, she found many other examples of married daughters helping their parents. But when she spoke in this voice, she did so in terms of a concern of the elder generation, support in old age. Daughters were just as valuable as sons because they were just as reliable, not because they were of equal value as women in any abstract sense.

In contrast, as we have seen, Songling looked forward eagerly to the day she would have a daughter-in-law of her own to relieve her of domestic burdens (even though when this eventually occurred, her son's marriage did not ultimately lighten her load). One day in 1996, I went with Songling to visit Xuelan and Sicong. The topic of an impending divorce in Moonshadow Pond came up. The daughter-in-law in the family was apparently in bad health, and her new in-laws claimed she had deceived them about the state of her health before the marriage. Songling told Sicong that she thought this was a valid reason for divorce.

"These issues are not reasons at all [mei you liyoude]!" Sicong exclaimed in reply. "They [the authorities] won't care if a daughter-in-law had good or bad health. First, they will ask the family to submit to mediation and try to reconcile. If that doesn't work, and if their affections are alienated [ganqing polie], then the couple will be granted a divorce. That's what the law says."[55]

As Songling presented the case to Sicong, it was clear that she was more sympathetic to the groom's family, because she thought the bride had turned out to be someone who would not be a hardworking daughter-in-law. Their ensuing discussion was fascinating to me as Songling's ideas about the reasons for divorce, based on the priorities of rural family life and of the family conceived as a corporate entity, contrasted with Sicong's explanation of contemporary law, in which the nature of the conjugal union between husband and wife takes priority.

Of course, not everyone in Moonshadow Pond embodied as full a range of ideological positions about family life as Songling. One might indeed say she embodied in one person the diversity of views held in the village at large! Nonetheless, she is certainly a good example of the range of ways people thought about family obligations in Moonshadow Pond. This range of views on the one hand included seeing the family as a hierarchical unit, one in which the needs of the conjugal bond were secondary to the needs of the family as a whole, especially elders. On the other hand, there were moments when Songling's views included a critique of the family as male dominated and oppressive to individual and specifically women's needs.

We have seen others in this chapter express some or all of these views, from Miaoli's complaints about mother-in-law oppression to Yuping's ideas that silently listening to the older generation's demands is more virtuous than complaining about them.

Aihua also articulated a range of ideas and views about family obligations. She bemoaned the fact that she had not herself been educated, and envisioned herself as a bureaucrat or office worker if she had only had the chance to become fully literate. She reveled in the opportunities created by the revolution for her as she became team leader, and she decried the ways of the old society in casting daughters out as infant brides or servants. She often told stories about the violence of male dominance in the old society and about how women who were seen as straying could be beaten up by the local ruffians.

Baoli's mother, she told me, was one such woman. Before Liberation she was out in the fields one day and began to sing "mountain songs," a popular form of call-and-response folk song. When another man answered her in song, the local ruffians went to beat her up for her scandalous behavior; only the intervention of her mother-in-law saved her from a savage beating. According to Aihua's story, Baoli's mother was so disappointed in her husband for not saving her from the bullies that she left China altogether to go live with her son, who had migrated to Burma. Indeed, Aihua had a large collection of stories about women's degraded conditions in the old society and about the oppression of male rule.

By the same token, Aihua had high and rather traditional expectations of her own daughters-in-law and grumbled about their demands on her. After all, she pointed out, she had done her share, raising her four grandchildren, and now it was time for her to take a back seat and relax a bit.

Finally, Ailing had gone to work in the city in the early years of the reform era, and she painted a critical picture of the extra privileges her brothers received growing up during the collective era. She chose her own mate, and after returning to marry in Moonshadow Pond she continued to work as a teacher's aide in school. One day, she complained to me that she did all the work at home and that her husband was "very lazy" and didn't help out enough. But then after saying these things, she immediately found it wise to add an addendum. "Nowadays," she said, "younger women don't know how to *chi ku* [eat bitterness], and they complain out loud about their husbands and in-laws. But I keep it all inside and don't get angry."

Like Yuping, Ailing added a testimonial to the virtue of not complaining and silently enduring one's burdens to her story about herself. Perhaps she added her remark because she had internalized this idea, or perhaps Ailing simply felt compelled to add this, because she felt that the idea of endurance without complaint still held traction in the wider community.

As mentioned in chapter 1, contradictions in social contexts often give rise to the expression of contradictory ideas, as even one person may hold inconsistent models of how the world should and does work. Furthermore, as we also explained in that chapter, ideas about moral obligation can be inherently contradictory, since they may place demands on people that cannot all be satisfied at the same time. That Songling, Aihua, Aihong, and other Moonshadow Pond women articulate contending ideas about family duty should therefore not be surprising. Not only are the demands on women as daughters, wives, and daughters-in-law themselves often in conflict, but further, these women have lived through major legal changes, as well as economic and social transformations.

Nonetheless, for the time being, acquiring a daughter-in-law is still anticipated as a necessary stage in the life of families. The daughter-in-law's entry into the family still adds to its status and is also anticipated eagerly by a mother-in-law hoping that the daughter-in-law will lighten her burden. It is therefore unlikely that the "virtue" of hard work without complaint associated with that role will be completely jettisoned as one standard of value.

CHAPTER 4

Everlasting Debts

"In the old society, people could not afford to complete a burial, so they left their relatives' urns in the hills. . . . Then during the Cultural Revolution, when things were really chaotic *[luan]*, some kids opened up the urns and scattered the bones all around."[1]

It was the spring of 1996 and Songling and Aihua were discussing death ritual in the old society, during Maoist times, and in the present. In southern Chinese death ritual, the bones of the deceased were traditionally exhumed and reburied in large ceramic urns several years after the initial burial.[2] Songling was explaining why one could find both unopened and opened urns on the hillsides that ran through Moonshadow Pond.

A few days after the discussion with Songling and Aihua, I asked Aihua again about the abandoned urns. She told me that at the time of the Cultural Revolution, her son, who was still a child, went up to the hills with his friends and smashed some of the urns. Aihua continued with her story: "A friend came home and told me about this. So I went to the hills with some spirit money and some incense sticks. I asked the ancestors to forgive my son because he was just a small boy. Later on, we found our own ancestors' bones there [her husband's grandmother, mother, and father], and about six years ago we gave them a proper final burial."

Mourning, memorialization, and care of the dead: no one would dispute that these have long played a dominant role in China. Here was Aihua, who had considered herself a good Communist, portraying herself in the midst of the Cultural Revolution asking forgiveness of the ancestors and even burning offerings to them. All this at a time when old customs and culture were supposed to be "smashed"!

Funerals are still a core ritual in Moonshadow Pond, although they have been altered, recreated, and revised several times through the twists and turns of the Maoist and reform eras. In this chapter, I ask what the role of funerals is in village life now and how residents of Moonshadow Pond understand them. It goes without saying that funerals in China are connected to moral obligation. But to what extent? Many have found other factors at work in the time, energy, and attention that rural Chinese put into funerals, such as the fear of ancestral retribution, the desire to counteract the inauspiciousness of death, or the coveting of status among the living. To understand contemporary funerals in Moonshadow Pond I guided my investigation by focusing on two interrelated dichotomies that often appear in analyses of Chinese mourning practices: (1) a contrast between a focus on historical continuity in ritual practice versus a focus on change and invented traditions, particularly practices dating from or changed by the Maoist era; and (2) a conflict over whether "performance takes precedence over belief," or in other words whether proper procedure and display are ultimately more important to the mourners than any specific ideology or motive that may underlie mourning rites.[3] In particular, descriptions of funerals as emblems of status among the living alternate with those that place primary emphasis on funerals as expressions of moral debt to the dead.

In understanding the motivations and meanings behind village funerals, we must also ask, to what extent are these funerals mere replications or revivals of "traditional" rituals? Some analysts have argued that what looks like the revival of tradition is nothing of the sort. They assert that the original meanings of traditional rites are lost because the old elements are only selectively revived. Such meanings are "recycled" in new combinations to fit contemporary needs and meanings.[4]

It is true that rituals are certainly never mere museum pieces. But as I hope to show, funerals in Moonshadow Pond do reflect certain formats and themes with a long history in China. At the same time, these long-lived themes also draw on contemporary raw materials, including new class relations and transformed gender roles. They also draw on the lived experience of community members and, by implication, elements of not only the present era but for many community members both the Maoist period and the "old society." Understanding this most central of rituals as either mere revival or complete invention misses the relationship between revival and invention itself. Even "invented" traditions must draw on available cultural materials, and revived traditions inevitably become part of ongoing social relations and cultural meanings.[5]

Nonetheless, certain encompassing values and motives do endure in Moonshadow Pond funerals. As we explored briefly in chapter 2, the idea of moral debt is a central motive and value in Moonshadow Pond funerals, and villagers express this value whether they draw on religious rites with a long history in China, the most popular choice now, or on the secular rituals of the socialist state, the only option allowed during the most intense years of Maoism.

This chapter argues that the motivation of moral obligation behind funerals is ultimately given more weight by villagers in Moonshadow Pond than is procedure. This does not mean that procedure is irrelevant. As we shall see, villagers often proclaim that proper procedure and the "show" of funerals is motivated by a strong desire for status in the community, but this status accrues to the mourners precisely because these elaborate displays are viewed as demonstrations of filial devotion. Mourners are not merely doing the "right" thing in the "right" way. They are also showing that they remember the kindness of those whom it will never be possible to fully repay. Moral indebtedness subsumes other aspects of Chinese death ritual, even those aspects to which it is often contrasted at other levels. In this case, "conscience" (liangxin) is therefore an "encompassing" aspect of Chinese funerals.

I begin this chapter with a review of approaches to understanding Chinese death ritual from imperial through Nationalist, Maoist and reform-era China. In the case of funerals, the Maoist state was not the first political authority that attempted to radically alter ritual practices. To understand funerals as they are now practiced in Moonshadow Pond, we need some knowledge of earlier attempts by the Chinese state to intercede in local ritual practice. The delineation of acceptable ritual practice was an ongoing process of the imperial state,[6] even though some argue that the degree of imperial control was not as total as that of the Maoist state.[7] The Nationalist regime also attempted to assert a "presence in local communities" through specification of acceptable ritual procedures[8] as well as campaigns against popular religion.[9]

The attempts by the Maoist state to alter popular rituals, however, were certainly the most far-reaching and dramatic. Just as in the last chapter it was impossible to talk about family roles without considering the impact of political changes, so too in the case of funerals some discussion of the role of the party-state is necessary. Still, although the state has been able to effect transformations in outward ritual expression, as this chapter shows, there has also been considerable continuity in the underlying cultural categories that villagers bring to bear on their understanding of death ritual.

We conclude this chapter by looking at villagers' reactions to Bright Ling's mourning observances for her father. These departed considerably from the grand funerals that have become popular in recent years, and we ask whether villagers accepted her observances as an appropriate expression of moral debt.

APPROACHES TO CHINESE DEATH RITUAL

Death ritual unsurprisingly serves as a focal rite in a culture in which the ancestral line is a critically important organizing principle. A great array of both historical and ethnographic scholarship seeks to investigate death ritual in general and funerals in particular in China. Summarizing this research here would be impossible, but there does seem to be consensus about a number of key features. To begin with, funerals in Chinese culture do not end the relationship between the living and dead. They begin an exchange relationship in which the living must fulfill obligations to the deceased, often repaying them for their support and love while alive.[10] The centrality of obligation to one's ancestors in China seems to have predated the Confucian writings about filiality or the development of Buddhist notions about repaying the kindnesses of parents.[11] (Archaeological evidence from the Shang period as far back as 1500 BCE finds sacrifices to the dead.)[12]

Yet, it is also apparent that successive philosophical and religious additions to China's cultural core created new rationales in articulating the value of exchange with the dead. The Confucians "saw caring for the dead as a filial duty."[13] As explained in chapter 2, concepts of repayment *(bao)* and profound kindnesses that create long-lasting debts have long been central in Chinese culture.[14] In ancient China, the idea that repayment did not end with death was already prevalent. Dead souls who were not cared for could go "hungry" and perhaps create problems for the living. Beyond the notion that the dead must be attended to, however, Confucian ideology elaborated no specific notion of an underworld. There is no hell in the Confucian tradition. Indeed, "the post-mortem locale of the dead remained obscure."[15] Furthermore, the Confucians did not enunciate any idea that in caring for the dead, one might be expiating their sins.

Buddhism added not only the presumption that death rituals repaid parents, especially mothers, for their sacrifices in their children's up-bringing but also the requirement that trained intermediaries were needed to aid in this effort. As the notion of a punitive underworld became embedded in the Chinese concept of an afterlife, the intervention of Buddhist clergy became a necessity if the deceased were to avoid suffering for his or her sins.[16] Moreover, by the Song period (960–1279 AD), Buddhist liturgies for the dead not only supplemented preexisting notions of repayment but also converged with Daoist funeral liturgies, with a strong emphasis on summoning back the dead soul so as to transform and deliver it.[17]

There is considerable evidence that Chinese funeral rites have long contained a "hybrid" quality.[18] These funeral rites have employed Confucian notions of filiality and Buddhist ideas about salvation and reincarnation. They have also utilized "indigenous ideas about yin-yang, auspiciousness and inauspiciousness of times, places, and activities that were vaguely associated with shamans and geomancers; and ideas about ghosts of ancient indigenous origins but modified over time by Buddhist and Taoist concepts of the fate of the dead."[19]

The motivational sources for the exchange with the dead in Chinese funerals are also varied. On the one hand, there are the inevitable feelings of obligation to the deceased, who devoted themselves in life to their progeny.[20] On the other hand, the Confucian emphasis on love of parents[21] might have also created strong emotions that could be partially calmed by "extravagant funerals" and "a deep reservoir of self-sacrificing practices ... providing opportunities for self-denial that could help quench sorrow."[22] Indeed, there is a great debate within the Chinese intellectual tradition about the relationship of ritual and emotion. An earlier emphasis on the way that ritual channels emotion gave way by the late Ming period (late sixteenth to mid-seventeenth centuries) to the idea that ritual was a sincere expression of emotion and, in the case of funerals, a sincere expression of grief.[23]

In either case, the inevitably strong feelings aroused by the death of family members, particularly parents, might certainly help explain why Buddhist teachings about repaying the kindnesses of parents resonated so strongly as they developed in China.[24] While Confucianism paid primary attention to the father-son relationship in its discourse on filiality, sons' emotional ties to their mothers were often felt more strongly than those to their more distant fathers.[25] Funeral services mediated by Buddhist clergy promised, among other things, to expiate mothers of the pollution of childbirth and sins of sexuality and therefore had strong emotional appeal.[26] Although some analysts suggest that patrilineal ties receive greater elaboration than matrilateral ties in death ritual, strong emotional bonds to one's mother may also strengthen the patriline.[27] As Margery Wolf has explained, a son's ties to his new wife were usually viewed by other family members as potentially divisive of agnatic unity, since these ties could pull a husband away from obedience to both father and mother and from solidarity with the joint family and even with the lineage as a whole. Ties to the mother, in contrast, helped keep married sons within the folds of the multigenerational family.[28]

As a result, the emotional lure of saving one's parents, especially one's mother, from underworld torture was an extremely appealing carrot as Buddhist funeral rites spread throughout China. The widespread appeal of the Mulian story, frequently reenacted at rural funerals by the attending monks, is one indication of the resonance of this emotional pull. Mulian is an extremely filial son who journeys to the underworld in order to rescue his mother, whom he is unable to save until he accepts the Buddha's advice to feed seven generations of ancestors in a yearly ritual that utilizes the help of Buddhist clergy as intermediaries.[29]

In addition to the carrot of delivering one's parents from underworld torture, however, there was also a stick to the popularity with which Buddhist elements penetrated Chinese funeral ritual. This was the fear that sure punishment would await those who did not follow through on their obligations to the deceased. In Buddhism, this punishment could occur after death, in the underworld. But in popular culture, there was also fear of retribution in this life. The degree to which feelings of obligation trump fear of retribution seems to vary both historically and in contemporary times, from field site to field site.[30]

Despite the importance of strongly internalized feelings of obligation and filiality in Chinese funerals, however, there is no doubt that there were equally compelling motivations that had little to do with notions of obligation to ancestors, desire to relieve them from otherworldly suffering, or even fear of their retribution. Certainly, using an elaborate funeral to confirm and confer status has a long history in China.[31] Ethnographic accounts refer to status competition between lineages in their ability to put on an elaborate funeral[32] while the low status of the poor was often confirmed by their inability to provide proper burials.[33] And in the postcollective era, as economic disparities have widened within rural communities, some analysts have focused their analysis of funerals in rural society on the role that they play in exhibiting economic power.[34]

The importance of funerals in status competition has led some analysts to conclude that "orthopraxy," or proper procedure, is more important than "orthodoxy," or proper belief, in Chinese death ritual. As James L. Watson states:

> When considering Chinese funerary ritual the question of audience becomes very complex. Who judges, and thereby validates, the performance? the deceased? the community? the gods, ancestors, and guardians of hell? or the performers of the rites themselves? . . . Most villagers make it clear by their actions that the general community, represented by neighbors and kin, constitutes the most important audience. . . . It is the proper performance of the rites—by specialists, mourners, and community members—that matters most to everyone concerned. . . . The internal state of the participants, their personal beliefs and predispositions, are largely irrelevant.[35]

But what is "proper procedure?" Here, the issue of state-society relations looms large. Some historians argue that for many centuries the Confucian literati considered Buddhism heterodox.[36] It is also clear, however, that as Buddhist practices spread among the population, these strict Confucian notions became unenforceable, even among the literati. Sponsorship of Buddhist and Daoist death rituals by literati and officials was common during the Song dynasty.[37] Then, in the late Ming and early Qing dynasties, certain elements within the gentry class tried to reactivate purely Confucian funerals using the text *The Family Rituals,* supposedly authored by the neo-Confucian Zhu Xi, as a guide.[38] This advocacy of purely Confucian funerals has been explained by the historian Timothy Brook as stemming from the gentry's need to consolidate lineages and the old rural order in the wake of commercialization and the emergence of new wealthy classes who were not dependent on land.[39] Buddhist funerals emphasized personal familial bonds, but Confucian ritual placed more emphasis on the lineage.

Nonetheless, as Brook finds, even at a time when large portions of the gentry class were advocating the abandonment of Buddhist ritual at funerals, many other elements of the gentry continued to use both Confucian and Buddhist elements in their own practice. In addition, Buddhist practices continued to be an important element in the funeral rites of many other classes, including peasants, merchants, and even landowners who did not have gentry status.[40]

In Maoist China, many elements of funeral rites that were practiced before Liberation were successively banned, as the state promoted primarily secular memorial services, insisting that most popular practices were both personally and socially wasteful. Memorial services organized by an individual's *danwei* ("work unit") became the standard. Although there was some tolerance for customary death rituals in rural areas during the 1950s, the Cultural Revolution (1966–76) swept away most vestiges of previous practice, even in the rural areas. During this time, the slogan "destroy the four olds" *(po si jiu)* was used to fuel attacks on lineage halls, gods' images, and ritual specialists.[41] Maoist campaigns viewed the discourse against "superstition" as a necessary form of class warfare.[42] In one north Chinese village studied by Andrew Kipnis, "residents were forced to cremate instead of bury their dead . . . [and] weeping, gift giving, and interclass attendance and *ketou*ing were forbidden at funerals."[43]

After the death of Mao Zedong in 1976 and the beginning of the era of reform in 1978, the rural areas were soon allowed to revive many traditional rituals. This "revival" of traditional rites often involved a process of research, finding scraps of previously performed rituals and putting them together in new ways or in ways that were imagined to adhere to their previous forms.[44] Frequently, altered or completely new elements were added.[45] In one village studied by Xin Liu in north China, disagreements and fighting characterized local discourse about rituals. Liu attributes this state of affairs to the absence of a "dominant local authority" such as the former gentry class or Maoist cadres, who in the past would "secure meaning and significance" of rituals.[46]

In contemporary rural China what constitutes "proper procedure" in any given locality may therefore not be immediately obvious. Is "proper procedure" the revived "traditional" rites? Would a villager who conducted a secular memorial service as endorsed by the state or a "traditional" rite as revived in the local area be following proper procedure? And in any event, is it correct to assume that villagers actually do place greater emphasis on procedure than on the ideological system and emotions that they believe should underpin mourning?

Evidence from urban China, where secular memorial services still prevail, is inconclusive. Some studies suggest that interest in caring for the dead has not dissipated despite radical changes in rites. For instance, Martin Whyte notes that urban residents exhibit great concern over ensuring a proper resting place for the ashes of the deceased (as burial is no longer allowed in urban areas). He also notes that offerings placed at the sites of ash boxes during death anniversaries and the Qingming festival (when family members traditionally sweep the graves of their loved ones clean) are common.[47] These gestures suggest to Whyte that orthodoxy is as important as orthopraxy, since an ideological orientation survived even after a forced change of procedure.[48] On the other hand, William

Jankowiak's study of urban Inner Mongolia found many respondents who maintained that they undertook a traditional funeral rite only because of an elder's request, and not because it was necessary as a form of reciprocity with the deceased's soul.[49]

Our analysis of contemporary funerals in Moonshadow Pond will attempt to address these questions of procedure versus ideology, as well as the related issue of the interplay of status and remembrance. I begin with a description of Hakka funerals as I observed them in Moonshadow Pond. It is based first and foremost on four complete funerals that I viewed between September 1995 and May 1996, as well as videotapes of two additional funerals. Although videotaping of funerals is not standard procedure by any means, it is not considered out of the ordinary anymore, especially for a family with some means. While I was in Moonshadow Pond, I was able to view on videotape a funeral that had occurred in a nearby town. I also left funds with Songling and Baoli for the complete videotaping of a funeral in Moonshadow Pond, should one occur after I left the village in May 1996. When I returned to Moonshadow Pond in the summer of 1997, I watched the videotape of the funeral of Songling's uncle, which had occurred the previous winter. This was an invaluable source of information. I saw this video numerous times in the presence of other community members and had many chances to ask questions about elements of the ritual. In addition to the funeral and funeral tapes from the 1990s, I also learned when I returned in the summer of 2006 and spring of 2007 of a few significant changes, which I will discuss later.

In trying to gain an understanding of what I saw in Moonshadow Pond, I turned primarily to Moonshadow Pond residents: my main interest was to see the funerals as they did. My interest in funerals may have prompted people to speak about them in my presence, but there is no question that the size and quality of important life-cycle events such as weddings and funerals was a central concern for villagers. Even when I did not hear a particular conversation myself, others would inform me about the local scuttlebutt, and weddings and funerals were frequently on the list of topics.

I supplemented my discussions with ordinary villagers with interviews of Buddhist monks and some written accounts of Hakka funerals, especially in regard to symbolic references that were new to me. The summary that I will provide, however, follows the outlines of funerals as I saw them in Moonshadow Pond only. If a particular ritual element was mentioned by a specialist or scholar but did not occur in Moonshadow Pond practice, I did not include it. I opted not to describe just one particular funeral but to summarize the most standard elements, since funerals did indeed follow a very similar format in Moonshadow Pond.

Before we begin, one aspect of terminology needs clarification. When villagers talk of funerals, they make a distinction between two kinds. When monks are called in to help the soul in its journey through the underworld, a funeral is referred to literally as "doing benevolent acts" *(zuo haoshi)*, a term which means religious rites for the deceased.[50] A secular funeral is described as a "memorial service" *(zhuidao hui)*. Terms in this chapter such as *traditional* or *customary* refer to the revived religious rites that involve Buddhist monks and a concern with the soul's fate. Such terms do not imply, as we shall see, that these rites have been resurrected from the pre-Liberation era without change.

The Format of Rural Hakka Funerals

One day during my fieldwork, Songling told me that a woman in the village had had a stroke and was near death. She had already been moved to the lineage hall, said Songling, because most people would like to die in the hall with their descendants surrounding them. In fact, Songling told me, she had heard that in the past people would not be allowed to have their funerals in the lineage hall at all if they had not first been moved there before actually passing away. It was still the case in Moonshadow Pond, she said, that most people would be moved from their own houses to the lineage hall to spend their last hours.

After death, several days will pass before the actual funeral rite. During this time, the immediate family of the deceased must hire ritual specialists, solicit help from close lineage mates, and pay for the ritual paraphernalia that they will need to use over the next few days. Meanwhile, the body is prepared for the coffin and clothed in special funeral garb. A paper soul house is constructed and put on display to be burned as an offering to the deceased at the end of the funeral. Funeral scrolls with condolence messages and floral wreaths are sent to the family of the deceased and are exhibited in the lineage hall. Notices will be tacked up on the outer wall of the lineage hall and also sent to relatives and friends outside the village informing them about the death as well as the time for the funeral rites. Even before the day of the funeral, individuals begin arriving at the lineage hall in order to pay respects. They also donate a small sum of money *(xiang yi qian,* literally, "incense-rites money") to help the family of the deceased pay for funeral services (these donations are recorded by volunteers).

The day of burial and the primary funeral rites can be divided into two main parts. In the morning, a service dominated and led by village elders emphasizes respect for the deceased and the symbolism of family and lineage unity. At the end of this service, the emphasis changes with the addition of Buddhist clergy. The Buddhist segment of the funeral is focused on the travails of the deceased's soul as it journeys through the underworld and is judged.

The use of Buddhist clergy as a necessary component of funerals has, as stated earlier, been an important component of funerals in many parts of China for centuries. Certainly, among Hakka populations in southeast China, it has long been critical[51] and judging from other ethnographic observations in this area, it has been widely revived.[52]

In the first part of the rite, a master of ceremonies begins by notifying heaven, the ancestors, and the soul that the ceremony is about to begin. A local ritual specialist (not a member of the Buddhist clergy) is also on hand to assist in preparation of ritual objects and to let various participants know what they must do and when.[53] Since much of this part of the funeral consists of making offerings to heaven and the ancestors, in particular taking care of the immediate needs of the deceased's soul, they must be present. Furthermore, for the soul to stray too far from the corpse before burial is considered dangerous. The primary mourners don their mourning garb: brown jute for the descendants of the deceased who remain in the patriline, white-cotton cloth for the descendants of the deceased, such as a daughter's children, who belong to a different lineage. (Other variations in mourning garb also distinguish different generations of mourners.)

Female mourners and male mourners are initially separated. The women kneel behind a screen and engage in ritualized wailing at the beginning of the service. They later emerge when the time comes to pay respects to the deceased. For the remainder of the service, female and male mourners are not separated, a difference from pre-Communist times.[54]

Throughout the first part of the funeral rite (in the morning), the master of ceremonies leads the mourners and other attendees. He calls forth in successive order the direct patrilineal descendants of the deceased, other descendants of the deceased, and finally community members and friends as he instructs them on when and how to come forward and pay respects through bowing or kowtowing to the spirit of the deceased. He also takes charge of lighting incense and offerings libations, paper objects, and food to the deceased throughout the ceremony (the local ritual specialist also helps out with technical details here).

PHOTOGRAPH 8. Reading a funeral eulogy in 1996. On the right side of this photo, one can see a portion of the paper soul house, including the female servant.

Three documents are read in the course of this first part of the funeral rite. The first document *(aizhang)* lists the descendants of the deceased. A second document *(dianzhang)* relates the good qualities of the deceased in a formulaic way (there is actually a standard text used for males and another for females). The third document is a eulogy that speaks about the individual life of the deceased. A representative of the local council of elders *(laorenhui)*[55] reads this eulogy, a postrevolutionary innovation that did not exist in funerals before Liberation.[56]

The location of the rite in the main hall of the lineage temple, the marking of the descendants of the deceased through special mourning garb, and the fact that those in the generation prior to the deceased cannot attend, are all elements of the funeral that emphasize patrilineal identity and respect for familial hierarchy. Only toward the end of the morning ceremony, with the first appearance of Buddhist monks, does the emphasis begin to shift from commemoration of the deceased and attention to the immediate needs of his or her soul to a concern with the soul's passage through the underworld.

After the morning service is over, all official mourners (those wearing

PHOTOGRAPH 9. Circling the coffin. The son and grandson of the deceased circle the coffin while holding the soul tablet and a photograph of the deceased at a 1996 funeral.

mourning garb) pose for a photograph in front of the soul house. The coffin is then carried out of the lineage hall. Leading the way are the direct descendants of the deceased; a son or grandson carries a soul tablet, and another descendant carries a photo of the deceased. The soul, for the time being, is thought to inhabit this tablet, which will be placed in the grave along with the coffin. The descendants circle the coffin, led by the Buddhist monks who chant sutras to comfort the survivors. Some of the female mourners then kneel around the coffin and burn spirit money for use by the deceased in the underworld. Finally, a funeral procession of all the mourners escorts the coffin to the bottom of the hills on the outskirts of the village. The leader of the procession scatters spirit money along the route to keep away dangerous spirits who might be attracted by the inauspicious nature of the event. In the last few years, this parade with the coffin has become more noisy and elaborate, as most families now hire a band to play in the morning before the ceremonies begin and also to noisily escort the coffin during the procession from the lineage hall.

When the mourners and coffin reach the village outskirts, all but the closest family members return to the village. Until 2005, the principal mourners then ascended the hills to bury the coffin. When the burial was complete, a monk recited auspicious words for the mourners while he

PHOTOGRAPH 10. Burning paper spirit money for the deceased. Some of the female mourners surround the coffin and burn spirit money at the conclusion of the morning portion of a funeral ceremony, 1996. A monk leads other mourners in chants.

distributed grain, an overt symbol of fertility. The mourners then returned to the lineage temple, where a big feast was held for both family and community members who took part in the morning rites.

After 2005, one change was made to this sequence. The township government insisted that the remains of the deceased be cremated following the morning funeral services. The parade of the coffin to the outskirts of the village still occurs. But instead of carrying the coffin to the hilltop for burial, the mourners are now met on the highway by a truck, which brings the coffin to the county capital for cremation of the remains. After cremation, the ashes are placed in a funeral urn. Two possibilities are open to the family of the deceased that modify the traditional practice of secondary burial but retain some of its features. The family may bury the urn of ashes in the ground, just as if it had been the coffin. When sufficient funds have been secured, they can then place this urn in a tomb—just as they would have done had they practiced traditional reburial, except that this urn now contains ashes instead of bones. Or the family of the deceased can skip the second stage and place the funeral urn in a tomb that has already been built. For instance, a family may build an elaborate tomb for both parents, in which case there is already a final resting place for the urn of ashes after the second parent dies.

PHOTOGRAPH 11. Funeral procession, 2007.

Despite the modification in burial practice in 2005, the afternoon's proceedings on the day of the funeral continue as before. After the midday banquet, the monks lead the mourners in a day and night of ritual. According to several monks whom I interviewed and who helped explain to me the text that they use in this ritual, the purpose of this rite is to lift the burden of transgressions from the deceased and to help the soul journey through the ten chambers of the underworld, where it will be judged. The monks invite the gods back to witness the soul's passage (including both Buddhist and local deities). They also invite the soul back, give it a bath, and offer it wine. The monks use offerings to dispatch hungry ghosts who may be hovering around the ceremonial area.

The "monks" who are invited in here are not the celibate, reclusive monks of tradition. These monks call themselves by the term "lay disciples" *(sujia dizi)* as opposed to "Buddhist monastic monks" *(sengjia dizi)*. One monk said to me, "Serious monks should practice abstinence, but we do not. This is because of the flaw of the policies of the old days [referring here to Maoist policies], such as removing and breaking down the temples, which forced monks back to secular lives. Due to these policies, we gave up quite a number of other rules, and are allowed to marry and have offspring." He added that the text they chanted was not "genuine" scripture *(zhenjing)*. Rather, he said, it is what they called "persuasion scripture" *(quanshi wen)* and was written in accord with "the customs of the Hakka people."[57]

Not all villagers accept the notion of an underworld, but those who do accept this cosmology believe that the monks can help the soul in its journey but cannot radically transform its fate. If the soul has merit, it will be rewarded; its fate is ultimately based on its actions in life. During the afternoon and evening rites, however, the monks' chants can help the deceased pass the inspection of underworld judges. At a certain point in the ceremony, the monks actually place a number of stamps in a book to indicate that the deceased has successfully completed this underworld bureaucratic review!

The Hakka are like other Han Chinese in conceiving of a place called the Western Kingdom (or Western Paradise), where the soul might go to avoid the endless cycle of reincarnation. But as elsewhere, these death rituals emphasize helping the soul find a fortuitous incarnation in its next life rather than avoiding the cycle of endless rebirths altogether. Although seemingly contradictory to an outsider, popular conceptions of the soul locate it in three places after death: the grave, the underworld, and the ancestral tablet in the lineage hall.[58] The day of the funeral sees a focus on the soul in two of these three aspects. The initial focus, during the burial rites, is on the soul in the grave. After the burial, during the afternoon and evening rituals, the focus shifts to the soul in the underworld. A focus on the soul as ancestor becomes more prominent in graveside rituals in later years, after the reburial of the bones as well as in ancestral rites in the lineage hall, but it is not prominent during the funeral rites.

As the evening progresses, some of the monks' chants also pertain to the identity of the deceased or the circumstances of his or her death. If the deceased is a woman, the monks will certainly recite the Blood-Bowl Sutra. This is supposed to counteract the pollution of pregnancy, menstruation, and childbirth; it also is meant as a way of teaching the living about the mother's sacrifices in the pain and suffering of childbirth, breastfeeding, washing and changing the baby's clothes, and sleeping wet while the baby was dry.[59] A monk said to me: "Women have pregnancy and menstruation. This pollutes the rivers and wells. The blood bowl is used to make these clean. This is also used to teach the sons and daughters to respect their mothers and to know how their mothers raised them." After the sutra is recited, the monks pass out wine. This was explained to me by the same monk in this way: "Sons, grandsons, relatives, and friends will drink this up to bring luck to the mourners and to relieve the mother of her burdens."[60]

PHOTOGRAPH 12. Burning offerings to the deceased. Mourners burn the paper soul house and other objects on the night after the funeral (note the paper bed and dresser in the background).

If the deceased died as a result of illness, special chants will be used to cure it posthumously. Other chants exhort the living to be kind and help others, to be filial, and to get along in the family; they also comfort the deceased. During the late-night hours, the monks tell a number of famous stories, including the story of Mulian.

By three or four in the morning, the funeral ritual is at an end, although monks can also perform longer rites if the deceased's family and friends are willing to pay for it. Paper objects and spirit money are burned in order to transmit them to the deceased in the underworld. The inventory of these paper objects always includes a house with two servants. It may also contain many other objects, such as paper beds and dressers, and paper versions of modern consumer items such as televisions and even audio equipment. The spirit money is supposed to help the deceased pay off any remaining debt for the incarnation that they have just completed. Finally, the gods that had been invited in are sent away, and the monks recite sutras to counter the inauspicious climate created by the death.

Until the township government enforcement of cremation rules in 2005, many years would pass before the family could complete this death ritual by reburying the bones of the deceased in a funeral urn and placing that urn in a permanent tomb with good *fengshui,* assuming the members had the economic means and the unity. Even now, however, some time may pass between the time of cremation and the completion of a permanent grave in which to place the urn containing the ashes of the deceased. Nonetheless, since yearly worship at the grave of one's ancestors continues indefinitely, one can also say that, in a certain sense, death ritual is never really complete.

Conscience

In chapter 2 the use of the concept of *liangxin* was explored in a number of different contexts. This stress on conscience, memory, and obligation certainly plays a key role in the mourning and remembrance of the dead, especially one's parents and grandparents. As mentioned in that chapter, the importance of remembrance is not necessarily connected to acceptance of the notion that a person will have an afterlife and that the soul will travel to an underworld after death. For instance, my neighbor Red Chong said to me one day, "I believe that when you die, you are just a pile of flesh and bones." He was chatting with two other male friends who heartily agreed that belief in spirits was "superstitious." "But," one of them continued, "to commemorate your roots is not the same as worshipping gods."

Of course, for some people, the fear of supernatural sanction does play a role as an impetus in commemorating the dead. Several villagers recited the story of a fellow villager's brother as an example. He returned from Taiwan without first stopping at the village to pay respects at his ancestors' tomb. Instead, he took a trip to a number of scenic spots, such as Guilin. When he finally did return to the village, he was struck with an illness for the next two weeks.

In another case, a family that had entered into a spate of bad luck was criticized for not being filial enough toward the ancestors. In the first two weeks after the Lunar New Year, most families visit the graves of their ancestors and make offerings. Miaoli's extended family, including her parents-in-law, husband, and husband's brother, rarely participated in these events. "They are not *xiuxin,*" said Songling to me one day during my fieldwork in 1996. (As discussed in chapter 2, the word *xiuxin* can be literally translated as a cultivated or renovated heart and mind, but it is used in conversation to refer not only to acting charitably or mercifully but also to accepting the responsibility of doing what one is supposed to do and seeing it through to the end.)[61] Songling continued in speaking about Miaoli's family: "You never see them visiting their ancestors' graves." Then she quoted from an old proverb—"What goes away in daylight comes back in the dark" *(Guang zhong qu, an zhong zhuan)*—to explain how by refusing to honor their ancestors with offerings, they ended up with no return on investment. If alternatively, Songling implied, they would go to their ancestors' graves in broad daylight and make offerings, Miaoli's family would later see good things come back to them, even at unexpected times.

Instead, Miaoli's family continued to be plagued not only by bad luck, but by tragedy. One day, in the summer of 2006, Miaoli's husband succumbed to high fever after working in the searing summer heat to transplant rice. Thinking he could manage himself, he declined medicine to bring the fever down. By the time he was hospitalized it was too late, and he died a few days later. Two months after this, his grieving and distracted father was hit by a truck as he bicycled through a busy intersection, and he also died.

On the New Year's Day after the death of immediate family members, visits to their gravesites are customary, and Miaoli was careful to tell me over the next New Year (when I had returned to Moonshadow Pond in 2007) that she had placed offerings at the graves of both her late husband and her father-in-law. But she also told me that she still did not believe in spirits or an afterlife, and that she thought such ideas were superstition. Miaoli was one of the few people in the village who did not state that commemoration had a value in itself, even if one did not believe in a spirit world. Rather, she told me, she had finally decided to do these things because "people say you should."

The importance of remembering the dead and performing proper funeral rites is not reserved solely for one's own ancestors. In some circumstances, the importance of memory and exchange with the dead may be applied to those with whom one has no direct familial tie, as long as one is reciprocating previous help. Auntie Xiuling, now an elderly woman herself, told me how she had once donned funeral garb and cried at the funeral of a childless widow who had helped take care of her own children. Some women in the village told me that they had heard people say that if no one cried at your funeral, you would be unable to speak in your next life. This was not something they said that they subscribed to personally, but merely reported in the category of dangers that there was no point inviting, even if the chances were slim! By mourning and crying at the widow's funeral, Auntie Xiuling was expressing gratitude for the help that she had received from the widow, and these mourning procedures could also help the widow's soul to avoid dangers in her next life.

Status

"*Mianzi* is worth a lot of money," said Yangsheng, the local funeral specialist. Although not a monk himself, he was frequently employed by mourners to help organize worship, giving instructions to both mourners and official masters of ceremonies and preparing ritual paraphernalia during funerals. I had gone to speak with him about what appeared to me as the enormous cost of death ritual in the village.

As explained in chapter 1, the word *mianzi* is normally translated as "face," but it most commonly refers to one's status in the community. There is no doubt that in Moonshadow Pond, just as in rural China of the pre-Liberation era, funerals often become templates on which families can assemble their social skills and material resources and through which, once these skills and resources are called upon, their status in the community is judged and ratified.

During the funeral, the family of the deceased is very much on display. Villagers frequently make comments about the size and quality of the funeral arrangements, including the number of guests attending the morning rites, the quality of the band and singers invited for the morning rites and the funeral procession, the number of people invited for the midday banquet as well as the quality of the food, and the estimated amount of money spent. An ensemble of classical instruments called *bayin* (literally, "eight instruments") as an added feature in the afternoon, several monks to aid in the afternoon and evening rites, and a large number of paper objects to be burnt as offerings later that night can also add to the grandiosity.[62] Since many guests bring monetary gifts on the day of the funeral or the days that precede it, villagers will often speculate about the total amount of cash received as gifts, and they say that if a large number of people attend a funeral, it shows that the family has more connections *(guanxi)*. If local officials are among the guests, this can also enhance status, but officials cannot make up for a poor turnout.

Historical accounts lead us to conclude that acquiring the services of Buddhist clergy for funeral rites was very difficult for the poor during the nineteenth century. Both Justus Doolittle and J. J. M. de Groot, observing southeast China in the late nineteenth century, noted that Buddhist specialists were more likely to be found at the funerals of mercantile families, other wealthy families, and some literati than among the poor.[63] Neither of these observers dealt with funerals among the Hakka. The available evidence, however, indicates that in the past, the Hakka poor of Meixian could provide for themselves only an abbreviated form of Buddhist funeral rites. According to the *Mei County Gazetteer,* a range of Buddhist funeral rites existed in the pre-Liberation era.[64] They could last as long as seven days and eight nights, or they could simply consist of asking a monk to read from the *sanjiu ku* (three deliverances from suffering) for a few hours. This part of the Buddhist service is the one most directly concerned with securing the soul's safe passage through the underworld and delivering it from suffering.

The funeral rites in contemporary Moonshadow Pond can hardly rival the more extensive rituals practiced by the elite before Liberation. Nonetheless, it seems fair to surmise that the full day and full night that is now so common to Moonshadow Pond, coupled with the large banquet and elaborate offerings for the dead, is certainly more extravagant than the ceremony that could be mustered by many of the residents' poor ancestors. Postfuneral spending on an elaborate tomb also adds to the competition. The size and elaborate nature of the tombs in which funeral urns are placed are also a source of comment amongst villagers.

A large number of descendants to mourn the deceased also adds to the status-enhancing qualities of a funeral. This, however, can be manipulated in a number of ways. For instance, through the institution of "dry daughters" and "dry sons" *(gan nuer, gan erzi),* the number of individuals wearing the funeral garb of descendants can be increased. Dry daughters and dry sons are individuals who are "adopted" for ritual purposes or to establish a link between families, but they remain with their natal families and have none of the responsibilities or rights of actual descendants. In Moonshadow Pond, dry daughters or sons may be included in a New Year's banquet with their adoptive family, and they may even be involved in friendly relationships throughout the course of the year. Sometimes they are adopted as children because they are sickly or demanding babies, and the ritual adoption is supposed to help displace their troublesome characteristics. Unlike descendants, they have no rights in property, nor do they have material responsibilities to care for their adoptive parents while they are alive. Nonetheless, they can be included as principal mourners in funeral rites and therefore have responsibilities toward these parents after death. Thus, at the funeral of Songling's uncle, who had seven grown daughters and no sons, there were actually four men wearing the garb of direct male descendants—three dry sons and one matrilocally married son-in-law.

Even the number of gamblers at a funeral is a measure of a family's social connections. Since the beginning of the economic reform period and increasingly in the 1990s, funerals have become magnets for mahjong

PHOTOGRAPH 13. Monks, gamblers, and mourners at a funeral, 1996.

players and other gamblers. Although descendants of the deceased cannot gamble (since they are mourners), other villagers quickly fill the lineage hall where the funeral services are to be held. They gamble throughout the day and night of the funeral as well as on the many nights and days preceding the actual service. One is thus often treated to the rather startling discrepancy of Buddhist priests conducting funeral services in the midst of noisy tables of mahjong players.

Gambling at funerals is not new. The Qing emperor Kangxi criticized the practices of feasting, gambling, card playing, and drinking at funerals, indicating that these practices were popular in the late imperial era as well.[65] Gamblers now come because they can; they believe correctly that the public-security bureau will never break up gambling in the context of a death ritual. Villagers say that gamblers prevent the funeral environment from becoming "cold and desolate" *(lengqing)*, and the families of the deceased therefore welcome gamblers because they add to the crowd and to the general air of excitement. Indeed, Red Chong contrasted the funerals of the 1950s and 1960s negatively with those of today in reference to gambling. "Back then, it was very cold and desolate in the lineage hall," he told me. "Now people come and gamble, so the family members of the deceased won't have that cold and lonely feeling."

Gambling as a way of drawing crowds to a funeral and to counteract the loneliness of death has also been noted by the anthropologist Alan Klima in his research on death and exchange in Thailand. As in China, although gambling is illegal in Thailand, funerals are legitimate spaces for gambling, and the large numbers of gamblers who are drawn to a funeral not only provide company for the family of the deceased, but for the dead person's lonely spirit as well.[66] Klima points out that during these occasions it is not always easy to discern the giver from the receiver. The family of the deceased receives the "gift" of "society," or a large number of people to counteract the loneliness of death, but at the same time, they must repay by making sure the gamblers who stay up all night are given food and drink.[67] Similarly in Moonshadow Pond, gamblers and those who come out for the general excitement will stay in the lineage hall most of the night in the nights before the burial. In return, the family of the deceased will prepare congee and soup for everyone each night at midnight.

Certainly, in Meixian, if a large number of guests do not come to a funeral, bystanders will critique it later on, saying that the funeral was not renao ("bustling and busy"), an element considered necessary for the success of a wide variety of Chinese ritual activities. That funerals are not "happy" occasions does not separate them from the celebration of more fortunate occasions, such as weddings, in the necessity of this element. Interestingly, the anthropologist Adam Yuet Chau found an equally strong emphasis on renao in his fieldwork in northern rural China. He translates the term literally as "red hot sociality"[68] and goes on to say, "Re means hot, heat, heady, emotional, passionate, fervent, or feverish,"[69] while "nao means to stir up and connotes a wide range of excitement: rambunctious, agitated, hustle bustle, playful, busy, noisy, conflicted, exuberant, colorful, to express dissatisfaction, to vent, to plague, to turn upside down, to be naughty, to make a scene."[70] As Chau tells us, renao is the desired goal in staging many public events in rural China.

Many villagers in Moonshadow Pond told me that if they did not have sufficient funds, they would borrow money in order to organize an elaborate funeral for a parent. "If you don't do this," one woman said to me, "people will say you are not filial." Indeed, even a fairly average funeral by local standards, with monks to perform services, and ten or fifteen tables of guests at the banquet after the burial, could amount to almost ten thousand yuan in the mid-1990s, about three times the average income of a wage earner in the village at that time. So clearly this was a very significant amount.

The importance of providing a good show, however, does not impede the expression of a fair share of ironic detachment. At the funeral of one old man who was known to be a drunkard and had bad relationships with all but one of his grown sons, several spectators poked fun at the funeral wailing. "The tears are fake," said one neighbor; "everybody knows he was an old wino who couldn't get along with his children when he was alive."[71] Indeed, there is a popular saying in Meixian about people who are not filial while their parents are alive, but who after their death attempt to create a sensation by a grand show of worshipping.[72]

Villagers even told me about funerals they had observed for which the ritualized wailing was performed by people hired from the outside.[73] I never saw a funeral with "mourners for hire" in Moonshadow Pond, and my sense from what people said about this is that villagers did not think it was appropriate. Wailing for one's own ancestor, even if not heartfelt, however, was expected—even if people were able to stand back from this and make fun of it in other people's families.

Sarcasm and humorous commentary about funeral rites are frequently extended to comments about the monks themselves. These monks are extremely well remunerated for their part of the day-and-night-long funeral ceremony. "Look at these monks," said one villager to me. "This new class of monks is not like the old monks. The old monks could see through the vanity of worldly things. They lived in monasteries on the mountaintops. Not these monks! They cannot survive up on the mountains. They'd miss their televisions, their motor scooters, and their gambling. The old monks had no aspirations, they were separated from . . . the affairs of the world. Today's monks are insincere." Stories of the sexual and marital escapades of various monks were also commonplace, and one monk who officiated at local funerals was known to have a mistress. (In fact, many of the monks who came to perform these rituals were the offspring of former monks who were forced to return to collective farming and who eventually married and raised families during the Maoist period. These "monks" were often married themselves—hence, the famous case in the village of the monk who had left his legal wife and was living with another woman.)

During the late afternoon of the funeral service, the monks often take a break from the more serious observances and put on a show in which they balance and juggle various objects. Children throw them red packets of very small change during this show. At the funeral of her grandmother, this practice prompted one villager to make fun of yet another additional opportunity for the monks to make money. As bystanders threw red packets toward the monks, she quipped, "Give one *jiao* and your family will fight; give ten *jiao* and your family will unite!"[74]

In one case, the expense of funerals was enough to prompt one elderly woman to convert to Christianity. Mingxie, the only identified Christian in the village, had joined a church in the county capital. Explaining her motivation for conversion, she told Songling, "It's much easier and cheaper, the funerals are cheaper! You don't have to spend a lot of money, you just go to the church once a month or so and don't need to buy a lot of offerings, and for the funerals you don't need to invite a lot of people, you can just have a service in the church."

While this old woman's conversion and her reasons, the expense of funerals, was a singular case, it is fair to say, as noted earlier, that such expenses are hard to avoid despite people's ability to poke fun at their own social conventions. A large and expensive funeral, however, is not enough to ensure that a family will gain status or even reconfirm their previous status. A very interesting example of this problem occurred in Moon-shadow Pond upon the death of a ninety-one-year-old matriarch with four married sons. Two of her sons had prospered through businesses that created ritual objects that are customarily burnt as offerings to ancestors and gods, including lifelike paper replicas of cars, televisions, bedroom furniture, and other coveted consumer items, as well as spirit money and clothes.[75] During the course of the preparations for the funeral as well as the funeral itself, the brothers were unable to work together. For instance, a formal announcement of the funeral was sent to the fourth brother, who lived nearby in the county capital. He was insulted by this behavior, since he claimed that it showed that his own brothers were treating him as an outsider, an interpretation shared by other villagers. Furthermore, little red envelopes of money, which are usually dispensed to people who help out during the funeral, contained only two *yuan,* instead of the ten *yuan* which was typically given at that time. The family exhibited both a lack of unity and a lack of generosity during the entire affair, and despite their wealth and the fact that they spent a considerable sum of money on the funeral, other villagers were critical of them.

"Their good name has amounted to nothing" *(you ming dengyu ling).* This phrase was frequently used in the weeks following the funeral. Indeed, villagers compared this funeral unfavorably to the funeral of Red Chong's mother, held several weeks earlier. Although Red Chong was his mother's only son and although his family was not nearly as prosperous as the four brothers just mentioned, many villagers came to mourn when his ninety-one-year-old mother died. And in the course of preparing for the funeral and conducting it, relations between Red Chong's family and all the villagers were exemplary. A funeral is not only an event in which filiality is on stage, but also an event where a family's dealings with the community at large are paramount.[76]

The funeral of Red Chong's mother was particularly interesting because, as mentioned earlier, Red Chong, a good Communist, frequently stated that he personally did not even believe in the concepts of an afterlife or reincarnation. From the beginning, he asserted that the funeral for his mother was primarily a matter of *lian* ("face") as well as a matter of honoring his mother's wishes.

Concerns with status and memory clearly intersect here. When I asked neighbors how they would have reacted if Red Chong had decided not to undertake a grand funeral for his mother, they all replied that it was a matter of filiality. "Whether you believe or don't believe," said Aihua, "you still have to do these things. Otherwise people will say that you are unfilial. . . . Even if you don't have the money, you'll borrow the money." The expression of filiality is therefore one of the primary aims of an expensive funeral, and it is also one of the reasons that orthopraxy seems to be so important in Chinese funeral rites. As will be explored shortly, however, despite general statements to the contrary, villagers were willing to make exceptions in some specific cases to the idea that a funeral must be expensive and grand, provided that they felt satisfied that filiality and remembrance were expressed in some other way.

I will further address the issue of the relationship between funerals as indices of status and as expressions of the morality of remembrance in the sections below. This issue is closely related to questions about the relative weight given to orthopraxy (proper procedure) as opposed to orthodoxy (proper ideological content). Before I can adequately address this issue, however, I must first examine the question of continuity in Moonshadow Pond funerals. Only after this can we explore the latitude given for nonconformity. Finally, we must assess the role of the state, and consider the degree to which it has influenced the villagers' discourse about obligations to the dead.

A CONTINUOUS TRADITION?

Death ritual is part of a deeply internalized sense of social obligation that does not end with an individual's death. It also plays an important part in the confirmation or establishment of a family's status. These two aspects of death ritual are nothing new in Chinese culture. Many villagers recounted stories from the old society in which a family literally went broke because of the financial requirements of a funeral. Aihua, in her good Communist recounting of tradition, often pointed out to me that the great expense of funerals most frequently caused villagers in the old society to sell their land off to landlords. Uncle Li, who had been shunned during the Cultural Revolution because of his higher-class background and who was less likely to recount the past in officially legitimated ways, also recalled that "if you didn't have a big funeral, people would laugh at you."

Just how continuous has this tradition been? Are we witnessing the resurrection of an interrupted tradition, or has there been a greater continuity than we might have suspected at first glance? Can we speak of continuity in ideological or emotional orientation with changed rites? Or conversely, do seemingly traditional rites actually work within the community to express new meanings? In order to answer these questions, we need to look at the economic, political, and social context of these revived rituals.

I should note that there was never a complete interruption of tradition. During the Maoist period, different elements of the tradition were dropped at different times. Reburial of the bones was not performed from the 1950s until after the reform period was underway in the early 1980s. Former monks and nuns were expected to work as ordinary members of production teams and most of them married; they were only allowed to ply their trade after the economic reforms. But on a few occasions in the early 1960s, these monks did officiate at local funerals, and the paper objects that were burnt as offerings to the dead soul, including the house for the dead soul, were also used occasionally.

For instance, Songling's husband, Baoli, participated in such a funeral for his father in 1963 and showed me two old photographs of the funeral. In one (photograph 14), the descendants dressed in their mourning garb pose in front of a paper soul house. In the other, taken after the morning service, the mourners as well as guests pose with the coffin prior to escorting it to the hill for burial. Songling told me that Baoli went to great lengths to pay for this funeral. He had to pay not only for the construction of the soul house but also for the photograph itself and for two former monks who officiated at the ceremony. In order to do this, Baoli sold silkworms as well as wood that he had collected from the surrounding mountains, sideline economic activities that were not legal at the time. The event was particularly significant for Songling because it occurred a year before her marriage to Baoli, and it left them with such

PHOTOGRAPH 14. A 1963 funeral. Mourners pose before a paper soul house.
Note the male and female servants on the right and left sides of the house.

meager economic resources that they were unable to invite even a single
table of guests to their wedding. Nonetheless, she contended that for the
sake of *mianzi,* the sacrifice was worth it (another way of viewing this
would be to say that death *mianzi* even trumps wedding *mianzi*).

During the Cultural Revolution, there was also some secretive reciprocity with the dead. Indeed, Aihua's story at the beginning of this chapter is a perfect example of this. Although a long-time party member, she
felt it necessary to burn paper money to the ancestors whom she felt her
son had wronged when he destroyed the funeral urns on the hilltops. Villagers told me that old women were also somewhat immune during the
Cultural Revolution. A few would make offerings to village ancestors
and gods during New Year—they were not taken seriously because of
their age and were therefore shielded from criticism.

Certain elements of tradition remained in public rites throughout the
entire Maoist period, at least in the cases in which the deceased was from
a "good" class and was not the object of political struggle. For instance,
Uncle Kewen was one of the few villagers who had the status of a
"worker," because he was employed in a leather factory in the county
capital and did not work the land. He showed me a photograph of his

mother's funeral from 1968. Unlike the funeral of Baoli's father that took place five years earlier and before the Cultural Revolution, this funeral had no soul house or monks. It was conceived as a memorial service. Yet, Uncle Kewen told me that heaven, the soul, and the ancestors were still notified at the beginning of the service, and he said that paper money was secretly burnt. In the photograph, the mourners are clearly wearing traditional mourning garb that indicates that they are descendants of the deceased.

Aihua told me that during the same period, as a coffin was led to the mountain for burial, it was not uncommon for an individual to scatter bits of paper in advance of the procession to keep away the malevolent spirits. Songling reported that even wailing occurred in some instances, although this also depended on whether the deceased was in a "good" or "bad" class.[77]

There was never a complete interruption of traditional practices, and even those practices that were suspended and banned were not halted long enough to go beyond some villagers' abilities to reconstruct them.[78] In contrast, the resurgence of traditional death ritual now occurring in the countryside takes place in a transformed social, political, and cultural context. For instance, while the rites are still central to a family's status, they now prop up that status in a new class structure, one that is unlike that of either the pre-Liberation or Maoist eras. In contemporary Moonshadow Pond, class is based neither on land holdings as it was in the old society nor on the hereditary class-label system of the Maoist period. Families now experience variable success in gaining access to economic resources based on a number of different factors: success in small business, appointment to bureaucratic positions, access to wage-earning opportunities in nearby or more distant cities, relationships with and access to help from overseas relatives, and so on.[79]

A marching band and singers, a day and night of Buddhist ceremonies, a large banquet with at least seventy or eighty guests, and several days of bustling activity (including gambling) are now the norm in Moonshadow Pond. This clearly surpasses the "cold and desolate" ceremonies of the Maoist era. And as discussed earlier, it also surpasses the grandiosity possible for even wealthy peasants in the pre-Liberation era.

In addition, death ritual from the pre-Liberation era has been resurrected in a new ideological context—one in which worldviews from the Maoist period have not been completely jettisoned but articulate in rather interesting ways with concepts with longer histories. The atheism of Red Chong and some of his friends is a rather good example of this. They based their endorsement of traditional rites on the importance of both *mianzi* and remembrance rather than on a belief in the spirit world. Indeed, Red Chong, who like Aihua was a long-time party member, went even further by enunciating a kind of post-Mao syncretism. On the morning of his mother's funeral, as the monks prepared for the long series of rites to follow, he said to me, "I think both Buddha and Mao were basically saying the same thing, 'serve the people.'"

As explained earlier, the addition of "secular or lay monks," modern eulogies, and the mixing of the sexes among the mourners for a good part of the ceremony all add new dimensions to the resurrected rites. Furthermore, the worldviews that villagers use to interpret the revival of death ritual in Moonshadow Pond are now informed by reference to several historical periods, as Red Chong's comment clearly illustrates.

Finally, these funeral rites appear to the villagers as an aspect of their *particular* identity, which can be seen by the way villagers link the revived death rituals to their identity as peasants *(nongmin)*. When Songling's sister, a nurse in the army, died of cancer in 1995, her work unit *(danwei)* in the county capital took care of all her funeral arrangements. The service was a primarily secular memorial service much like those described by Martin Whyte in his work on urban funerals in the People's Republic of China.[80] The service was held in a public building rather than in a lineage hall. In a room to the side of the main assembly hall, Songling's sister lay in a glass-covered coffin in her army uniform and cap. A piece of red cloth with a yellow hammer and sickle was draped upon her body.

During the service, the primary mourners, the deceased's siblings and children, knelt down on their knees wearing no mourning garb other than black armbands. Floral wreaths, sent by friends, relatives, and colleagues, were placed at the front of the hall. Above these wreaths hung a large piece of cloth from the ceiling, labeling the event as the memorial service for Comrade Lin.

Several additional touches were added by family members and were not part of the ritual as organized by the *danwei*. Family members placed a spirit tablet to one side of the wreath display, and prior to the commencement of the memorial service, Songling and her sisters wailed by the side of the coffin and burned some paper money. They also placed a table of offerings of fruit, buns, and meat by the coffin as well. When the service was over, Songling, her brothers, and her sister's sons and daughter returned to her sister's house with her spirit tablet.

Nonetheless, even with these features added, compared to most contemporary village funerals, this service was a short and primarily secular memorial. There was no soul house, the mourners donned no funeral garb, there was no long night of ritual led by monks, and there was no burial (since the corpse was to be cremated). A eulogy was delivered by the unit commander rather than by a representative of the native village, and, of course, Songling's sister was referred to as "comrade," a decidedly Maoist designation.

In speaking about this funeral, Songling and her husband explained that the funeral was "organized by the work unit" and asserted that this was the reason that it was different from village funerals. Of course, during the collective era, rural teams and brigades were also considered work units by the government, but the post-Mao dismantling of the collectives means that most villagers now work for themselves. They reserve the term *danwei* for government jobs that provide stable salaries and benefits, a work situation available to few rural residents. Songling could easily say, "We *nongmin* [farmers] don't have *danwei*." For her, the two terms were mutually exclusive. (Chapter 7 will probe more deeply into these distinctions.)

Songling and other Moonshadow Pond residents now associate memorial services *(zhuidao hui)* with *danwei* and therefore not with peasant life. Villagers now assume rural funerals will take the form of "doing benevolent acts" *(zuo haoshi)*. As mentioned at the beginning of the chapter, this implies the use of Buddhist monks and a focus in the ritual on the fate of the deceased's soul. What we might call the distinction between secular and religious is understood in Moonshadow Pond as the difference between memorial services and "doing benevolent acts" and as the distinction between the *danwei* and the peasant community.[81]

Although Songling saw customary funerals as an aspect of peasant identity, it does not follow from this that Moonshadow Pond residents were primarily *motivated* in their practice of such funerals by a need to assert this identity.[82] Rather, as I have pointed out, a number of motivations underlie Moonshadow Pond funeral practice, especially those of status and the morality of remembrance.

What weight do villagers give to these various motivations? Answering this question inevitably involves tackling the issue of orthodoxy and orthopraxy, or ideological orientation versus practice, in Moonshadow Pond funeral rites. Do the residents of Moonshadow Pond recognize any legitimate alternatives to the kind of rites that we have been describing in this chapter, rites that we might categorize as "modernized traditional"? Is remembrance of the deceased more important than the form of that remembrance? Or does "proper procedure" count for everything? To try to understand these issues in the specific context of Moonshadow Pond, the next section analyzes an individual case of nonconformity.

THE DAUGHTER WHO DID NOT CRY AT HER FATHER'S FUNERAL

The revival of "traditional" death ritual in Moonshadow Pond has also opened up a space for the return of older forms of nonconformity. The case of Bright Ling is a good example of this phenomenon. In the 1990s, Bright Ling was one of a handful of villagers who had graduated from college. After attending the local university in the county capital, she found employment in a bank. Thirty years old and unmarried but with a good job in a government work unit, Bright Ling was often the object of village gossip that speculated as to why she had never married. One theory was that Bright Ling's intense devotion to Buddhism meant that she had forsworn any interest in marriage, although Bright Ling claimed that she would marry if she met someone whose interest in Buddhism paralleled her own.

As already described, a popular form of Buddhism is practiced in Moonshadow Pond. Monks are called in for the funeral ceremonies. In addition, the village Buddhist temple that was closed during the collective era has now reopened. But village Buddhism in Meixian is of a very different sort than the more orthodox and philosophical form of Buddhism that attracted Bright Ling. Aside from the integration of Buddhist elements into village funerals, visits to the Buddhist temple in Moonshadow Pond are of primary interest to elderly women who go to request good fortune for their immediate families. "The average person," said Aihua, "goes just four times a year to the Buddhist temple unless there is a special need."[83] These occasions for worship are thought of as an attempt to gain and pay back for good fortune. The gods in this village temple are a combination of Buddhist deities, such as Guanyin, and popular non-Buddhist deities, such as Caishen (the God of Wealth) and Guandi. When making offerings, meat is allowed as an offering to a number of the non-Buddhist deities. The village practice of Buddhism is therefore quite syncretic and is oriented toward obtaining practical results.

Bright Ling, in contrast, was passionately involved in the activities of a Buddhist temple in the county capital. This temple attracts a number of educated urbanites who visit in order to take instruction in Buddhism, recite sutras, and sing songs together as a congregation. Followers consider recitation of the Buddha Amitabha's name and vegetarianism as ways to amass virtue, and those followers who ultimately decide to live in the temple give all their property to the temple rather than to their descendants.

There have always been heterodox alternatives to orthodoxy in popular Chinese religion.[84] Although these alternatives were varied, they were based on voluntary ties rather than on membership in a particular family or community. In their approach to death ritual, they focused on "immediate forms of salvation outside the ancestral line."[85] Like the temple to which Bright Ling belonged, these religious movements emphasized both congregationalism and sutra recitation as well as immediate salvation through recitation of the Buddha Amitabha's name. Unlike the majority of rural peasants, those who participated in these movements placed little importance on the continuing interaction between the dead and living.[86]

In her approach to death ritual, Bright Ling followed in the footsteps of this older tradition. When her father died, Bright Ling chose rites that were meant to release her father's soul from its attachment to the living, rather than to generate a new set of exchanges between living and dead. She eschewed the elaborate and status-enhancing death rituals described in this chapter. Rather than undertaking an expensive funeral ceremony with its feasts, array of paper offerings, and crowds of gamblers, Bright Ling contended that calmly reciting sutras by the side of the coffin would be sufficient, and she called in a few nuns to keep her company in this recitation. To do more, she claimed, would obstruct the dead soul's ability to depart peacefully from this world.

Bright Ling also shared another characteristic with individuals who were attracted to heterodoxy in imperial China. They were often people who "for one reason or another were not fully involved in the 'natural' network of social relationships based on family, kinship, and community and who therefore had to make their own arrangements."[87] As an educated, unmarried woman in her thirties, Bright Ling was also a nonconformist in Moonshadow Pond. She could not easily mingle in the networks of most women her age who were married and interacted with each other, their children, and their in-laws.

Of course, although Bright Ling's religious practice and social situation shared some characteristics with followers of heterodox cults in imperial China, there are clearly some important distinctions. First, most scholars of Chinese religion insist that the word "heterodox" be reserved for those religious movements that the state sees as threatening to the social order.[88] This was clearly not the case here. The temple to which

Bright Ling belonged was approved by the local government and allowed to operate openly. Bright Ling was clearly a nonconformist but was hardly viewed as dangerous.[89]

In fact, and rather ironically, many of Bright Ling's ideas about the differences between her religious devotion and the religious practice of the villagers were not in opposition to the ideas of the state but actually dependent on the very vocabulary of the party. Although the Communist state and party originally construed all religion as a form of *mixin* (superstition), this position changed in reform China. The state now differentiates religion *(zongjiao)* from superstition, and separates religion from popular practices such as New Year's observances, ancestral cults, the worship of various folk spirits, and the practices of geomancers and shamans.[90] As such, Bright Ling's devotion to a more theoretical form of Buddhism than that practiced in the village was more in line with the state's view of acceptable religion than that of the villagers. "Buddhism is the mother of philosophy," Bright Ling once told me, "and Buddhist practice contains knowledge, not blind superstition like that which exists in the villages." Bright Ling also criticized the "monks" who were regularly employed for village rites as frauds who were just out for money.

I expected that villagers would not validate Bright Ling's choices regarding her father's funeral because they did not conform to the revived religious rites that had become so important as a measure of status and an expression of filiality in Moonshadow Pond. This was true of her initial decision not to move her father's coffin to the lineage hall. It was too much of a bitter pill to swallow, and her uncle finally persuaded her that the coffin must be placed in the lineage hall before burial. The rest of her plan, however, was preserved in its simplicity. When I asked villagers about Bright Ling's refusal to honor her father with large-scale funeral rites, most replied that her recitation of the sutras was an acceptable alternative (although not one that they themselves would choose). "She still commemorated her father," one neighbor told me. "As long as you commemorate your ancestors, it's not really that important how you do it. It's not as if she did nothing."

The villagers' reactions to Bright Ling are suggestive. They continually emphasized conscience, memory, and commemoration as the most essential elements in funeral rites. This emphasis could find room for someone such as Red Chong, who denied the existence of a spirit world altogether, or someone such as Bright Ling, who chose nonstandard rites. This is not to suggest that standard rites are not preferred or that status accruing from elaborate traditional rituals is not highly desired. But ultimately, what Donald Munro calls "family feeling" is even more important.[91] Despite a strong preference for proper procedure, villagers were willing to give a certain amount of leeway to someone who did not follow these rituals, as long as they felt that the deceased was commemorated in some form.

To use the analysts' terms here, "orthodoxy" is more important than "orthopraxy." Red Chong decided to go ahead with a traditional rite, but Bright Ling did not. She chose a format without physical manifestations of her father's lineage or descendants, without guests, feasts, gamblers, or ritualized wailing, without even a twenty-four-hour "show" by a group of hired monks. Nonetheless, villagers respected her choice as a form of commemoration, even if it was one that they would not themselves select.

STATE, PEASANT, AND ENCOMPASSMENT

The revival of popular religious practice in reform-era China has prompted many assessments of its implications for understanding contemporary relationships between state and local society. Despite the changes in local culture, of course, the state still has enormous power. It has powers to allocate resources and regulate action at both national and local levels, and state personnel can exercise considerable local authority on behalf of their own interests.[92] The state can also try to exercise ideological and persuasive power. Nonetheless, during the reform era, there has been an undeniable loosening of state controls over local ritual. Some analysts, therefore, see the return of local memory as an outcome of this rejuvenated ritual.[93] The revival has, in their eyes, helped "restore to local communities a sense of place marked by the singularity of their history and their ritual traditions."[94]

Certainly, this approach has some relevance to the case at hand. The lineage hall in Moonshadow Pond is now both physically and socially restored to the center of the village. The lineage tablets, each of which lists the name of a male ancestor and includes almost all such ancestors going back to the village founder, were hidden away during the Cultural Revolution. They have now been restored to the central hall. Funeral services, which take place in the confines of the lineage hall, thereby reaffirm the importance of the local lineage and its history.

The revival of popular religion in its rural context has been explained further as a positive assertion of peasant identity in contrast to the contemporary state's negative portrayals of peasants as "backward." Says

Andrew Kipnis in regard to his field site in north China, "Local non-peasants took up the post-1978 official rhetoric by scorning much of the (re)-invented ritual of Fengjia peasants as backward . . . and feudal. . . . In contrast, villagers who were 'peasant and proud' contested this objectification by flaunting their new ritual."[95]

In the present case, this argument only partially applies. True, Songling viewed religious funeral rites as part of a "peasant" class identity, but this does not mean that Songling saw "peasantness" as the chief motivation behind the return to such rites. In Songling's eyes, peasants have revived popular rituals because they *want to* and *can*. The state's loosening of control over popular rituals is important, but Songling did not speak of these rituals as an assertion of "peasant" identity as against pejorative state definitions. She spoke about them as a commemoration of the dead, status for the living, and protection of the deceased's soul.

Instead of viewing religious revival as a case of one-way assertion of peasant identity or community identity as against state definitions or limits, it might make more sense to see the revival of popular religious practice in rural China as an instance of interpenetrating categories and mutual influences. Peasants may use categories adopted from state discourse, just as the state or its personnel may use ideas originating in popular religion. Indeed, many analysts now refrain from viewing state and society as discrete and opposed entities, and this caveat is certainly applicable in the case at hand.[96] For instance, Songling's categorical opposition between peasants and people who are part of a work unit is clearly taken from the postrevolutionary order; it is inconceivable outside the parameters of Chinese Communist history and the class categories utilized by the party-state. And while the "Maoist" Red Chong undertook a "traditional" funeral rite for his mother, the devoted Buddhist Bright Ling dispensed with the popular and expensive religious rites now preferred by the villagers. In fact, despite her adherence to Buddhism, Bright Ling criticized villagers' religious practices as lowbrow superstition. The extremely religious Bright Ling came closer to anyone else in the village to accepting implicitly the orthodox party categorical distinctions between religion *(zongjiao)* and superstition *(mixin)!*

Local cadres, in contrast, who might be viewed as the most intimately connected to the modern state and whom one might expect to be wary of customary ritual, actually use it to enhance their own status and power. While their presence at a ritual may give status to its sponsor, they also gain face and prestige for themselves by appearing at these events. As in rural areas of north-central China, local officials "are not interested in cracking down on superstition because they do not derive any benefit from doing so."[97] To the contrary, both ordinary villagers and cadres gain mutual status benefits by their participation in local funerals.

I also submit, however, that there is a hierarchy of values here. Despite the interpenetration of state and locality and of concepts from pre-Liberation, Maoist, and reform periods, there are some encompassing categories. A combination of status and moral evaluations that is continuous with a long tradition of mourning in China still motivates mourners in contemporary Moonshadow Pond. But although status and questions of "face" are critical components of funerals in contemporary Moonshadow Pond and although a grand enactment of a "traditional" rite is preferable, the most indispensable element of mourning, from the villagers' point of view, is still commemoration and memory of the deceased.

If we return to the original dichotomies mentioned at the beginning of this chapter, those of continuity versus change, and orthodoxy versus orthopraxy, our answer should now be abundantly clear. Although villagers prefer certain kinds of outward ritual expression, their absence is not fatal (to use a particularly apt word!). Despite transformations over time, some of which were enforced by the Maoist state itself and a few of these ultimately incorporated by villagers into the revived traditional rites, villagers did not jettison their essential understandings of the most indispensable motives in mourning rites.

This is not to deny that the form and content of ritual bear some relationship to one another, but this relationship has always been dialectical rather than a form of one-way production. For example, as discussed earlier, when Buddhist elements were added to Confucian funeral rites, they were attractive precisely because they responded to existing dynamics within Chinese families, particularly to the bond between mothers and sons, which was underplayed in the existing Confucian rituals. Looked at from another vantage point, however, once added to funeral rites, these Buddhist elements helped reproduce the subjectivities and social roles within families—particularly the strong mother-son ties and suspicion of the in-marrying daughter-in-law—that upheld Chinese patriliny.[98]

In contemporary China, a change in outward form was enforced from above by the Maoist state. Religious rites for the deceased (zuo haoshi) were replaced (although never completely) by secular memorial services. Nonetheless, rural dwellers brought their own understandings to this outward form as long as it lasted, and these understandings were based on already existing ideas about moral debt to the deceased. Villagers ultimately integrated some elements of the secular memorial into the revived religious rites that are now almost universally practiced in the village. But they also accept the legitimacy of other forms of commemoration.

The morality of remembrance is therefore "encompassing" here, to use Louis Dumont's term.[99] It begins with conscience *(liangxin)* and reciprocates, at a minimum, through commemoration. In contemporary Moonshadow Pond, one's moral debt to the deceased is usually fulfilled through rituals that assure safe passage of the soul through the underworld and through a series of continuing exchanges with the deceased. Other elements of funeral rites, including the rites as an element of status competition and even villagers' questions about the sincerity of individual mourners or clergy, can be understood with reference to this encompassing value. Status accrues to those who at least *appear* to be remembering.

There is almost a kind of "overdetermination" to this outlook. As discussed in chapter 2, the deepest kindnesses, or *enqing,* can never be fully repaid. But as I have alluded to before, even if kindnesses can never be fully repaid, they most importantly can never be forgotten.[100] Among these kindnesses are the sacrifices of parents. Although Bright Ling did not cry at her father's funeral, she did commemorate him. No one could say, "She has no conscience."

CHAPTER 5

The Moral Dilemmas of Return Visits

Songling told me two stories. The first was intended as a commentary on the social caste system of Mao's time and the ironic reversals in social status that occurred once that system was discarded in the reform era. The second was certainly intended as a cautionary tale and moral warning about neglecting one's ancestors.

> *A Bad Class Marriage:* When Qiufang decided to marry the Chen's son, her parents were so upset that they made her kneel in front of a portrait of Chairman Mao for an entire day! The Chen's son came from a bad class category, because he had overseas relatives, and Qiufang's parents were afraid that with this kind of connection, the rest of their family would be discriminated against. Finally, Qiufang ran away to the neighboring village where the Chen's son lived and married him anyway, but she did not see her natal family for seven years. As time went on, however, her family began to see that it really wasn't a bad match after all. Her husband's family began to receive a lot of money from their overseas relations in Indonesia. Now Qiufang's parents really like their son-in-law.

> *An Unfilial Visitor:* Xiuling's elder brother came to visit from Taiwan last year. But instead of first returning to his mother's grave to worship her, he decided to take a trip around China, and visited lots of scenic places such as Kunming. Later he returned to Meixian [his native place], and he was immediately struck down by a severe illness for over one week!

What is interesting in both these tales is the ambiguous role of the overseas Chinese relative—a source of despised status during the Cultural

Revolution, later an attractive source of economic benefits, but also a foreigner who may neglect the moral obligations to ancestors incumbent upon all descendants.

The reform period made it possible for a host of dormant links between Moonshadow Pond residents and their overseas Chinese relatives to be revitalized. Overseas connections, considered to be politically damaging during the Maoist period, became highly coveted by families, villages, and local governments in the reform era, especially in southeast China, which had experienced high rates of emigration in the first half of the twentieth century. But as the stories above illustrate, these reestablished contacts with overseas Chinese kin are accompanied by a number of new ironies and anxieties: ironies relating to the status of those with overseas connections, as well as anxieties about what is to be expected from these visitors.

With the death of Mao Zedong and the onset of the reform era in the late 1970s, China's political leaders changed their attitudes and policies toward links with the outside world, including connections with overseas Chinese. As mentioned in chapter 1, the class-label system was abolished, and those descended from landlords, rich peasants, and other "bad classes," including those with overseas Chinese connections, were no longer pariahs. But as relatives from abroad have returned to visit their village kin, new sets of questions arise. What is to be expected from these visitors from overseas? What are the ground rules for relationships between those who emigrated and those who were left behind? How are the actions and decisions of those who return to be judged? And how do these returns affect relationships among villagers who stayed behind?

This chapter examines the return visits of these overseas relations and explores the implications of these visits for an understanding of villagers' ideas about moral obligation. We will also examine the moral dilemmas that return visits can engender. While only 11 percent of Moonshadow Pond families have an overseas Chinese connection, their impact is felt in many ways: through the fanfare that may accompany their visits, the donations they may give to local projects, and through the way villagers deal with the differences between those families who do have such connections and those who do not.[1]

In the anthropological literature on China, particularly on southeast China, a number of ethnographies have already investigated the connections between emigrants and their native villages. Many of these works focus not only upon the economic impact of emigration, remittances, and investments by overseas kin, but also on the impact of return upon local communities. They ask how emigration, remittances, and return affect class structure and infrastructure[2] as well as whether they unravel or help to strengthen traditional cultural forms, such as the lineage.[3] A number of recent works also examine the allure of transnational Chinese culture for those who remain on the mainland.[4]

Although the issues above will be considered in this chapter as well, the focus and point of departure differ from these previous studies. First, this examination also adds a new dimension to the treatment of return in the Chinese context because previous ethnographic studies of overseas return focus on pre-Liberation China or on Hong Kong, or they deal with the role of remittances but not with actual return.[5] Further, since my focus throughout the book is on moral discourse in Moonshadow Pond, I look here at return from the point of view of those who remained behind in the village, especially their expectations about returnees and about villager interactions with them. A frequent theme in the literature on return home worldwide is that returnees must wrestle with contradictions between imagined and actual homelands.[6] It is less often pointed out that those who remain behind must also sort out multiple and often contradictory images of homecomings.

As we shall see, Moonshadow Pond residents construe their visiting foreign kin in several ways. Villagers expect them to remember their family and commemorate their ancestors. But, as illustrated in the second story at the chapter's beginning, they may also view returnees as foreigners whose priorities are not congruent with those of the villagers. Further, while overseas kin are viewed as potential benefactors, as we also see in the first story, both their public and private contributions are subject to a variety of interpretations, and these contributions can also generate new social frictions. When villagers discuss their expectations about the obligations inherent in the various roles overseas kin can assume, they articulate a number of competing moral visions. When this occurs, they make judgments about visiting overseas kin *and* about other villagers who interact with them. Thus, the return "home" creates a complex and contested moral space. I conclude this chapter with the story of one overseas Chinese visitor, "the old man from Taiwan." When people in the village interacted with him and spoke about him, many of the contradictions in the role of the overseas Chinese—as benefactor, kinsperson, and foreigner—were brought to the fore.

Before going further, an explanation of terms is necessary. There is some debate about whether persons of Chinese descent who live outside mainland China should be called "overseas Chinese" or some other term such as "diaspora Chinese," "persons of Chinese descent" *(huayi)*, or simply "Chinese people" *(huaren)*.[7] I use the term "overseas Chinese" because it correlates with the terms used by the villagers of Moonshadow Pond to refer to their overseas relations—*huaqiao* or "overseas Chinese," and *haiwai qiaobao* or "overseas compatriots." Furthermore, although relatives in Hong Kong are not technically "overseas," and Hong Kong was unified with the People's Republic of China (PRC) in 1997, I include Hong Kong relations as "overseas Chinese" in this essay. Until 1997, Hong Kong was not only part of a separate political entity, but also part of a vastly different cultural, economic, and social world. After 1997, and despite increasing economic consolidation between Hong Kong and mainland, there are still "two systems": different legal frameworks, political structures, currencies, educational institutions, and more. Relatives who return from Hong Kong to the village are treated in much the same way and are the objects of similar sets of expectations as those coming from more distant areas, and letters from lineage, village, or township leaders addressed to "overseas compatriots" are also sent to Hong Kong relations.

HISTORICAL ANTECEDENTS

To understand the significance of return migration to mainland China, one needs first to understand the fluctuating role that diaspora has played in Chinese life for the last several centuries. Although contemporary Chinese migration and return migrations are influenced by present-day structures of the world economy, it would be wrong to view these movements as new phenomena.[8]

During the early decades of the Qing dynasty (1644–1911), the Chinese state banned emigration. Indeed, the Qianlong emperor stated that emigrants had "deserted their ancestors' graves to seek profits abroad"[9] and emigrants who returned were often executed in order to deter others from leaving.[10] However, in the waning years of the Qing dynasty, the imperial court, much like the reform-minded Communist leaders of the post-Mao era in China, realized that emigrants might provide an important source of wealth that could be used profitably to enhance Chinese development. By the 1880s, imperial policy towards emigrants had reversed itself, and by 1902, the Qing government was actually sending envoys to Southeast Asia to encourage the Chinese merchants there to invest in China. By the Republican period in the 1920s, overseas Chinese remittances "helped balance the trade deficit of China in the 1920s."[11]

The use of the word *huaqiao,* or "overseas Chinese," also began in the waning days of the Qing dynasty. As Wang Gungwu points out, the word *qiao* is "an ancient word whose main meaning is 'to sojourn, or reside temporarily away from home.' The first clear use of the word . . . occurred in an official document in 1858. . . . Up to this time, a whole range of other terms, some most uncomplimentary, were employed to describe Chinese who resided overseas."[12]

Between the downfall of the Qing dynasty in 1911 and the establishment of Communist rule in 1949, many areas of southeast China, including Meixian, witnessed large rates of emigration. According to the official *Meixian Gazetteer,* there were over six hundred and thirty thousand overseas Chinese of Meixian origin by 1985. These emigrants and their descendants were spread over five continents and forty-six countries, although about half of them were in Indonesia, and a large number of the remaining group were in other Southeast Asian countries.[13] Considering that at the time this figure was reported the population of Meixian was not much more than seven hundred thousand people, this is certainly a significant number of emigrants, since the number of Meixian Hakka living abroad was considered to be almost equal to the population of Meixian.

In Moonshadow Pond, emigration during the turbulent first half of the twentieth century was often viewed as the only alternative to destitution. Emigration from Moonshadow Pond, as from most parts of Guangdong Province, was heavily gendered.[14] Most of the emigrants from Moonshadow Pond were male, and most went to India, Thailand, Burma, or Indonesia. Often they never returned, leaving wives behind as virtual widows. Later, at the time of Liberation in 1949, a few men emigrated because they had been soldiers in the Nationalist Army and feared retribution. These men went to Taiwan rather than to Southeast Asia. Finally, in the wake of land reform instituted by the new Communist government in the early 1950s, a few more villagers emigrated. In this case, the émigrés were individuals who were in "bad class" categories, mostly those who feared that as former landlords they might be beaten or even executed, and these individuals made their way to Hong Kong.

As in earlier historical eras, the Communist government went through several changes of policy toward emigrants and their families. During the 1950s and early 1960s, relatives of overseas Chinese were able to receive some remittances, but return visits from emigrants were not encouraged and rarely took place. The possibility of emigrating also ceased (and indeed little legal emigration took place until the reform era). During the Cultural Revolution era (1966–76), almost all contacts between overseas Chinese and mainland kin were severed. Overseas Chinese who returned, such as refugees from Indonesian political violence, were "attacked for their bourgeois values and wasteful practices."[15]

In Meixian, local policies closely paralleled national policies. During the late 1950s, the Bank of China branch in Meixian set up procedures that made it easy for overseas Chinese to remit funds to their relatives.[16] As the Cultural Revolution erupted, relations with overseas relatives were viewed as foreign connections to be attacked, and remittances were condemned as "rotten capitalist money."[17]

"If you had an overseas Chinese relative," one villager told me, "they might even accuse you of being a spy. So most people, if they had any connections, just kept it a secret." Many villagers pointed to a popular slogan of the period—"self-reliance and arduous struggle" *(zi li geng sheng, jian ku fen dou)*—as an example of wrongheaded ideals. "Imagine if overseas Chinese could have invested in China all along," one resident told me. "We would certainly have been better off by now!"

After 1978, the policy was reversed again and contacts with overseas Chinese began to be actively encouraged.[18] Confiscated property and bank accounts were returned to overseas Chinese.[19] In Meixian, not only was property returned, but the class status of overseas Chinese was "rectified."[20] Formal class status designations were no longer in use in China by 1984, yet at that time the Meixian government still went through a process of eradicating from past records the class status of households with overseas Chinese relatives. They removed the designations of landlord and rich peasant from these records, and these families were even issued official documents certifying the change in their class status.[21]

Unlike some contemporary rural areas in Fujian Province which have seen a resurgence of emigration in recent years, Meixian has not re-emerged as a place of exodus to foreign lands. As mentioned in chapter 3, young adults from Moonshadow Pond now journey for employment to the much closer urban centers in Guangdong. Meixian was also too far from Hong Kong to be a site of a significant refugee stream during the Maoist era. Hence, emigrants and their families who visit Moonshadow Pond are usually those who left before Liberation.

During these return visits, emigrants may donate to a village project, and these contributions are often marked by banquets and ceremonies in honor of the donor. Indeed, when villagers speak of the return visits of their overseas kin, they often refer to acts of beneficence. I therefore begin my examination with an analysis of the way villagers discuss overseas visitors in their role as benefactors, and of the contradictions within these images and the social relationships they attempt to describe. After examining returnees as benefactors, I describe villagers' understandings of their visiting kin in terms of two other models: villagers view returnees as family and lineage members with unbreakable ties to ancestors and living relatives, but they also view them as foreigners who may no longer honor these ties. Throughout my analysis, I emphasize the competing and contradictory desires and moral judgments that return visits engender amongst villagers.

RETURNEES AS PUBLIC BENEFACTORS

"When a *huaqiao* [overseas Chinese] returns to the area," a villager said to me one day, "he almost always takes the local-level officials out for a big meal and also gives them *hongbao* [little red envelopes in which money is placed]." While gift-giving is an important part of social interaction throughout Chinese society,[22] villagers in Moonshadow Pond view this kind of behavior as an especially prominent feature of overseas Chinese, primarily because so many returning *huaqiao* have more financial resources than their lineage mates.

In this section, we examine the ways in which villagers view returnees as benefactors who extend a helping hand beyond the needs of their immediate family. All villagers are aware of the significant role that overseas Chinese play in economic revitalization. They often compare different regions of Guangdong as well as different villages in their own area in terms of the frequency and strength of their connections with overseas Chinese. Indeed, compared to its neighboring villages in the township, Moonshadow Pond residents have relatively few overseas relatives. The township in Meixian of which Moonshadow Pond is a part has the highest proportion of families with overseas Chinese connections in the county.[23] But in Moonshadow Pond, only twenty-one out of 184 families (11 percent) say they have an overseas Chinese connection.

But while only 11 percent of Moonshadow Pond families have a direct connection to Chinese living abroad, several recent village projects involving road and bridge building and the repair of the local primary school, main ancestral temple, and branch temples, could never have been completed without their help.[24] Donations from overseas donors to public institutions and projects are now deemed so important that cadres and even ordinary village residents are involved in trying to solicit them.

Villagers often organize themselves into committees whose goal is to recruit funds from overseas Chinese in order to garner support for these development plans. Among other things, they write letters to overseas Chinese with village connections in order to solicit funds for these projects. These letters are written in formal language and often allude to progress in nearby villages as a way to goad donors into caring about Moonshadow Pond.

For instance, a 1994 letter written to raise money for the elementary school and signed by several members of a local committee to support the school stated that other local schools had received abundant help from overseas compatriots and that their own local school lagged behind, leaving teachers dissatisfied and students unmotivated. At the end of the letter, potential donors were encouraged to think of the large task ahead as one in which they would "build a tower by gathering sand" *(ju sha cheng ta)*, or, in other words, accomplish their project with the help of many small donations.

Success in seeking help from Chinese overseas is an important measure of a local cadre's competence. Big Gao, who was the head of the production brigade from the late 1970s until 1993, listed his accomplishments in soliciting help from overseas Chinese as one of the major achievements of his term. The projects he worked on included raising funds to fix one bridge, building another bridge, improving flood protection around some parts of the river, road construction in the village, and acquiring new desks and benches for the primary school.

At the township level there is now an office dedicated to returning overseas Chinese and two cadres are delegated with the official responsibility of playing gracious hosts to returnees and soliciting overseas Chinese donations. If an overseas Chinese returns and is residing in the district during the Lunar New Year, then township cadres will make sure to visit on New Year's Day. Returnees are also usually invited by local township cadres for a banquet at a local restaurant that specializes in Hakka food and that is conveniently located near the township offices. The hope, of course, is that returnees will also reciprocate at some point by donating to a village project.

When I asked villagers why they thought overseas Chinese would contribute to the village, they often mentioned what might be called a "primordial" connection between overseas Chinese and their ancestral villages. People are expected to have emotional connections *(ganqing)* toward their native villages that will automatically generate an interest in contributing. "Your native village," explained Baoli, "is your root *[gen]*, and it is only natural that you would want to help." Traditional Buddhist notions are also attached to these explanations. For instance, the notion of *gongde,* which means "beneficent works," is often cited in discussions of overseas Chinese donations. Charitable giving is supposed to have good repercussions not only for oneself and one's family, but also for one's descendants.

Curiously, there are actually two notions of morality inscribed in these explanations. The idea that it is only natural that one would want to help one's native village, or the village of one's ancestors, explains correct behavior as something that is simply inherent and that merely needs to be cultivated in order to be expressed. In the analysis of formal Chinese systems of thought, this approach has often been viewed as characteristic of the "Confucian" approach.[25] However, the second idea—that good works in this life can achieve "merit" in the cosmological ordering of things—is connected to Buddhist forms of thought and ascribes the motivation to help one's native village not as a natural inclination, but as something at least partially executed by the desire for an otherworldly reward.

Interestingly, my own status in the village was anomalous in this regard. During each extended field stay, I thought it was important to give back to the community at large by making some donation to the village. In the spring of 2007, my husband and I decided to set up some basketball hoops on the paved area in front of the old school house. Basketball is now extremely popular in China and this court soon became a favorite spot for youngsters on their way home from school. Villagers were very happy with this donation and often compared our contributions with that of other *huaqiao,* even though we were foreigners with no kinship ties to the village. The fact that this was not our ancestral village and that we therefore didn't have a primordial connection to the village was used discursively to praise the donation, but it was sometimes also used to reflect negatively on *huaqiao* who, though related, had taken no interest in making donations to village projects.

Not all aspects of giving are viewed positively. Beyond the idea that a person may bestow gifts to the village because of primordial connections, or to achieve religious merit, or (in my anomalous case), as reciprocity for hospitality, there is also the acknowledgment that giving can increase the status or *mianzi* of the giver. Villagers view this phenomenon somewhat ambivalently. They welcome donations but on occasion they may deride the pride that can motivate them.

For instance, just a few miles up the road from Moonshadow Pond was the home of a former smuggler who had grown up in the Indian Chinese community. In India, he had run afoul of the law and had therefore returned to his native village in China, where he built a house for his elderly mother. Despite his former occupation and an unsettled family life, including strained relationships with his own sons and three former wives—none of whom returned with him—he endeavored to build a solid reputation in his ancestral home by making generous public and private donations. After several years of giving, however, he experienced financial troubles. Both his family members and unrelated villagers explained his predicament as stemming from the fact that he "loved 'face' too much" *(tai ai mianzi)*; in other words, that he was too concerned with raising his status by public giving, and therefore went bankrupt.

This ability of overseas Chinese to dispense money and other gifts contains implications for villagers' moral evaluations of each other as well. There is much to be gained from cultivating relationships with wealthy visitors, but villagers will harshly judge a person who fawns upon an overseas Chinese visitor with whom he or she does not have a close family connection purely for the purposes of personal monetary gain.[26] Many like to quote an old saying—"last night you were just a three-pound dog, but today, you are my third great uncle"—as a way of expressing the rapidity with which relationships change when a person suddenly becomes rich. The expression refers to a Hakka story about a man who was very poor, and so poor that he was also very skinny. People called him "three-pound dog" to imply just how skinny he was. But then he went to Southeast Asia and came back with all kinds of goods and beautiful clothes (presumably he gained weight too). Everyone started treating him respectfully and talking about their connections with him.

The most extreme example of taking advantage of the deep pockets of overseas Chinese was that of Aihua's nephew "Ironpot," who got his nickname because he used to eat rice while watching it cook as a child. Ironpot was an insatiable gambler whose fortunes, as one might expect, were marked by dramatic turnarounds. One of his most frequent tricks was to go to the county capital, not far from the village, and lure overseas Chinese into a variety of gambling games and card tricks. Because of his skill at both gambling and deception, he easily won many of these games, effectively emptying the pockets of the visitors with whom he played. But the hapless victims of his gambling talents were strangers. He would not have been able to take such advantage of returnees to his own village.

RETURNEES AS KIN

Writing about Chinese conceptions of kinship, the anthropologist Charles Stafford has said, "Mere physical departure should not be allowed to threaten the underlying, and fundamental, unity of kin."[27] Certainly, as discussed in chapter 3, the ideology of patrilineal descent is still strong in Moonshadow Pond as is the identification of lineage identity and place. As such, Moonshadow Pond residents expect returning *huaqiao* to travel to their home village and make offerings to village gods and ancestors before going anywhere else. This applies to both men and women. While men's names are recorded for posterity in the lineage history, the daughters and daughters-in-law of the lineage are also expected to honor the remote ancestors of their fathers and husband, as well as to visit the gravesites of their own parents and grandparents.

When arriving in the village for the first time, or returning after a long absence, a returnee is expected to proceed to the entrance of the village and make offerings to the village gods who protect it. Visiting kin should then proceed to the ancestral temple, and after that, ascend the hills surrounding the village to worship at their more immediate ancestors' graves. Family members from the village usually expect returnees to host a small banquet for their closest relations as well. However, villagers feel that long years abroad may diminish returnees' sense of connection with their ancestors. They like to tell moral vignettes about the eventual fate of people who ignore this ritual and who are struck with misfortune or ill health, much like the hapless individual in the second story that begins this chapter.

"*Huaqiao* who are not born here don't have a concept about their ancestors," Baoli said to me one day. He was equally perplexed by his elder brother, a former Nationalist soldier who fled to Taiwan in 1949 and who now returned to visit every few years. Why had his brother bought a flat in the city when everyone knows that when you grow old you will want to return to your native village? This proved, Baoli asserted, that his brother had a very strange way of calculating things (*da gui suanpan,* literally, "use the abacus in a strange way"). Baoli contrasted his brother unfavorably with his widowed sister-in-law in Taiwan (his other brother's wife). Although this sister-in-law resided in Taiwan, and never visited the mainland, she sent money every Lunar New Year to Baoli and Songling so that they could buy offerings to give to the ancestors on her behalf.

The ideal of remembering the ancestors easily connects to the notion that *huaqiao* have a responsibility for their living relatives as well. Villagers often write letters to relatives with whom they have not been in contact for years, and whom they may never have met. (Indeed, while I was in the village I translated into English several letters written to second-generation relatives who could not read Chinese.) Some letters are attempts to reestablish ties, while others are more direct pleas for help. The latter may occur when a family member has been struck with a serious illness and overwhelming medical expenses, or in the context of wanting to build a new house.

This expectation of help from returning kin also contains the roots of discord among those who remain behind. My notes are filled with examples of disputes that center upon money remitted from abroad. Usually the problems begin when one family member claims that other family members are hoarding remittances that were supposed to be dispersed. At other times, a family member will complain that an overseas relation is helping one branch of the family more than others.

"The closer someone is to you, the more they act like a stranger" *(yue qin yue jian gui),* said Baoli's daughter Meiying when she tried to assess why her Taiwanese uncle had not been particularly helpful to their family when he returned for a visit. Yet these expectations and reactions to returnees are just a more extreme example of general tendencies at work in contemporary rural China. As Ann Anagnost points out, there is still a strong egalitarian current which runs through the Chinese countryside.[28] This current is influenced by ideas of reciprocity operative in the countryside before the Communist era (which encouraged banqueting and contributions to ritual functions on the part of the elite), as well as by the continued influence of the Maoist period with its emphasis on destratification and radical egalitarianism. Anagnost points out that while the official press is skeptical about customary means of satisfying reciprocity norms such as banqueting, it encourages contributions to village infrastructure. Expectations regarding visiting kin remain high from all quarters.

In her book on social relationships in urban China, Mayfair Yang relates a story about a woman who never returned to her native place precisely because she dreaded the number of gifts she would have to bring.[29] Ruolan, for instance, who introduced me to the village and to Songling and Baoli, sometimes came to Meixian without visiting Moonshadow Pond precisely for this reason. She wanted to avoid bringing gifts or at least minimally hosting a small banquet.

One must keep in mind that post-reform changes in the Chinese economy exacerbate the disparities that can be created by overseas remittances. During the Maoist era, when relations with overseas kin were almost completely severed, there were few ways one family could become vastly richer than another. Flaunting wealth would in any case make one politically suspect and could even be dangerous, especially during the Cultural Revolution era. In addition, there was simply little way for a person to differentiate himself or herself economically from fellow villagers. Everyone worked for the collective. One's labor contribution was measured in work points recorded by the accountant of each production team, and a large part of the payment was in staples rather than in cash. One could earn more by working longer hours, or perhaps collect more work points by taking on more taxing and more highly valued jobs within the production team. A family might also bring in more work points if most family members were able-bodied workers rather than young or elderly dependents. Beyond this, there was little a family could do to differentiate itself economically from others.

In the contemporary reform economy, however, the need for cash has grown exponentially—as have the opportunities to use money to differentiate oneself from others. Competition for the attention of overseas visitors must be viewed in this context as well.

Not surprisingly, while Moonshadow Pond residents expect and desire assistance from their own relatives, visits by these returning kin help nurture an undercurrent of grudging resentment among families. Again, to take Ruolan's case, her avoidance of some return visits to Moonshadow Pond was not only to avoid expense, but to avoid being drawn into the competitive claims and jealousies of those she did or did not help. Many of the elderly women whom Ruolan knew were all too happy for small gifts of cash—anything to decrease their daily dependence on their grown children, a topic explored in chapter 3. But how could Ruolan give to every person she knew every time she visited? Many different people could claim some degree of relation to her in some way, since Moonshadow Pond was her father's native village. Even a small cash gift bestowed by her to one person, if heard about by others, would inevitably produce jealousy.

"That is why, if I don't have any business, I just don't come here!" she exclaimed to me in the spring of 2007. The headache of small or petty jealousies was sometimes easier to avoid by simply not returning.

Such jealousies were not purely about finances, but also about more symbolic kinds of status. In ways that remind one of the famous Trobriand kula trade, in which the identity of an object's previous owner increased its value, many people told me that the same item given as a gift was much more desirable than if one had purchased it oneself.[30] On a different occasion, when Ruolan actually did visit Moonshadow Pond, she gave three gold bracelets to three older women with whom she was friendly. A fourth woman felt snubbed, and mentioned these gifts to several others. Likewise, Songling's daughter told me how her mother-in-law wanted to say that I had given her a gold bracelet, and she would gladly give me the money to purchase it—as long as her mother-in-law could later say it was a gift from me.

Of course, in addition to the status achieved from displaying relatively small gifts, there is also the question of much larger amounts of financial assistance. Some gifts can help a family build a house, buy an expensive consumer item, or start a business, and thereby have a significant impact upon their economic circumstances. While almost all residents of Moonshadow Pond have experienced increasing prosperity in the post-Mao order, they have also witnessed the emergence of much greater economic differentiation between families. Overseas connections are not the sole explanation for this, but they do play a role. Villagers know which families have overseas connections and they know which of these connections have added to the economic well-being of the family. Pointing to the success of Jiawen in his village medical practice, Aihua said to me, "Of course they are well off. Not only is their business successful, but also Jiawen's mother has connections with her uncle's family in Thailand and her brother's family in Hong Kong. *We* had to make it without any help from *huaqiao*."

Ironically, Jiawen's family was ultimately so successful that they didn't really need help from overseas relations. By 2007, Jiawen's son had also opened a village medical clinic. The family was very prosperous. One day, Jiawen's elderly mother Chunyu pulled me aside with a secret to tell me. Chunyu was in her eighties, and not literate, so she knew only that I was from "America." She also knew that she had some distant relatives from America as well. "Don't let them know where I am," she whispered in my ear. "I've heard they aren't doing very well, and if they find me they might try to get money from me!" Though this example was the exception, I found it a humorous inversion of the assumed positive side of having overseas relations.

In most cases, however, the willingness to help their own family and kin is still the most prominent value by which villagers assess the moral caliber of returnees. We can see this emphasis quite clearly in the case of one particular category of kin—those men who fled China in the wake of the Communist victory, because they were Nationalist soldiers. In Moonshadow Pond, four emigrants fit this description. All of these individuals except for one had abandoned wives and families in their retreat, married again, and started new families in Taiwan. Although they had virtually no contact with their families throughout the Maoist period, they were able to reestablish connections during the reform era initiated by Deng Xiaoping. (Indeed, the subject of former Nationalist soldiers who return to the mainland to visit children and first wives has recently been a popular subject of television dramas and movies in both the PRC and Taiwan.)

In the case of Moonshadow Pond, one of the abandoned wives fled the village and started a family elsewhere. This was Baoli's sister-in-law. She left her own son in Moonshadow Pond, and to this day different cousins, including Baoli, all take credit for raising him. In other families, however, the wives who remained behind did not remarry, but remained in their in-laws homes to raise their children. All of their husbands have returned to the village at least once, some living in the village with their adult children for several months at a time. And all of these returnees have sent back considerable remittances, enough to distinguish their Moonshadow Pond families economically from those of many other villagers. When I asked villagers about whether these men should have remained faithful to their first wives, no one said they believed they should have. What was important, they said, was that they should remember from where they came and help their abandoned families.

In certain ways, the standards used to evaluate returnees as kin, the expectations and the disappointments, are not all that different from the standards that would be expected from any economically successful kin. But unlike kin who return to visit from cities within China, *huaqiao* are different *because* they are foreign. This creates a number of conundrums for the villagers. Can one expect perfect filiality and familial devotion from those who have lived and acculturated to foreign customs and culture abroad? Are there limits to familial loyalty?

RETURNEES AS FOREIGNERS

The villagers' questions about whether returnees understand ancestral ideology is a good example of how returnees come to be seen as embodying at least some foreign attributes. Although some returnees may reside in the village for several months at a time and may gradually acclimate themselves to the pace of village life, other visits may be brief, lasting only a few days, and the visitors may stay at a hotel in the nearby county capital rather than with relatives in the village. This choice is explained as resulting from the returnees' inability to adjust to life in the countryside after years of a much easier life abroad. Indeed, residence abroad is viewed as having a profound and irreversible impact upon returnees. For instance, villagers were surprised that I traveled by bicycle since returnees rarely travel that way. They assumed that the *huaqiao* reluctance to use a bicycle was an attitude picked up from living abroad. Similarly, as we have already discussed, the failure of a few returnees to give priority to ancestral ritual was also explained as a result of long years abroad.

Huaqiao foreignness is also embodied by their legal status and by their ideological orientation toward state and party. Legally, *huaqiao* have a somewhat "liminal" status. When they first visit they must register with a special *huaqiao* office in the local public security bureau. However, unlike the Cultural Revolution period, access to their relatives is unrestricted, and they can stay in China for longer periods of uninterrupted time than ordinary foreign visitors. Spending time with these foreign kin exposes villagers to heterodox opinions that may implicitly or explicitly critique party hegemony. I have heard visiting relatives criticize local newscasts, newspapers, and other media as both narrow and slanted. One villager told me that he had never thought about how limited the daily newscasts were until his uncle visited from abroad and complained about them.

Since it is much harder for villagers to leave China than for *huaqiao* to return, returnees often function as a window on the rest of the world. It was not uncommon for villagers to ply a visitor with hours of questions about Taiwan, Hong Kong, or whatever other far-flung country from which he or she was visiting. One might view this give and take as an element of larger processes of cultural globalization or transnationalism.[31] But if it is part of a transnational process, then it is the localization of the global that is most notable here.[32] Whatever stories are told, and however returnees decide to comport themselves, they are quickly pulled into the local world of gossip, moral judgments, and status evaluations. In this case, it is important not to overestimate the "global" or "transnational" side of this process.

Likewise, it would also be possible to view returnees as a potential political threat because they occasionally articulate views that are critical of state power or of the state media. However, in Moonshadow Pond, at least over the short term, it would be jumping to conclusions to view returnees as having any kind of unsettling effect on state power at the local level. In fact, as discussed above, returnees often legitimize this power by treating officials to banquets and plying them with gifts and money in attempts to either gain favors or at least insure an uneventful visit. When returnees donate to a visible public project such as a school, local cadres are always present at the ceremonies acknowledging these gifts and thanking the donors. Obviously, the marginal legal status of returnees is also significant. Despite any ideological heterodoxy returnees may inject into the local scene, their actual behavior does little to challenge local or national political structures, and even supports them.[33]

THE OLD MAN FROM TAIWAN

The discourse about returnees as benefactors, kin, and foreigners, and the sometimes contradictory motivations and obligations that villagers see in these roles, was colorfully articulated in discussions about the singular figure of Old Guosheng.

Old Guosheng was the former pilot in the Nationalist Army mentioned in chapter 2. For several years he had been returning regularly to Moonshadow Pond for a few months each year. As someone who had spent most of his adult life in Taiwan and was now comfortably retired on a pension, he was well endowed financially by village standards. As I mentioned earlier, a potential benefactor in the midst also sets gossip and stories in motion, as well as negative moral evaluations about those who are seen as trying to curry their favor in order to get personal financial rewards.

Not surprisingly, stories frequently circulated throughout Moonshadow Pond about individuals who were ostensibly trying to gain favors from Old Guosheng, sometimes by impugning the motives of others, and saying that only they could really be trusted. Whether any of these stories was true is less important than the fact that they existed. The idea that people would say bad things about others in order to gain the favor of a wealthy returnee had traction, even if the particular accusations may have been without merit. Aihua, for instance, told me in very disapproving tones how she thought that Skinny Hong had connived to get financial help from Old Guosheng through precisely this type of ploy.

By the same token, those who actually did receive help from Old Guosheng were expected to remember it. For instance, a woman in the village who had a job cooking for Old Guosheng decided to quit her job because she was tired of his infamous bad temper. Since he had supported her beyond her salary, including paying her daughter's tuition for high school, many people said she should have stayed longer and swallowed the insults.

The obligations of overseas Chinese as kin and their status as foreigners was also an element of the discourse that surrounded Old Guosheng. Old Guosheng's case was somewhat different from ordinary overseas visitors because he built a house in the village in order to reside there for several months each year. But unlike the others, he returned to his native village in order to *avoid* his family in Taiwan rather than to reconnect with abandoned family members in China. Old Guosheng was unable to get along with any of his sons or with his wife back in Taiwan, and the rest of his Taiwan family made only one short ceremonial visit to Meixian during his many returns there. Although Old Guosheng had a sister in Meixian who lived in the county capital, not far from the village, she also had little to do with him. Villagers noted that he had no close kin to care for him, and that he had to pay people from a different sublineage to tend to him when he became seriously ill.

Old Guosheng's presence in the village, therefore, was viewed ambivalently, since it was the direct result of his failure in familial relationships. Old Guosheng had contributed funds to a number of village projects, such as to the village school. He was, after all, descended from the same ancestors as everyone else in the village. He could not be viewed as a total outsider, nor could his contributions to the village as a whole be pushed aside. But while he was treated respectfully, he was also the focus of negative gossip, much of it relating to his bad temper and familial relations. "Old Guosheng has money," people would say, "but he does not always *zuo ren*" (an expression that literally means to "act like a person," but really means to handle human relationships properly). The respect old Guosheng may have garnered as a result of his wealth, as well as the implicit status he granted to the village by returning to it and therefore honoring his "roots," was diminished considerably because of his bad family relationships. His lack of family connections, in turn, tended to emphasize his foreignness.

By the time I returned to the village in 2007, Old Guosheng had passed away. His village house, which, unlike other new houses, had been built in the traditional architectural style, now lay abandoned and was slowly decaying. In the end, this house, with no family members to take care of it, was a visual reminder of his ultimate social separation from his village of birth.

THE CONTRADICTIONS OF RETURN

The opportunity to reunite with overseas kin is welcomed enthusiastically by the residents of Moonshadow Pond, but it has also created an unsettled space of discourse. In this space, desire for status and material wealth is both expressed and satirized, expectations of family loyalty are both fulfilled and sometimes shattered, returnees are both kin and foreigners. Returnees, in this sense, embody a number of contradictory expectations and images.

A common expression in Hakka refers to a visitor as someone who is *hen you xin,* a phrase translated in chapter 2 as simply meaning someone with a heart/mind. In actual discourse, this phrase is really used as form of praise, a way of saying that a person cares so much that he or she has taken great pains and traveled great distances to see their host. Because the act of visiting is seen as taking time and trouble, Hakka take great pride in an ethos which stresses that all visitors must be treated well. Local residents like to boast that a specialty of Hakka culture is that "we treat guests well."

There is an egalitarian aspect to this pride in being good hosts. Any guest who has taken the trouble to visit is said to have shown that he or she is *hen you xin,* and must therefore be treated with hospitality, regardless of his or her social or economic status. In theory, at least, this hospitality must be bestowed simply because the guest has taken great pains to come. Villagers often told me that treating guests well is a matter of "face" *(mianzi).* And many residents of Moonshadow Pond said that hospitality was part of being Hakka, it was the way they wanted to be perceived by the outside world.

However, return visits play into the production of "face" or status in ways that go beyond providing a venue for a family to display its hospitality. First, the higher the status of the visitor, the more "face" *(mianzi)* is gained by the host.[34] The host basks in the reflected glory of the visitor, and material gifts from that visitor further add to the status of the host family. As we have seen, gifts from overseas visitors not only add to the family's status by increasing its wealth, but they also embody the relationship of recipient and giver, adding to the recipient's relative status in the village.

Those who are slighted suffer in two ways, since they lose not only materially, but also in one arena of status competition. Yet as we have also seen in this chapter, even here there is a complex play of moral and status evaluations. Those who have no overseas connections can always boast that they didn't manipulate relationships merely for material benefit. Further, while returnees are welcomed as kin and benefactors, their foreignness can lead to transgressions of local moral expectations, especially in the familial realm.

Thus, returnees become enmeshed in a web of local judgments about both themselves and their hosts. The Hakka ethos of hospitality is suffused with all kinds of expectations, especially when it involves overseas kin. Glorious as any visit may be in itself, it also becomes the template on which villagers articulate a host of competing expectations and desires.

CHAPTER 6

Property Rights and Wrongs

Before her son was married, Songling had often imagined his wedding. If all went well, he would walk across the threshold of the family home with his bride. Fireworks would explode to keep out the unsavory spirits and elderly women would gently nudge bride and groom through the subsequent ceremonies. Meanwhile, children and onlookers would be free to walk in and out of the house and enjoy the spectacle.

But to whom did this house actually belong? As Songling often reminded me, houses belonged to ancestors and descendants. This rule applied equally to recently constructed houses and to older dwellings. Once I asked Songling about Weiguo and Jieguo, the two brothers in the village who had each secured remunerative and secure jobs in the county capital due to their good party connections. They were rarely at home and had amply furnished apartments in town. Yet they had built two of the biggest houses in the village.

"Why don't they sell their houses?" I naively asked. "They're hardly ever here."

"They don't see it that way at all," Songling corrected me. "Their houses belong to their families, to their sons and grandsons, and having such nice houses also gives them a lot of *mianzi* ['face,' or high status] in the village."

Even during the heyday of the collective era, family residences were not regarded as belonging to the collective, the state, or to individuals. A house belonged to an unbroken family line that stretched both backward and forward in time. The only exceptions were the homes of land-lords and other "bad" classes. After Liberation, poor peasants occupied these homes and the landlords were evicted.

"But it was dangerous," Songling told me. "If you lived in the house of someone else's ancestors you could have all kinds of misfortunes. People who lived in these houses would burn spirit money to the ances-tors of the former owners every year [so that the ancestors would not be angry]. They even did this secretly during the Cultural Revolution."

In the mid-1980s, even these "bad class" houses were legally restored to their original owners and their postrevolutionary occupants compen-sated with funds so they could build new homes. Because the compen-sation funds were barely enough to even lay a foundation, I expected that the people who had to vacate these houses would describe their evictions with distress and would be bitter about the small amount of compensa-tion they received. But to my surprise this was not the case. One expla-nation of this muted reaction is that the restoration of homes to former landlords occurred during a surge of new home building and economic expansion in the village. Since most of the landlords' old homes, like all of the old homes in the village, were in very bad condition, the evicted residents of these homes were simply doing what they would have done anyway—moving out of old decrepit houses and building new ones.

Nonetheless, the meaning of living in a home that did not belong to one's own ancestors was certainly not a negligible part of people's reac-tions. Families that had moved into landlord and other bad class houses and then vacated them voiced sentiments similar to those of Songling about these homes. "As long as we prospered in the landlord's house," Skinny Hong's son-in-law told me, "the prosperity we enjoyed was not ours." He continued, "This wealth wasn't ours, so we really couldn't pass it on to the next generation." His sentiment—that houses belong to ances-tors and descendants—predated Liberation and has persevered through all the twists and turns of the ensuing decades.

But this certainly is not the only conception of property in Moon-shadow Pond. In addition to houses, property in Moonshadow Pond in-cludes both land and productive resources, and it has been a frequent area of contentious debate. Listening in on village gossip and visiting people in their homes, I learned about a number of ongoing property dis-putes. These disputes served as vehicles for the articulation of several dif-ferent concurrently held ideas about property—notions from the old so-ciety, Maoist, and reform eras—and they included conflicts not only over private versus collective rights in property, but also disputes over individual versus familial rights in property. Most importantly, each of these contending approaches to property also implied different ideas about the obligations and rights of villagers to each other. Hence, arguments about property were also a form of moral discourse, since they ultimately entailed differing expectations about obligation.

In this chapter, I examine property disputes in Moonshadow Pond. My aim is not to determine whose argument was legally correct in a particular case, especially because property rules have changed over time in reform-era China, and villagers do not always make their decisions solely on what they think is lawful. Rather, my aim is to discern the various moral stances behind different property claims.

I conclude the chapter by looking at the case of Slippery Cheng, "the man who sold the collective's land." As we shall see, Slippery's case served as a template for the articulation of several different ideas about property. But in the end, when people spoke about his case, their evaluation of how he conducted his social relationships was as important to their judgments as ideas about the legal validity of his claims.

SCHEMAS ABOUT PROPERTY

Nothing was more central to the Chinese Communist revolution than the relationship of peasants to land. Mao Zedong gathered support from peasants by promising to return the land to them and to break the power of large landlords. Later, collectivization removed individual landholdings from these very same peasants, and invested it in communes, production brigades, and production teams. With the reform era, land was returned to the peasants for use, although, at least in theory, the land still belonged to local collectives and was not private property. These changes in property regimes were harbingers of transformations in the overall political regime, with collectivization attached to the Maoist order, and the break up of collectives ushering in the beginning of the reform period.

In contemporary China, the decollectivization of rural production has led to divergent claims to property and has even fueled violence in the countryside. In some areas of rural China, peasants have been "compensated" for their land in minimal amounts by public authorities. They often learn later that this land has been given to local real-estate developers or factories. These enterprises often generate huge tax revenues for local governments, profits for the private interests who manage them, and payoffs for the officials who make the deals possible.[1] In one case in southeast China, a corrupt local official "sold" collective land to a private individual. He pocketed the earnings and then disappeared from public sight, leaving villagers to vent their anger on the new "owner."[2] Lack of clarity about land ownership and repeated transfers and "sales" of what is still legally collective land has even led to physical fights between parties who often claim the same plot of land.[3]

In Moonshadow Pond nothing so dramatic has happened, but disputes about rights to property and the nature of these rights have occurred. Reform-period changes in rules about land tenure have ushered in confusion and contention about what rights people have and who has them.

The background to interpreting these disputes is the rural reform program initiated in the early 1980s, better known as the Household Responsibility System. This reform guaranteed land-use rights to individuals while ownership rights remained with the collective.[4] The collectives in which ownership rights resided varied. They were teams, villages, or townships[5] and the duration of household land contracts with collectives also varied from place to place.[6] Nonetheless, since the rural reforms, every version of the Chinese Constitution has reiterated the principle that land belongs to the collectives, even though rural residents receive use rights to this land.[7]

Yet some individuals in Moonshadow Pond have acted and spoken since the reforms began *as if* they owned the land, and even as if they could pass their land down to their descendants as they could with their houses. Other forms of productive property such as machines, ploughs, and farm equipment have also become a focus of contention. With decollectivization, many of these resources were taken over by individuals who charged fees for their services, but other community members have asserted that such equipment is still a collectively owned resource.

I should note here that property rights in any society are not easily ascertainable by a quick visit to legal statutes or laws. Rather, many analysts prefer Harold Demetz's notion of property as a "bundle of rights . . . [that] disaggregates . . . into three kinds of rights—control, income, and transfer—and explicitly acknowledges that there are a variety of ways in which such 'rights' might be enforced, ranging from formal law to social custom."[8] It is all the more confusing, then, to figure out these rights in a society that has undergone dramatic changes in property regimes over the past half century.

These momentous changes in property regimes in China have obviously added to the diversity of concepts that villagers bring to their discussion about property. But we should keep in mind that multiple schemas for understanding laws and regulations are common in societies that have undergone much less dramatic change in property regimes and legal structures than has China. In their study of commonplace understandings of law in the United States, Ewick and Silbey found that people hold a variety of models about how the law works. Using the concept of schemas to describe this, they write, "Examples of schemas include the interactive rules of a criminal trial, the concepts of guilt or innocence, and the obligation born of a promise or contract, in addition to commonplace proverbs and aphorisms asserting such truths as 'possession is nine-tenths of the law.' "[9] When their interviewees talked about the law they used "multiple interpretive schemas."[10] Sometimes they spoke of the law as beyond individual control, while at other times they described it as something that could either be manipulated or worked around.[11]

As noted in previous chapters, Moonshadow Pond villagers draw on different and sometimes contradictory ideas, from several different historical eras, in assessing their obligations in a variety of domains. With regard to ideas about property, several competing schemas also seem to be at work as villagers try to sort out contending claims. These schemas can be loosely categorized as falling around two main ideas. One is the notion that "property belongs to the collective." By contrast, many people act according to a different schema, one that can be summarized by the notion, "if I work on the land, it will eventually belong to me and my descendants." However, even the notion of "property belonging to the collective" is not so simple. Under the rubric of understanding property as belonging to a collective are included the notions of production team property, brigade property, village and township property, and national property.

Arguments about who has rights to different kinds of property are an ongoing part of daily life. In addition to arguments over specifics, more general moral codes about reciprocity in social relations influence people's evaluations of property claims. A claim that people object to can seem even more out of line if the claimant is additionally seen as violating a personal obligation or forgetting a kindness from the past. In this postcollective era, there seem to be no definitive answers about ownership.

Finally, conceptions of the role of law in these claims also vary. Thus, the idea that "the law is objective" is contrasted with another generally held notion that "good social relationships" can enable a person to circumvent the law. Added to this is another schema that we might characterize simply as "greasing the wheel can get a person what he or she wants," or, in other words, that bribery is more important than the law.

During my visits to Moonshadow Pond, I saw all these ideas put to the test as property was claimed and claims were also disputed.

During the 1990s, Moonshadow Pond residents were locked in an ongoing series of disputes about property and ownership. For instance, Baoli and Small Gao, the daughter of Baoli's closest friend, had regular altercations with the local council of elders. The elders claimed that Baoli and Small Gao's rice-threshing operation really belonged to the village and that they had taken it over illegally and hoarded its profits. Skinny Hong and Aihua were also locked in a dispute about land on which Skinny Hong had built a house. Aihua thought the land still belonged to Team 2 and could not be taken out of use by building a family residence there. Then there was the dispute between Aihua and Skinny Hong regarding his second son. This son manufactured tiles on land that Aihua claimed was not properly contracted and which still belonged to the production team. Finally there was the case of Slippery Cheng.

In the spring of 1996 a story began to circulate in Moonshadow Pond that Slippery's cousin from Taiwan intended to build a house on the land that Slippery had been allocated during decollectivization. This cousin, Long Beard Li, had returned to Mei County several times to visit. On each visit, so the story went, Long Beard had "married" a different woman much younger than himself. (This phenomenon, in which an older overseas Chinese man takes on a younger mainland mistress is a social issue that has recently gotten much attention in China.) As the story of Long Beard circulated through the village it created a firestorm. Had Slippery *sold* the land to him? How *could* he sell it? It wasn't really *his*. *Whose* land was it anyway? Didn't it still belong to Team 2? If it was sold, shouldn't the profit go to all the team's members? Didn't the township government have to approve such a sale anyway? The salacious underpinnings to the story—Long Beard's most recent mistress, who some said was also pregnant—added to the liveliness of the swirling gossip.

All these property dispute stories circulated over the course of my fieldwork. Everyone had some opinion and no one hesitated to jump into the argument while passing the time on store benches and in living rooms. No issues were definitively resolved, but at least I began to understand more about why these disputes were taking place. People brought to these disputes a consciousness about property relations formed out of both pre-Liberation customary notions and from the experience of living under a collective system for several decades. I will come back to each of these stories, especially Slippery's. But to appreciate their significance, I need to digress. As stated above, land and property were the central issue of the revolution itself, and they are always central in the lives of peasants. Their lack of land had been fundamental to peasant support for the Communist revolution. And land reform, collectivization, and the break-up of the collectives all had profound impacts on Chinese farmers, including those from Moonshadow Pond.

The move from revolution to land reform, collectivization, and finally the dismantling of the collectives is a piece of Chinese history reviewed extensively in the literature. I need not move the readers through all the details of this history. But it is important to be familiar with the way these national events were experienced locally; specifically the way they might have influenced contemporary understandings of property and land on the part of village residents. It is with these questions in mind that I summarize below the post-Liberation upheavals in China's rural property regimes as they were experienced in Moonshadow Pond.

FROM LAND REFORM TO COLLECTIVIZATION IN MOONSHADOW POND

The Land Reform Law of the People's Republic of China, issued in 1950, was the impetus for land reform in Moonshadow Pond, as it was throughout China.[12] In Moonshadow Pond, as in many other villages, the movement began with the formation of a poor peasant meeting group.[13] Gathering in secret, in order to prevent wealthy landlords from receiving advance warning and then plotting a counterstrategy or hiding their wealth, the group began to identify the landlords and rich peasants in their areas. Work teams sent by the party from outside the village also helped select membership for the poor-peasants association, individuals who came from the poorest families in the village.

All this took place in about one year, between 1951 and 1952. At the end of that year, every family had been categorized into classes derived from the new national law on land.[14] Landlords and rich peasants not only possessed land of their own, but also rented to others. They were distinguished only by degree. In Moonshadow Pond, landlords were those who could produce more than fifty *dan* of rice from their fields (one *dan* is equivalent to fifty kilograms). Middle peasants had land of their own plus some productive assets, such as water buffalo, but they did not rent to anyone. Finally there were poor peasants who owned barely any land, and tenants who had no land. There were other designations as well, though they were less common in the countryside—these included capitalists, merchants, small peddlers, and workers.

At the time, since redistribution was the goal, middle peasants were left alone while poor peasants and tenants were to divide land that had formerly belonged to landlords, rich peasants, and the corporate holdings of lineage groups. Members of the poor-peasants meeting group broke up into teams of three. They measured the land and put up a sign with the name of each household head. A land certificate was issued that listed the household head, the number of people in the family, and the amount of land that was held. Very often, the name given for household head was that of a woman rather than a man, a source of great pride for Aihua, who became an enthusiastic party member. Even now, some of those old signs are still present in the village, and Aihua liked to show me the one with her name.

Meanwhile, the work teams sent down to the village encouraged the poor-peasants association to attack the landlords and rich peasants and to raise consciousness among the ordinary peasants about their exploitation. This tumultuous period was not without violence. In many villages throughout China landlords were executed. In Moonshadow Pond, one individual was sentenced to death but managed to flee. At the very least, landlords were publicly criticized, and in Moonshadow Pond, as in many other villages throughout the country, their homes were ransacked and belongings confiscated. Landlord and rich peasant houses, along with their lands, were distributed to the poor peasants.

According to the *Mei County Gazetteer (Meixian Zhi)*, the county had about 101,911 households at the time of land reform in the early 1950s. Nearly 4,400 of these received the designation of landlord or rich peasant, and they were said to hold 12 percent of the land. But, in addition, corporate lineages were assessed as holding 41 percent of the land, and many of those who managed this land for the lineages were also the objects of "struggle."[15] This is not surprising when considered in light of what we know about prerevolutionary Guangdong, where some scholars estimate that lineage estates owned 40 to 60 percent of the land.[16] The *Mei County Gazetteer* also indicated that of the 1,549 landlords and counterrevolutionaries who were "struggled," 103 were imprisoned and six received death sentences.[17] Others fled the country or committed suicide and do not show up in these official statistics.

In Moonshadow Pond, most families fell into the category of poor peasants, tenants, or middle peasants. But four families received bad class labels. Songling's father, because he owned and operated tanneries in the village and also had a leather business in town, was categorized as a capitalist. Three additional families were categorized as landlords. At first, these landlords were to be executed, but then orders were sent from above that their lives were to be spared. It was too late, however, for one of them. After being categorized as a landlord, he committed suicide. His son, who had been a soldier in the Nationalist Army, fled to Taiwan, leaving a wife and mother behind in the village. A second individual who was categorized as a landlord fled with his entire family to Hong Kong. The third landlord was Baoli's uncle. He was actually the manager of the Song's corporate lineage land and did not own much land.

Lineage land, as mentioned earlier, was indeed a problematical category. The Song lineage had branches in the village, and, as chapter 1 explains, the second lineage branch (*fang* 2) had two subdivisions—the descendants of five and seven brothers respectively. Each of these subdivisions held collective land that could not be partitioned for inheritance purposes but was instead held corporately. This land was rented to poor or landless peasants, who gave up part of their produce in return for use of the land. The proceeds financed yearly observances at the branch founders' graves, and also paid for banquets held after these yearly ceremonies. Although such corporate lineage land was supposed to be divided and redistributed amongst poor peasants and tenants during land reform, the managers of these estates were not technically landlords. But in the case of Baoli's uncle, he was accused of appropriating some of this corporate property for himself and he was given a death sentence.[18] Fortunately for him, he managed to escape from the village before the sentence could be carried out, and he fled to Burma, where a number of his nephews lived.

There were other individuals in Moonshadow Pond who received bad class categories that were not based on their landholdings or wealth, but instead connected to their political activities. As mentioned in the previous chapter, three men had served in the Nationalist Army and fled to Taiwan, including Baoli's brother. Even now, villagers speak about the counterrevolutionary plots to assassinate Communist officials which took place at that time. According to one of the stories, a band of Moonshadow Pond youths plotted to kill the township head, who had just come to power. A battle ensued at the outskirts of the village between these youths and other youths who supported the Communists, and two of the Communist supporters were killed. Elders say that the plotters then drank wine infused with their own blood and swore to stick together, much like the members of blood brotherhoods in the old society and in contemporary gangs. Most of the plotters were eventually captured, including one of Baoli's cousins. It was his father who had been categorized as a landlord and who fled to Burma. But while the father had managed to flee the country, his son was not so lucky and he was executed for his counterrevolutionary activities.

As occurred throughout China, no sooner had land been redistributed then a process of collectivization began. The land reform and the struggle against landlords in Moonshadow Pond had all taken place in barely over a year's time, from the end of 1951 to early 1953. But by 1954, the party was urging peasants to form mutual-aid teams, and in 1958 Moonshadow Pond was swept along in the tide of collectivization known as the Great Leap Forward. It became part of a commune comprised of twenty villages. Within Moonshadow Pond, five or six work groups were each served by a canteen that distributed free food. There was no longer any attempt to record working hours or types of work, because sheer revolutionary will and the fervor to take China forward in a "great leap" was supposed to motivate people. As in other parts of China, Moonshadow Pond peasants were encouraged to contribute to the country's industrialization by smelting their own iron and steel.

The disastrous results of this period on a national scale have been well documented.[19] In Moonshadow Pond, many of the younger and most able-bodied workers spent all their time in the hills surrounding the village trying to smelt iron from pots and pans. The ripening rice crop was left to rot on the ground, since only women with small children were left behind to harvest it. For the first forty days of the public canteens, people ate to their hearts' content, but then the food started to run out.

While death from starvation occurred in many parts of China, hunger was alleviated to some extent in Moonshadow Pond because overseas relatives sent care packages of cured meats. Those without such relatives suffered more.[20] Their bellies and legs swelled up and they became extremely weak as edema caused by the lack of food *(shuizhong bing)* advanced.

By 1961 the radical egalitarian and voluntarist line underlying the policies of the Great Leap Forward had been discredited by disasters on the ground. Peasants in Moonshadow Pond were each allocated a plot of land on which they could grow their own vegetables. The rest of the land still remained with the collective, but the management of labor was decentralized to production teams. Moonshadow Pond was divided into six production teams and became part of a production brigade of fourteen teams. Team leaders like Aihua were responsible for organizing daily work, and team accountants such as Baoli recorded the number of work hours and type of work completed by each person. They were also free to decide on a team basis how they wanted to reward work. If a particular job was onerous or physically hard, they might reward it with more work points to motivate people. Yields from work were forwarded to the brigade, and payments in kind and cash were passed back down to the team and team members based on their relative work contributions.

Aihua and Baoli often spoke of the difficulties they experienced administering this system, since it required them to be aware of what each team member was doing every day in order to record their work points. But the system did establish some relationship between work and reward. Except for the most radical years of the Cultural Revolution, an individual who worked for longer hours or on more strenuous and difficult jobs received more work points and therefore extra pay. And if a production team as a whole produced more, then they earned more as well, especially if their production exceeded the amount they were required to give to the state. According to Aihua, Team 2 produced more than many other teams. Therefore, each individual's work points were worth more as well, since the team was dividing shares of a bigger pot.

Aihua often spoke proudly about the accomplishments of Team 2, as well as her own accomplishments, regaling me with stories about the number of loads she could haul each day to earn extra work points. Though a strong defender of the collective system, she was also a strong advocate of the idea that reward be related to work, and she had no tolerance for policies that based one's pay on politically correct attitudes as opposed to productivity. Aihua was especially critical of the changes implemented during the "Four Cleanups" campaign of 1965 and the ensuing Cultural Revolution. For her, the Cultural Revolution represented a period when political ideology and motivation counted more than the work one actually accomplished. When Aihua talked about this period, she made fun of the woman who had temporarily replaced her as team leader. "She was so short and weak, how could you compare her ability to work with mine?" Aihua would dismissively chuckle. "She was getting more work points than me because she was considered to be more progressive politically!"

Although Aihua disapproved of this system of calculating pay in terms of political fervor, she was a strong supporter of the collective system in general, and she spoke with pride about the accomplishments of the era as a whole. "Look at these fields, they're all level now. Our production team did that; an individual family couldn't have done that," she told me one day as we walked through the village. When Aihua took me to see a small reservoir built in the mountainous outskirts of the village, she beamed with satisfaction as she talked about the effort and achievements of building this reservoir in the late 1950s. She would frequently point to the stone irrigation ditches that controlled the water flow through the village fields, noting that prior to Liberation the village had nothing more than gullies of mud to direct the flow of water.

Even Skinny Hong, who had little praise for the Communist system or era, viewed the collectives as a necessary phase. One day, Ruolan's cousin visited Songling and Baoli's house. She had returned from a visit to India, where her sisters lived in an overseas Chinese community. The cousin described the poverty she had witnessed in India in a very vivid fashion. Skinny Hong was standing outside Baoli's house chatting with some others at the time and half listening to the cousin's accounts. "Without the production teams," Skinny Hong inserted, "we would have been in the same position."

A NEW PROPERTY REGIME

Though its achievements included leveled field land, irrigation canals, and reservoirs, even the most dedicated Communists began to find the collective system difficult to administer on a daily basis. Both Baoli and Aihua talked about the endless hours they spent as accountant and team leader respectively—deciding what had to be done each day, how many work points each task should be awarded, and keeping track of each team member's hours of work. In Moonshadow Pond, when the orders came down to divide the land among the village families, it was welcomed by almost everyone.

On the eve of decollectivization, the state officially recognized three types of property: state, collective, and private. In the state's eyes, urban property was primarily state property, while individual incomes and houses were private property. Rural farmland, on the other hand, was primarily considered the property of the collective.[21] So when peasants "divided" the land in the early 1980s, they were essentially dividing use rights to property that was still considered collective property.

In Moonshadow Pond, each production team in the brigade divided its land into six categories based on their use in agricultural production.[22] Although shares of land were allocated to each individual alive at the time, there was also care taken that every family received land in each of the six categories. If someone wanted to build a house, he had to apply to the township government for permission, and by law (if not in practice), no one was supposed to build a house on paddy land.

Each individual then signed a contract with the township that specified his or her land allotment. In the early years of this new system, peasants paid a tax in grain and were also required to sell some of the surplus to the government at a set price. But over time, peasants were allowed to use money instead of grain for this tax, and in 2005 the tax was abolished altogether. In the original contracts that the residents of Moonshadow Pond signed with their townships, however, the regulations were quite strict. Not only did peasants owe a yearly tax on their land, but the contracts stipulated that they were not allowed to sell their land, or to even rent it. For instance, Songling's 1984 contract articulated explicit rules about her paddy land, stating that she could not "neglect it, build houses, excavate for bricks or merely, according to one's wish, change what is cultivated there."[23]

These contracts stipulated an amount of land for each person, but did not specify a specific place. As Laurel Bossen observed in Guangxi Province, where she conducted fieldwork, the claims of peasants to land during the reform period were "essentially claims to shares, not to any specific plots . . . there is no official system of recording household land claims and transactions. To a large extent, a family's and individual's rights rests on the attitudes of the community and personal authority of the team leaders . . . family farmers have little written proof of their claims to particular plots of land."[24]

Despite the lack of individual legal claims to specific plots of land, the shape of the land and its use changed rapidly in Moonshadow Pond. In Team 2, as explained in chapter 1, some of the lesser-grade land was divided into lots. Then each family drew a number, and this determined the location where they could build a new house, although there was some subsequent trading. Small stores begin to spring up in these new houses as well. Baoli's nephew had a small shop right across the street from us, and Skinny Hong ran a little store across the street from the school. Soon there were all kinds of small shops peppering the village, including restaurants, a gas station, two tailors, a hairdresser's, a shop that produced ritual objects for funerals and other ceremonies, and the doctor's office and dispensary. Forest and mountain lands were also divided. In Moonshadow Pond, this land became village land. Anyone cultivating fishponds or using the land in other ways would contract it from Moonshadow Pond itself.[25]

In theory, allocations were to be readjusted every few years to take account of changes in the membership of the production team. If a woman married out, she would lose her share. Or if a family added to their numbers through the birth of a new member, they would gain a share. But in Moonshadow Pond, as throughout China, this practice of readjustment became difficult to implement. While in some areas of China the collective structures remained strong enough to implement a periodic readjustment, in other areas new arrangements were ad hoc.[26] For instance, peasants going to work in the city would have to make their own arrangements to be sure that their plots were cultivated.[27] Often, the person taking responsibility for the land might simply pay tax on that parcel. In other cases, they might actually pay cash rent to the original occupant.[28]

In Moonshadow Pond, administrators made several attempts to take account of changing population and family composition in allocating land. Readjustments occurred in 1984, 1990, and finally in 1997. The addition of new team members through birth, and the fact that some land had been taken out of use for highway construction, meant team members received less land in 1990 than they had received in the initial redistribution in 1980 (0.35 instead of 0.50 *mu* per person). But the unalterable facts on the ground meant that these readjustments became more difficult to make as time passed. "How can you reallocate this land?" Uncle Wei said to me one day in 1995. "People have planted fruit orchards, built houses, and started fishponds. You just can't readjust anymore."

Sure enough, in 1997 team members all signed thirty-year contracts on the land, a move that was encouraged throughout China. But this time, the land allocations were not altered from those at the last readjustment, despite changes in land use patterns and residence. Thirty years is a long time, and Moonshadow Pond residents reacted in different ways to this state of affairs. Baoli still insisted that the land belonged to the government and not to the ancestors. "It can still be adjusted or even taken away," he said. But Aihua expressed a more typical view when she said, "The land is just going to stay the way it is now and get passed between family members."

Others expressed the view that the land could never be taken away after individuals had invested so many of their own assets in it. For instance, Songling's friend had contracted some "dry land" from the administrative district. She had put a great deal of effort into it and now grew a variety of fruits including pomelos and tangerines. "She's put so much work into it," Songling told me, "this land will definitely be hers one day." Skinny Hong also expressed himself succinctly with regard to the land he had been allocated. "After thirty years, the land will be mine."

CONTENDING VOICES AND CONTENDING CLAIMS

While individuals had thus begun to stake private conceptual claims on the land, they also held on to other perceptions that seemed to contradict the notion that land was now essentially family property. Not forgotten in the new scheme of things was the issue of *hukou,* or residence. Many expressed the opinion that if one migrated to the city and actually succeeded in acquiring official residency papers there, then one should give up claims to land in one's ancestral village. This contradicted the idea that land had essentially become heritable family property.

For instance, Songling's sworn sister Xuelan had been a peasant with a rural residence for most of her life, and she contracted land from her township after the reforms. She and her husband invested in and cultivated an impressive pomelo orchard. But because both held government jobs, they were able to officially change their residence to an urban one. Urban residency held future advantages for their children who might want to live in the county capital and send their own children to urban schools, which were presumed to be better. But changing their official residence also meant that Xuelan and her husband would have to give up their orchard. They could keep their house but were no longer allowed to be included in the allocation of fields in their village.

This fluid situation meant that individuals often held contradictory ideas about property. While Songling could say on one day that contracted land would become impossible to lose, on another day she might point to the impermanence of land rights under the new system. Interestingly, the conceptual contradiction between seeing land as still somehow under the collective rubric and also acting as if it would remain in one's family forever was mirrored by other contradictions in the discourse about the collective. For instance, the reforms had actually replaced the older terms of commune, production brigade, and team that implied collective organization with township, administrative district, and villagers' small group. But many people still used the older terms when speaking of these groupings.

Indeed, disagreements about what remained of the collective were at the root of many of the ongoing conflicts between people. In everyday life, collective organization is still a presence. For instance, in the spring of 2007 I witnessed households from Team 1 (now called Villagers' Small Group 1) gather to decide to whom they should rent their team fishponds. The money from the rental was to be divided among group members. On another occasion in 2007, one of the members of the local villagers' committee spoke specifically about the contradictions in compensation. He pointed out that if agricultural land was taken by the government for road building, then the entire team would be reimbursed. But if a person's house was in the way of the proposed road, only that person would receive reimbursement. This makes sense in terms of the law—since as stated earlier, even in the collective era houses were regarded as private property. Nonetheless, the villagers' committee member complained about it and insisted that compensation should go to the entire team.

As we will see shortly, the breakup of collective management coupled with the maintenance of collective ownership inevitably created misunderstandings over who had rights to particular assets. But as I have also indicated, these misunderstandings were not purely about legality. In sorting out claims and counterclaims to property, people inevitably invoked their past history with each other as well as their ideas about obligation and memory.

What were some of the ongoing conflicts surrounding property in Moonshadow Pond? One involved Baoli's threshing-machine business. The roots of this dispute lay in the electrification of the village many years earlier. When electricity came to the village in the late 1970s, the six production teams jointly invested in a number of new machines. Chief among these were machines which husked rice, a process that used to take much more time when done by the *long gu,* a large circular stone that one had to pull round and round as it squeezed the rice kernels from their husks.

But when the Household Responsibility System was instituted, what was to become of these jointly owned machines? Baoli was in a good position to take advantage of the opportunity that was presented. As mentioned in chapter 3, Baoli and Big Gao were close friends and related in a myriad of ways. So with the coming of the responsibility system, Baoli and Big Gao's daughter, Small Gao, decided to rent the rice-threshing machines from the six production teams to which they jointly belonged.

Things started out smoothly. They paid a yearly rent to the six production teams in addition to Sneaky Tao, in whose shed the machines were kept. But after seven years, Sneaky Tao wanted a share of the profits. After all, he said, the machines were in his shed. Baoli and Small Gao used this opportunity to make their move. Big Gao built a new shed for them on land he had been allocated during the breakup of the collective. Baoli and Small Gao then reasoned that they shouldn't have to pay rent to the production teams. "The machines have either been completely replaced or fixed," Baoli told me. "So now we just pay the electricity tax to the administrative district, we don't think we have to pay rent on the machines anymore."

Others clearly disagreed. One day in 1995 Baoli and Small Gao came to work and found a lock on the door of their shed. The elders' council *(laoren hui)* had put the lock there, claiming that the machines belonged to everyone in the six production teams, and that they should all realize some profit from Baoli's operation. "We don't have to listen to them," Small Gao told me. "They don't have any authority."

And indeed, she was right. Though village elections had already taken place in other parts of China, there was still no elected village committee in Moonshadow Pond until several years after this incident. Had there been such a committee, it might have had more authority than the elders' council to mediate this conflict. Further, the existing administrative district officials for Moonshadow Pond and the adjoining village were reluctant to get involved, as were township officials. The elders' council jumped into this authority vacuum, but they had no real mandate.[29] Baoli and Small Gao managed to have the lock removed. People grumbled on both sides, but Baoli and Small Gao continued with their business.

Baoli and Small Gao's response to the altercation was not an unusual one in the moral universe of Moonshadow Pond. A common feature in the discourse about disputes in Moonshadow Pond was to cast blame on a third party, accusing them of surreptitiously manipulating people in order to sow the seeds of conflict for one's own interest. In this case, Baoli and Small Gao deflected criticism by just such an accusation. They protested that Skinny Hong had stirred up the elders' council to act against them for reasons of his own.

Skinny Hong, they said, didn't like their business because their shed was opposite his store and the threshing operation made noise. Further, they claimed, Skinny Hong was using the elders' council to target them for another reason as well. He wanted to deflect attention away from his own conflict with the collective. Skinny Hong had been allocated extra land from Team 2 to build a small shop for his son, who was disabled. Instead of a small shop, he built a large house with the shop occupying merely a portion of the first floor. Everyone seemed to have some complaint about it. Strings of accusations followed in which the issue of land and property became enmeshed not only in disagreements over collective versus personal assets, but also in over thirty years of personal relationships. Who had helped whom, and when? How could this person forget and without conscience go ahead with his plans anyway? This combination of notions about land as collective property, private property, and as a token of memory can be seen clearly in Aihua's response to the crisis.

Aihua claimed that Skinny Hong had violated the team's understanding and needed to provide compensation. The house Skinny Hong had built, unlike the shop, was not a temporary structure and the land was not part of the land originally allocated to him. Furthermore, Aihua pointed to yet another of Skinny Hong's sons, who was using production-team land to manufacture tiles. This land had not been formally contracted from the production team, she said, and this was not fair.

Yet for Aihua, Skinny Hong's violations went beyond defrauding the collective. Her feelings also centered around personal obligations that she felt Skinny Hong owed her family, obligations that stemmed from events during the collective era.

The recent disputes had rekindled thirty-year old memories in Aihua. As I mentioned in chapter 2, Aihua's husband, Uncle Wei, had stepped down from his post as party secretary of the brigade in the late 1960s, primarily because of accusations that he had accepted gifts from Skinny Hong. These accusations took place because, in Aihua's view, her husband had allowed Skinny Hong to work outside the team in order to earn extra money for his many children. Thus, Skinny Hong's refusal to recognize the jurisdiction of the production team in the present case was more than a legal issue for Aihua. It was a personal one, a failure to remember the sacrifices Uncle Wei had made on Skinny Hong's behalf. In the swirl of contemporary property conflicts, past memories and ideas about unrequited favors often shaped claims and counterclaims. Skinny Hong, said Aihua, was like a person who sent his dog to bite you after you had saved it!

In evaluating Aihua's responses, however, we should keep in mind that Aihua had always taken pride in the accomplishments of the production team and in her role as its leader. If there were a possibility of compensation for the team, she would find it. In any dispute between an individual and the team over land or other kinds of property, she would be likely to argue for team rights.

THE MAN WHO SOLD THE COLLECTIVE'S LAND

Until the matter of Slippery's land arose, team property in Moonshadow Pond that was "sold" fell into only one category—agricultural land that the government needed in order to build the highway that runs through Moonshadow Pond. In this case, every member of the production team to which that land belonged was compensated. The notion of team membership and entitlement was strong enough that several team members who now worked and lived in the county capital (but who still had rural residency papers), made sure to demand their share of the payment. These people included Songling's eldest daughter, Meiying, who had been left off the original list.

Ironically, people's interest in a piece of land and their notion of it as collective property increased dramatically when there was a possible individual gain associated with their relationship to it. For instance, Lanfang, also a member of Team 2, had taken over some land that was not considered prime agricultural land. Through hard work and stewardship, she made the land productive, growing several varieties of fruit trees, including pomelo, tangerines, and persimmons. No one contested her use of the land when she first began to cultivate it, because it had been agricultural wasteland. "But if they suddenly decide to build a highway through her land," Baoli told me, "then everyone will be demanding a share of the compensation, and saying that the land belongs to the team, and not just to Lanfang."

Not unexpectedly, when Slippery's case was raised in conversation the first time, it was in the context of team property—with reference to the idea that all team members should be compensated *if* his share of land was sold. On the day in 1996 when I first heard this story, Aihua was sitting in Baoli and Songling's living room, where everyone was discussing what they thought was the sale of Slippery's land. Aihua was outraged. How could his land just be sold? First, he needed permission. More importantly, team members and not Slippery were the rightful recipients of any payments for this land.

As mentioned earlier, the impetus for the gossip surrounding Slippery's case was the visit of his elderly cousin from Taiwan. Whisperings and then open discussion circulated around the village that Slippery had sold his share of team land to his cousin Long Beard for eight thousand *yuan*. This was a sizable sum in the context of Moonshadow Pond in the mid 1990s, certainly more than most factory workers could earn in a year. Further, this land was paddy land belonging to Team 2. As with all matters in Moonshadow Pond, several stories circulated simultaneously about the sale. Some said that Long Beard had bought the land so that he could donate it to the elders' council for a clubhouse. Others said that Long Beard wanted to build a house for his wife, actually a mistress who, some said, was even expecting a baby (more scandal still, since Long Beard was well into his seventies). Aihua said, "It doesn't matter what Long

Beard wants to do with the land. Slippery can't sell it without permission from the township government, and he can't keep the money himself; it belongs to all of us!"

Others chimed in with their opinions as well. If the land were used for a clubhouse for the seniors, wouldn't there be gambling there? Seniors would spend their days playing mahjong and this would be inappropriate for the land, because it was right next to the school.

People soon learned that the root of the problem was Slippery's inability to get a permit for building on the site. Every time he applied to the township for permission, he was denied, because the land was too close to the school. Slippery, people said, was the source of most of his own problems. He had originally been allocated "dry land" as well as the paddy fields needed for rice growing (and more thoroughly regulated because of its national importance). Home building was allowed on dry land only, but Slippery had traded his share of this with Sneaky Tao. Now he was stuck with the paddy land and unable to build anything on it. Slippery, at least according to the surmise of the villagers, was looking for any angle to rid himself of the land and get compensation. The eight thousand *yuan* would cover the thirty years of tax that he would still have to pay. (As mentioned earlier, this tax was later abolished, but only after these incidents took place.)

Such informal trading of shares was not unheard of, and this trading had added a layer of complexity to land rights that had little legal foundation. When paddy land was traded, the original user of the land would still be liable for grain procurement and other forms of taxes. He would have to come to an informal agreement with the person he was trading with, to make sure the responsibility of paying taxes was in the hands of the new land occupant. So Slippery's responsibility for the land tax on that particular parcel of land was already the product of his previous trade with Sneaky Tao.

The use of such informal agreements was springing up all over China at the time, and some analysts therefore concluded that the system of land tenure had evolved into a system that was private in all but law.[30] And yet, as I have already shown, in Moonshadow Pond, the limits of "private" and "collective" were actually being tested every day, and there was rarely consensus.

In the midst of the controversies over Slippery's land, the township government finally weighed in. The land, they said, could be used only for school-related activities, or it could remain paddy land. As the controversy proceeded, further confusion arose when Slippery then asserted that he had never sold the land in the first place and all the subsequent discussion was irrelevant.

To further complicate matters, many villagers believed that neither legal limitations nor administrative decisions were the real reasons Slippery could not proceed with his plans to build on that plot. Many villagers believed that he could easily have circumvented the law. It was not the law that stopped him, they said, but his poor personal relations with others in the village. "When he borrows money, he never pays it back," one villager told me.

Worse still was his treatment of his elderly stepmother. His father had married her when she was in her late thirties, at the time of Liberation. A bonded female servant *(binü)*, she had just regained her personal freedom at that time. Because she had no children of her own, she was now dependent on her stepchildren in her old age. A distant stepdaughter would send her money occasionally, but Slippery was "without conscience" *(liangxin)*. "He only feeds her rice porridge," said Aihua, "and when someone else gives her something, Slippery gets angry. He says that you think he hasn't fulfilled his responsibilities."

With money and good social relations, one should have been able to circumvent the letter (and even spirit) of the law. Villagers assumed that legislation and rules about land and property were social challenges, not necessarily legal ones. Though they often vigorously complained about the way the system enabled the rich to get their way, they also assumed that this was simply reality.

For his part, with all his plans rejected, Slippery now stepped up to defend himself. First, he claimed that there had been no land-related transaction between himself and his cousin. He had merely received an unrelated gift from his cousin.

In the summer of 1997 I finally decided to speak directly with Slippery about the ongoing dispute. "If we had money," Slippery told me, "we could 'buy the road.'" (This expression was often used to refer to the strategic use of payoffs to cadres and administrative officials to circumvent laws or regulations.) Further, Slippery told me, his cousin had never bought the land. Rather, he had planned to allow his cousin to use it. In return, his cousin would reimburse Slippery for the taxes that he would still be required to pay, precisely because the land tax was still Slippery's responsibility.

Slippery was emphatic about these points and he showed me all his documents. "Look here," he muttered, casting the documents before me. I started to peruse them. The first, a handwritten note signed by Slippery, stated that his cousin would be allowed to use the land. The cousin, in a second document, pledged to hand over eight thousand *yuan* to Slippery, on behalf of their brotherly connection and feelings *(ganqing)*. Another document followed with a slightly different twist, although I was not sure Slippery was aware of the contradictions he arrayed before me. In this document, Slippery wrote that he would allow the elders' council to use his land, providing that they assumed the responsibility for the land tax (this would presumably have nullified the necessity of the second document, where Slippery's cousin pledged eight thousand *yuan* for the same purpose). Finally, there was a fourth document. Here Slippery and his cousin pledged that the eight thousand *yuan* was entirely their own affair, unconnected to any transfer or use of land!

These documents, in chronological order, were obviously Slippery's attempt to work around the perception that the land had been sold. In fact, the final document tried to disconnect any transfer of money between Slippery and his cousin from the land, land tax, or any use of the land. Their obvious internal inconsistencies were either not apparent to Slippery, or else he felt no need to hide from me his apparent attempt to fit his actions *ex post facto* to the existing laws and regulations. Slippery was not insensitive to the gossip that swirled around him, nor was he unaware that there was still support in the community for the notion that land was still the property of the collective.

AN UNRESOLVED DISPUTE

Ten years after Slippery's dispute initially occurred, the situation had both changed dramatically and not changed at all. When I returned to Moonshadow Pond in 2007, I discovered that Slippery had died a few years earlier. So, what was to become of his land now? His cousin from Taiwan, Long Beard, was still alive, but since the land had never been legally transferred to him, he still had no authority to give it away for any purpose. Furthermore, Slippery's son now claimed that this land was his to use, and he showed no interest in giving it up, even though it lay unused. As mentioned earlier, since farmers had signed thirty-year leases on their land in 1997, many had begun to treat the land as family property that could be inherited, and Slippery's son felt he was on solid ground in claiming the land for himself now that his father had died. Finally, the village school adjacent to this plot of land had recently been closed by the local authorities because of the decline in births. Students from Moonshadow Pond now had to go to schools in surrounding areas, and the school building had been taken over by the local elder's council. They used it for gambling and gathering on most afternoons, so there was no longer any reason to build an additional clubhouse.

Meanwhile, Sneaky Tao had retired from any participation in village affairs and was well over eighty years old. But his son Small Tao was now the highest-ranking local official in Moonshadow Pond. He decided that the best use of this land would be to turn it into a badminton court. The front of the school had already been paved over, and my husband and I had contributed funds to turn it into a basketball court. Slippery's old land was directly adjacent to the basketball court, and Small Tao thought this would create a great center for local youth to congregate and play games. It might also be good for his reputation. Elections for village officials had finally been implemented in this corner of Guangdong Province, and Small Tao had a variety of plans on the books to demonstrate his effectiveness as a member of the villager's committee. Ironically, Long Beard was still alive and said he would like to "give" this land to the village so that it could be used for recreation. But clearly, it was not his to give away. Nothing could be done since Slippery's son now showed no inclination to part with his claim to the land.

Disputes over property in Moonshadow Pond therefore have continued to function as public forums in which contending claims were articulated, if not resolved. Support for the idea of collective property has contended with support for the idea of personal property, or property that will become family property and passed on to descendants. The idea of the law as objective has contended with the notion that good social relationships plus money can always find a way to circumvent it. Notions of obligations from the past are also added to the mix in assessing one's right to a particular piece of property.

While Slippery was alive, he was not able to simply dispose of "his" land in any way he chose. Had he lived longer, would he have had an easier time "selling" his land? As stated earlier, although agricultural land ownership still resides in the collectives, rules about the transfer of land use rights are now more liberal than at the time of Slippery's difficulties.[31]

But people's responses to Slippery went beyond their understandings of the limits of law alone. Ideas about Slippery's poor social relationships and lack of "conscience" also influenced people's rejection of the idea that Slippery could sell his land. This was certainly abetted by people's desires for shares in sales of team land, and a still surviving ideological investment in the idea of the collective order. Nonetheless, Slippery failed not only because he was not supported by law or because the idea of the collective was still held strongly by community members, but also because he had not met customary expectations about moral social behavior and fulfillment of obligations. The importance of meeting these social and moral expectations is also a key feature of economic behavior noted in other recent ethnographic studies of China.[32] As discussed in this chapter, ideas about moral obligation still influence the way residents of Moonshadow Pond evaluate the validity of a number of other property claims.

Take the case, for instance, of Baoli and Small Gao. Was their threshing machine their personal property from which they could profit, or did it belong to the collective? While some community members claimed they were taking over a collective asset, Baoli and Small Gao managed to continue using it for their private business.

Several factors might have protected them in ways that did not help Slippery. They had better personal relationships in general (as opposed to Slippery's mishandled ones). They also had better connections. Small Gao's father was once the brigade head, a striking contrast with Slippery's lack of connections. Further, some of those who objected to Baoli and Small Gao's use of the threshing machine (such as Skinny Hong) had their own conflicts with the collective. While Baoli and Small Gao certainly faced opposition on the grounds that they were privatizing a collective asset, they seemed to have avoided the universal offense to sensibilities that Slippery so unfortunately fell into, and they were able to hold on to their claim.

Of course, Baoli and Small Gao may also have benefited because a machine still seems less significant to community members than land itself. Despite changes in the rural economy, land is still the ultimate guarantor of survival in China's rural communities, and it also provides a fallback for rural migrants if they lose their urban jobs. While wage work can come and go, access to land at least assures one of food for subsistence. As Sally Sargeson points out in a summary of land policies in contemporary China, "The loss of land affects villagers in multiple ways. In poorer areas, access to land guarantees caloric intake as well as monetary income. It is the sole source of social security for most farmers, underpinning the intergenerational reciprocity that provides welfare for the elderly and support for rural migrant workers during cycles of recession and unemployment."[33]

As we have seen, Moonshadow Pond residents hold a number of ideas about property rights, both descriptive and proscriptive. In addition to the idea that past obligations and reciprocity can determine one's right to make a claim, there is the equally strong notion that putting work into land or another asset should solidify one's entitlement to it. And still surviving is the idea that land, as well as other forms of productive property, is a collective asset. These are assuredly more than mere interpretations of law. Each of these ideas about property is not only an assertion about what is legal, but also what is right.

Nonetheless, it is interesting to observe that as they work their way through the post-Mao economic regime, Moonshadow Pond residents still find a role for protecting the concept that at least some resources are collective. In our next chapter, we go beyond the issue of property to examine in more detail the moral implications of the conflict between collectivist visions and those based on the private accumulation of wealth.

CHAPTER 7

"Money Causes Trouble"

"Monks nowadays make a lot of money. That monk not only has a wife, but he has a mistress too, and he has built a separate house for her! But then again, as they say, 'money causes trouble' " *(you qian zuo guai)*. Baoli made this remark as we were speaking about a monk I had observed at a funeral that morning. As explained in chapter 4, there are a number of "secular monks" in Moonshadow Pond who officiate at funerals and other rituals, but who have not taken vows of celibacy. During the collective period, most monks were forced to return to secular life by the government and many of them married, but this has not stopped people from making fun of them for their lack of asceticism.

Baoli's expression, "money causes trouble," is also a useful way to begin this chapter, in which we focus on the way Moonshadow Pond residents articulate a moral commentary on growing differences in wealth amongst themselves and in society as a whole. Despite Baoli's use of a catchy proverb to describe the monk's escapades, there is no simple summary of villagers' ideas and expectations about the accumulation of private wealth. Its ideological value and role from the old society through Maoist times to the reform era has varied enormously, and its meanings at present are therefore numerous and contradictory.

I have already discussed aspects of this issue in previous chapters. For instance, in chapter 4 I described how an elaborate funeral display can create status for the family of the deceased and serve as a show of their filial piety. Yet, this same display in a funeral rite can amount to little if a family does not appropriately show its appreciation of people who help them with the ritual. In fact, a modest ceremony may garner more respect than an elaborate one in certain situations. Likewise, in the chapter on returnees I noted that access to the potential wealth of overseas returnees has different connotations depending on contexts. Villagers may harshly judge a person who tries to turn a distant connection into a close one just for the sake of personal gain. But at the same time, contacts and connections with overseas relations are prized in part because they can result in financial windfalls. Finally, the chapter on property disputes pointed to the multiple meanings of property in contemporary Moonshadow Pond, where ideas about collective property exist alongside ideas about property as residing within a family line. In all these cases, we see changes in the meanings and implications of wealth (and property) over time, as well as the simultaneous existence of seemingly contradictory concepts, since cultural ideas from different eras all play roles in shaping people's responses to the exigencies of contemporary life.

In what follows, I take a closer look at the meanings of wealth and the expectations surrounding wealth in Moonshadow Pond. As we shall see, divergent discourses about wealth and class circulate in the village. A person might emphasize class commonalities among villagers in one particular context, while in another context draw attention to wealth differences within the same group. In all these cases, people make both implicit and explicit moral judgments about the inequalities in contemporary society, as well as about the obligations of particular individuals with respect to their specific roles. At the end of the chapter, I will ask if there are any unifying expectations beneath the many voices villagers use to talk about disparities in wealth in the reform era. I conclude the chapter with a story that circulated around the village in 1996 (the story of Jintao's ring). The story is illustrative of moral discourse in the village with respect to its presentation of the moral obligations of wealth.

COMMODITIZED CONCEPTIONS

Most historians agree that entrepreneurial ideas have flourished in China for many centuries. As the historian Mark Elvin has pointed out, with respect to some commodities, even rural areas have been linked to a national market for almost one thousand years.[1] Elvin described Chinese peasants from the Song period through the imperial era as "adaptable, rational, profit-oriented petty entrepreneurs."[2] The anthropologist Hill

Gates has argued that petty capitalism appeared as an attractive alternative for working people in traditional China. They could not necessarily enter into the ranks of the bureaucracy, but they could at least hope to better their chances through entrepreneurial success.[3] Even popular Chinese religious practice has long reflected monetized thinking. As I described in chapter 4, mourners burn spirit money at funerals and at other occasions as well to help the deceased pay off debts for previous incarnations or to build up credit for favorable future incarnations.

The idea of profiting and earning money to better one's family circumstances and status is an old one in China. But this does not imply anything about the uses to which money is supposed to be put. If traditional Chinese society accepted the idea of striving to prosper and profit, it hardly endorsed an individualistic use of these assets. Wealth was supposed to be used to better the material circumstances and status of family and lineage.

The conversion of individually earned wealth from amoral to moral purposes by channeling it into family or lineage was a kind of conversion not uncharacteristic of many cultures. As the anthropologist Jonathan Parry points out, most societies have "two related but separate transactional orders: on the one hand transactions concerned with the reproduction of the long-term social or cosmic order; on the other, a 'sphere' of short-term transactions concerned with the arena of individual competition."[4] Parry further notes that the long-term cycle "is always positively associated with the central precepts of morality, the short-term order tends to be morally undetermined since it concerns individual purposes. . . . If, however, that which is obtained in the short-term individualistic cycle is converted to serve the reproduction of the long-term cycle, then it becomes morally positive."[5]

In southeast China, therefore, wealth that was plowed into family or lineage use was what Parry would refer to as "long-term" or "cosmic" use, since it bolstered the position of these central and enduring social structures. While wealth might be used to enhance family or lineage strength, class inequalities within lineages were historically downplayed by rituals and other mechanisms of lineage unity; these included lineage rites and lineage halls, as well as the use of assets from lineage corporate property to help poorer lineage mates to attain some education. As James Watson has observed, poor peasants in communities organized around a single strong lineage "had little reason to identify with poor members of other lineages, and it is doubtful that they felt any sense of class solidarity with outsiders. Primary loyalties lay unquestionably with one's own kinsmen because, without this lineage tie, the villager would have been simply another peasant fending for himself in a hostile environment. To ordinary lineage members, the lineage was more than an abstract kinship organization; it was an integral part of their personal identities."[6]

With the Communist revolution, of course, ideas about class were turned upside down. Not only did class become a primary identity, but as mentioned earlier, capitalists, landlords, and rich peasants received denigrating class labels that were passed down long after the material circumstances that led to these designations were eradicated. By the time the Cultural Revolution erupted, it was not only those categorized as "landlord" or "capitalist" who met with trouble; it was also dangerous to engage in any behavior that was imagined to be *similar to* that of a capitalist or landlord. As we saw in the story recounted in chapter 2, Skinny Hong was sent to prison camp because he was accused of exploiting workers on the construction project he organized in Jiangxi Province. The workers who accused Skinny Hong were from Moonshadow Pond, and Skinny Hong's actual class status was that of a poor peasant. But at that time, common ancestry and lineage ties did not protect Skinny Hong from his accusers. It was only after Uncle Wei intervened in his role as brigade secretary that Skinny Hong was released from jail.

Despite the class labels of the Mao era, however, it is important to remember that the vast majority of Moonshadow Pond residents lived out the collective era just as they had been labeled—as poor peasants. Most could look to the future with similar economic expectations. As mentioned in chapter 3, a young man who knew he would spend his life tilling the fields in the collective and eating the collective's rice did not have to wait long to get married. His future may not have been one of prosperity, but it was certain enough to go ahead with the marriage. There was no question of waiting until he had built a new house or acquired a job with a good salary, since neither of these were likely possibilities.

Ironically, the abolition of class labels in the reform era occurred at a moment when actual differences in wealth became more noticeable. But how are these changes characterized by Moonshadow Pond residents? When they look out at their village, do they see sharp class differences? Or do they still see their fellow villagers primarily as lineage mates and fellow peasants, whose differences in material circumstances are less significant than their commonalities and mutual obligations?

DISCOURSES OF SOLIDARITY AND SAMENESS

There are still many forces that encourage Moonshadow Pond residents to emphasize their commonality. It *is* a single-lineage village, and people still use the term *ziji ren,* or "one's own people," to refer to each other. In the reform era, lineage organization in many southeast Chinese villages has been given a new lease on life. With greater wealth and additional help from overseas relations, the refurbishment of lineage halls has become widespread.[7] In Moonshadow Pond, worship at the common lineage hall during New Year reinforces the symbolism of village solidarity based on the identity of villagers as *ziji ren* or lineage mates.

Indeed, the term *ziji ren* is often used in conversation as a way to mollify anger or tamper down discord amongst villagers. For instance, during my last week in the village in the spring of 1996, I invited a traveling acting and singing troupe to come to the village and give a performance. I hoped to thank villagers collectively for the help that so many individuals had provided during my research. It turned out to be a big hit, because no such performance had taken place in Moonshadow Pond for over thirty years. The entire village, as well as people from neighboring villages, came out to see the show, which was staged in the courtyard of the local school. It was even covered by the local newspapers and television. At one point, Aihua's nephew, the gambler Ironpot, became upset because no one had saved him a seat close to the stage. He began to grumble loudly, at which point Aihua immediately said to him, "Stop this! We are all *ziji ren* here. What is there to be upset about?"

On another occasion, some people complained that Aihua's younger son was charging too much for the pork he sold at his shop every morning and not giving people as much as they thought they were buying. One neighbor said, "He can do this when he sells his pork in town, but not here. The other day he measured one *jin* as 8.5 *liang* [instead of ten *liang*].[8] The customer caught him and he apologized; she then told him, 'We are all *ziji ren,* so you should not be doing this!'"

So, the idea of solidarity through lineage identity is still a strong one and is used in some circumstances to invoke the need for harmonious behavior or feelings. Collective-era organization into production brigades and teams was built upon preexisting lineage ties and added another layer of identity that stressed solidarity over division. As mentioned in the previous chapter, people may still refer to an area within the village in terms of the production team with which it used to be identified. For instance, the area where I lived was sometimes referred to as the Team 2 area, because most of the homes were built by Team 2 members on their team's land.

Ideas and mechanisms of solidarity, therefore, come from both traditional lineage organization as well as Mao-era collective structures. There is also a discourse of similarity in addition to one of solidarity. This discourse does not emphasize that people are linked organically in the same structure so much as that they are similar in terms of their class position. It describes villagers as rural folk who are no longer desperately poor and who can get by from day to day, but who lack power and wealth in the larger society.

The idea that all villagers share a similar status and condition as *nongmin,* or peasants, has some of its roots in the household registration system, an official system of classifying population that began in 1955 and which continues through this day. In 1955, the Chinese government instituted a policy of registering each member of the population as either urban or rural. Those who were categorized as rural received their rice through the collective. Those categorized as urban received not only their food, but other benefits as well, through their *danwei* or work unit. Of course during the collective era there was not much of a market, so access to goods and services was highly dependent on one's categorization as a peasant or an urban worker.

One's household registration *(hukou)* had major ramifications on where and how one lived. During the collective era, it was extremely difficult to change registration unless one served in the army, became a party member and official at a level higher than the commune, or managed to attain specialized education. One of the aims of this system was to control rural to urban migration, a major cause of urban slums in poor countries, and in achieving this end, the policy was successful. Throughout the collective period, peasant mobility to urban areas was very low, and China avoided the rural to urban migration characteristic of much of the developing world. Of course, this also meant that many rural people were essentially locked within their native villages, and a major means of upward mobility was lost to them.

In the reform era, however, restrictions on movement were lifted as tens of millions of rural people migrated to the cities of China for jobs in the booming manufacturing sector. These migrants were often referred to as the "floating population."[9] But despite this physical movement, most of these migrants retain their rural registration and are counted by the census as members of their rural families. Further, although changing one's status is somewhat easier than in the past, it is still difficult. In Moonshadow Pond, for instance, the brothers Weiguo and Jieguo had changed their residence before the reform period began because of service in the army and subsequent employment in the state sector. When team land was divided among families at the beginning of the reform period, they received none, for they were no longer peasants and members of the collective. Although they still have houses in Moonshadow Pond (as well as urban residences), their status is somewhat anomalous. They are lineage members, but technically they are no longer "peasants" or members of the collective.

Thus, the category of *nongmin* or peasant is created by state practices in China that have persisted for several decades. It is one basis of similarity that most residents of Moonshadow Pond certainly share, unless they are among the few villagers who have successfully changed their residency to "urban." But beyond official categories, many Moonshadow Pond families do share similar sets of circumstances.

One example of villagers articulating their sense of sameness and deemphasizing their differences occurred in the summer of 1997, when I conducted a survey of village households. I asked Baoli and Big Gao to categorize families in terms of their relative economic position. Big Gao had been the production brigade head from the late 1970s until the early 1990s, and was familiar with almost every family in the village. I was interested not in some absolute economic measure, such as household income, but in how people in Moonshadow Pond categorized each other. Giving Baoli and Big Gao a list of the 184 village households that then composed the village, I asked them to come up with their own set of categories to assess the economic circumstances of each house. When they were through, they had placed all but fourteen households in the resounding "middle." Furthermore, they placed 63 percent of their fellow villagers in the "middle" of this middle category, rather than categorizing them as "upper middle" or "lower middle" (see table 4). Ten years later Big Gao had passed away, but I asked Baoli to go through the same exercise. Even though he didn't look at the old material, the percentages came out almost exactly the same.

Baoli and Big Gao's decision to deemphasize economic differences was not unique. It echoed a strain of discourse I heard often in Moonshadow Pond that described the situation of most villagers as in the "middle." Another way people talk about this is to say that right now everyone's situation is *chabuduo,* or "not differing much." Most village residents no longer see themselves as poor, in part because "poor" in Moonshadow Pond is often described in relation to food scarcity, something that is no

TABLE 4   ECONOMIC STATUS OF MOONSHADOW POND HOUSEHOLDS
ACCORDING TO BAOLI AND BIG GAO

Economic Status	Households (1997)	Households (2007)
Xia (lower)	5 (3%)	5 (2%)
Zhongxia (lower middle)	14 (8%)	11 (5%)
Zhong (middle)	114 (63%)	124 (63%)
Zhongshang (upper middle)	38 (21%)	33 (17%)
Shang (upper)	9 (5%)	25 (13%)
Total	184 (100%)	198 (100%)

longer a problem. But few villagers would characterize themselves as rich, so the "middle" *(zhongdeng)* is the way they identify themselves and others.

It is important to point out that this middle is not a middle as understood in Western terms. As Aihua's second son said to me one day, "Eating, wearing clothes, and having a place to live are not problems anymore, but finding employment and getting your kids educated is still a problem." In his case, the land allocated to family members was enough to provide their rice and most of their vegetables, and his business of slaughtering pigs and selling pork provided the cash they needed to get by from day to day. Also, as rural folk, "homelessness" was impossible, since at a minimum families had their ancestral homes as well as the plots from their production teams for their new homes. But for Aihua's son, it was the problems looming on the horizon, paying high school tuition for his kids, or a possible sickness of his elderly parents, that were worrisome.

In contrast, Big Gao described the rise in living standards since the reform period this way: "Today's 'middle' is higher than landlords in the old society." When I asked Big Gao how he would explain this, Baoli interjected and said, "In the old society ordinary people just ate meat three times a year, during the Lunar New Year, the Dragon Boat Festival, and the Ghost Festival. Landlords were considered rich because *they* had meat three times a month instead."

Songling quoted from an old saying to describe the situation as she saw it for most people, "We're not dying of hunger, and we're not getting rich." In such statements, villagers place each other together in the same boat and rather than making distinctions among themselves, emphasize their common peasant background. For instance, Miaoli went to a school reunion and showed Songling the picture of her classmates who were now middle-aged. When Songling looked at the picture, she said, "You can tell who the peasants *[nongmin]* are. They are dark and look older than the people with a *danwei* [work unit]."

Likewise, when I visited the village where Aihua grew up, a young man said to me, "It's easy if you are an official to make money, but we peasants have to go out and earn money in Shenzhen or some other place." Interestingly, "peasants" in this statement are identified not by agriculture, the activity with which they were originally associated, but by their need to migrate to cities to earn cash. In the cities, they not only remain "peasants" because of their official registration, but in terms of self-identification. In addition, it is interesting to note that "peasants" and "officials" are also contrasted in this statement. But it should be pointed out that the category of "official" is a slippery and somewhat imprecise term.

Another common way that peasants are differentiated from others in discourses about wealth is by talking about their relative lack of connections, power, and influence in society at large. Wealth is sometimes referred to as something siphoned off by those who are in a position to borrow more money, and these are not ordinary peasants. Many stories circulated in the village about huge loans from banks to land developers who never paid back the money. This money was often described as "state money" that had been diverted into private pockets and which the country would never get back. Aihua put it this way, "The people who are rich are just the people who have borrowed more money."

Of course, emphasizing peasant commonality vis-à-vis officials and other economic elites is not always used rhetorically to glorify peasant solidarity. It can also be used as a means of emphasizing the necessity of social mobility away from peasant status. Songling's sworn sister Xuelan was one such person who had secured a good position in a *danwei* and Songling usually spoke about her achievements in doing so in glorified terms. Likewise, Aihua frequently lamented her lack of education. Her way of describing this most often was to say that she remained a peasant rather than having a chance to work in a *danwei*. And Songling often admonished her children in the midst of the rice harvest while they were small. "Are you afraid of this?" she would ask. "If you are, you better study hard!" In this case, referring to peasant activities like harvesting rice was used to goad her children into studying so that they could presumably surmount their peasant background.

Fear of jealousy is another openly acknowledged reason to avoid talking about differences amongst village residents. For instance, before I left Meixian after fieldwork in the spring of 1996, I created a small scholarship fund for the primary school. I initially thought that it might be used to help families who were in difficult economic circumstances to pay their children's school fees (these primary school fees were abolished several years later). Even though elementary school tuition was not high, it still added expenses twice a year that could be stressful for families who did not have much cash income. I soon discovered, however, that no one liked the idea of using the money for just a few families. The teachers thought this use of the funds would create conflict and jealousy among those who did and did not qualify. So they decided instead to use the interest on the fund to buy small yearly gifts for each student, creating an award to acknowledge something good about each one.

Reciprocal responsibilities to others are an additional reason for families to downplay their differences with one another. An example of this occurred in the winter of 1995, when my parents visited me in the village. Because they were from the United States, the rumor immediately began to circulate in the village that they had given Songling and Baoli the huge sum of ten thousand *yuan*. Actually, nothing of the kind had occurred, but after my parents' visit, Chunhua, the wife of Baoli's nephew, began to sulk. She thought the rumor was true and was insulted because none of the funds that she thought Songling and Baoli received had been shared with her own family. Emphasizing one's similarity with everyone else is therefore a good way of avoiding the inevitable accusation that one has enriched oneself while forgetting obligations to kin. Songling's eldest son-in-law put it this way, "China is still a backward country and therefore people are still poor. Therefore, if you have more than somebody else, he will be jealous. If you get something from someone, don't tell others, or they will be very jealous."

The idea that one person's prosperity is garnered by taking something away from other people in the community closely parallels the "image of the limited good" described many decades ago by George Foster in a classic essay on peasant cognitive orientation. At that time, Foster noted that in many peasant communities throughout the world people assume that "good things in life are in limited and unexpandable quantities, and hence personal gain must be at the expense of others."[10] Hence, Foster wrote, peasants deal with differences either by trying not to stand out or by recycling some of their wealth back into the community through "ritual expenditures."[11] Such expenditures attempt to neutralize the impact of standing out from one's community through acts of reciprocity, and as we have already seen in previous chapters, feasting at funerals and weddings are just two examples of this kind of expenditure in the rural Chinese context.

It might seem odd, however, that this parallel with Foster's example exists. After all, life in rural Meixian today is hardly that of the peasant societies described by Foster, communities that were relatively enclosed and not integrated into a larger capitalist economy. With many Moonshadow Pond residents migrating to large metropolises to work, and with everyone incorporated into a cash economy, one might wonder why an ethos connected to the idea of wealth as a "limited good" continues to exist.

Perhaps one factor which encourages the continuation of this discourse of the "middle," or the emphasis on similarity of economic position, at least on the part of those who remember the Maoist period, is an attempt to forget about the ill-fated class-label system. Certainly, those in the stigmatized categories were happy to see the end of these labels, which not only prevented them from accessing opportunities, but in the worst-case scenarios led to persecution and disruption of family relations.[12] For instance, Songling's father was labeled a "capitalist." He had also married twice and had a second wife and family in Chaozhou, a different area of Guangdong Province. During the Cultural Revolution he was marched through the streets of his other home with a white dunce cap, jailed for several months, and forced to write confessions each day. He stayed away from his family in Moonshadow Pond for almost twenty years after that, fearing that his disgraced status might pass on to them. So people like Songling, whose families received bad class labels were obviously happy to see the end of the class-label system.

While it is easy to see why people like Songling would want to forget about the class-label system, by the time it was abolished, it also had little support among those in good class categories. As Jonathan Unger explains, there were too many people in the poor peasant category for it to confer any real advantage by the 1970s, and almost three decades after the revolution the life circumstances of those in the bad categories were hard to distinguish from those who were labeled poor peasants.[13] Indeed, those in Moonshadow Pond who had received bad class designations now associated with their fellow villagers in ways no different from anybody else. These included Anlong's mother, whose husband was one of the Nationalist soldiers who fled to Taiwan and whose father-in-law was the landlord who committed suicide, and Songling's father, once labeled a capitalist, but who was now a frequent participant in discussions of village affairs with other members of the elder's council. Uncle Li, the old schoolteacher who was once shunned because of his class status, was another who now interacted freely with fellow villagers, although several people told me stories about how they had avoided him during the Cultural Revolution because of his class status. All these people were now part of everyday life in Moonshadow Pond, and no one defended the treatment they had received in the past.

An example of the discomfort people felt in talking about people's former class designations was revealed the time I asked Big Gao and Baoli to categorize Moonshadow Pond families. In addition to asking them to compare the economic status of families in the present, I asked if they could simply note down the original class designations of these families. They started to pencil these in, but after a discussion with each other and with me, they said they thought it was a bad idea to go back to these labels, and we should forget about probing in this direction. Baoli and Big Gao had both been categorized as poor peasants themselves. Nonetheless, they felt uneasy dwelling on references to the class-label system.

Discourses of solidarity and sameness within the village do not imply a vision of rural society as completely egalitarian, but they do emphasize the common condition of Moonshadow Pond residents vis-à-vis the outside world—as lineage mates and as ordinary rural folk who are no longer poverty stricken, yet not wealthy in terms of society in general. Indeed, many commentators have pointed out that the cultural distinction between peasants and urban dwellers in China has actually sharpened since the 1990s. Despite the fact that so many rural people have migrated to the cities, they take their peasant identities with them. Not only, as mentioned before, do they retain their rural registrations, but in addition they are often seen as culturally inferior to urban people. Says Hairong Yan, "In the post-Mao cities, it has become an epithet or a crude joke to call someone peasant *(nongmin),* a sign most potently suggesting ignorance *(yumei),* backwardness *(luohuo),* and a dire lack of civility *(bu wenming)."* [14] In addition, many economic analysts have pointed out that the distinctions between rural and urban incomes have become more severe in China since the 1990s. [15] These cultural and economic trends inevitably influence villagers when they emphasize their common condition.

However, at times Moonshadow Pond residents also talk about inequality amongst themselves in ways that deemphasize ideas about common bonds described in the previous section. For even if most villagers are still categorized as "peasants," they have not all shared the same economic fate.

Talking about inequality within the lineage is a more dangerous discourse than talking about commonalities. If some people are more prosperous or better connected than others, then what do they owe their poorer lineage mates? To bring these questions to the fore undermines images of solidarity based on lineage membership and similarity based on common peasant identity. While it is easier to avoid uncomfortable topics, it is also impossible to entirely ignore differences. Life-cycle rituals, life crises such as an illness, feeling snubbed by a richer relative, and even altercations with the law can bring differences out into the open and create occasions for comment. I will now consider these threads in discourse and then evaluate what they imply about moral conceptions in Moonshadow Pond.

VILLAGERS THEORIZE INEQUALITY

Officials Then and Now

Discourse about inequality within the village takes a number of different shapes, but certainly one of those is focused on the category of "officials." As mentioned earlier, the use of the term official or cadre *(ganbu)* as distinguished from peasant *(nongmin)* depends much on context. Even during the collective era, cadres who worked at the brigade level (below the level of the commune) were not state employees. Technically, they were peasants like everybody else. Later, when the communes were changed to "townships," the practice continued. Local people who work in the township offices have salaries, benefits, and days off; in short, they have work units or *danwei*. But village-level cadres do not have work units. In Moonshadow Pond, these cadres include a district party secretary, a district head, and members of a district committee. Moonshadow Pond is part of a two-village administrative district and its cadres are paid a small monthly sum by the township for their services. But their positions are not and have never been tantamount to a salaried job.

When villagers talk about these local cadres, do they think of them as officials or as ordinary villagers? Much depends on context. When reciting a story about favoritism or taking advantage of one's position, a village-level cadre might be referred to as an official, especially if he is understood to be the guilty party. For instance, Sneaky Tao's son Small Tao was now on the district committee and was the highest-ranking cadre in Moonshadow Pond. Although he received a monthly stipend for this work, it was not equivalent to working in a township office, where employees were part of a formal bureaucracy. Yet people might still refer to Small Tao as an official when complaining about the way he used his connections to obtain favors. They might also call him a "high-ranking cadre" to his face as a kind of half-joke and half-compliment. In other circumstances, however, village-level cadres were simply lumped in with other Moonshadow Pond residents as peasants and fellow lineage members. This was especially true when talking about villagers, such as Uncle Wei, who had been cadres during the collective era.

Speaking favorably about the behavior of cadres prior to the reform era can also be seen as a way of making unfavorable comparisons with the present. For instance, one day I was interviewing Uncle Wei about his ten-year term as brigade secretary, which began in the late 1960s. Uncle Wei emphasized that he had not used his post to help his sons.

"Cadres at that time were different from now," he went on to say. "Once they made a little mistake, they would be picked out and accused of corruption or plotting capitalism again socialism! Once you were caught, you would never have a chance to get back your good name, and sometimes even if you stuck to principles, people would accuse you of corruption anyway, and you had to resign after losing face. So, even though we had some power in our hands, we wouldn't dare abuse it." While Uncle Wei was speaking, Miaoli walked into their house. "Yes, if he had been a bad cadre," she said, "he would have been very rich by now."

In fact, Uncle Wei served most of his term without major accusations launched against him. But finally, even he had problems when he was accused of helping Skinny Hong get out of prison in exchange for favors. So after acting as brigade secretary for ten years, Uncle Wei finally stepped down.

Big Gao, who served as head of the production brigade from 1978 until 1993, had also been accused of corruption at an earlier time. He was first chosen as a brigade head in 1962.[16] But when the Four Cleanups Campaign of 1965 broke out, he was accused of stealing from the collective. The accusations sound small compared to the stories told of reform-era cadres. Big Gao was accused of stealing the fruit from the *longyan* ("dragon eye") trees he tended, killing cows for himself, taking extra pork and grain from the brigade, and selling brigade materials for private profit. He was also accused of accepting bribes, was ordered to return money back to the brigade, and was expelled from the party.

Describing these earlier events, Big Gao said, "They demanded that I pay back the money and if I did not obey, they said they would use force. I did not have any choice. I sold my bike, watch, winter coat, clothes, and everything, even my wife's and kids' clothes, and my wife's mother's bed. All these things were actually against the party's policies. But the other cadres insisted on doing this to me because they wanted to stand out in terms of their performance in the cleansing movement. Looking back at these events, I feel both sad and ridiculous."

To add to his humiliation, Big Gao was sent to jail a year later during the Cultural Revolution. He remained for three months although he was never charged. Ironically, he reflected later that it might have been the safest thing that happened to him. Another man who was not sent to jail was attacked by an angry mob and beaten.

Such was the fate of cadres accused of corruption during the Mao era, and both Big Gao and Uncle Wei could remember these events vividly. In contrast, many villagers insist that at present not only are cadres no longer falsely accused of corruption, but they were never accused of corruption at all. In fact, most people assert that nothing can be accomplished now without bribing officials. They use their own interactions with cadres as illustrations. For instance, Songling's friend Lijia spoke openly about paying several thousand *yuan* to get her son a job in a government department. "If you don't do this, college or no college, you just can't get a job," she said.

While Lijia's example was about a cadre at a higher level of administration, villagers also talk about their own lineage mates, cadres at the village level, as engaging in corrupt practices. For instance, Sneaky Tao, who had been a party branch committee member, was seen as not only using his influence to help his own son get an official position, but also as using dubious means to enrich himself. When a post for an agricultural technology specialist in the township came up, his other son got the job, even though many people whispered that his son was a driver who didn't know anything about agriculture. Likewise, when a car that belonged to the administrative district was burnt in a fire, many people suspected that Sneaky had actually taken the license out in advance, had the car destroyed, and then sold the license for a hefty sum!

These stories were only rumors, but the willingness of villagers to believe such stories, even about village cadres, is indicative of how they interpret the current motives and behavior of many officials. For instance, one village resident said to me, "The best kind of work nowadays is to be an official. Then you are guaranteed a great income!"

All in the Family

In the spring of 2007, I went with the members of the second lineage branch to pay annual respects at the graves of their founding ancestors.

After ascending the hills to visit the graves of the second lineage branch founder and his immediate descendants, we returned to their lineage hall. It was time for the annual banquet. There a discussion ensued about fixing some of the old graves, a project that had not been completed the year before and that needed more funds. The accountant for the second lineage branch stood up. Why not ask every descendant in the lineage branch to give twenty *yuan?* That would be enough to raise the needed funds. Uncle Wei stood up. "It's not fair," he said. "Some of our families have many descendants, but little money. Others have plenty of money, but few descendants!" Someone else stood up and asked Uncle Wei, "But how can we be sure those with more money will give more?" The argument went on for awhile. Finally, enough people came forward from the assembled group to donate and the money was raised.

Nonetheless, this small skirmish was illustrative of the fault lines within the village. Despite the notion of *ziji ren*—the idea that all villagers are members of the same lineage—they nonetheless confront class differences both between themselves and the outside world, and even among themselves on a daily basis. The example above concerned a symbolic matter, but often the differences are apparent in more urgent affairs.

Healthcare, for instance, is one of the most constant sources of worry in the reform era and it is an area where village residents can perceive vast discrepancies among themselves. Rural people do not even have the rudiments of health insurance, and a serious illness can be attended to only by seeking help from many people. In this climate, villagers immediately distinguish those families who have funds to draw on versus those who cannot. When an elderly woman in the village dislocated her back in the spring of 2007, she spent almost a week in the county capital's hospital. Her two sons who lived in Guangzhou pooled their resources, and she was able to get the treatment she needed. News of the total cost of her treatment also spread rapidly around the village. People said the family had spent over twenty thousand *yuan,* and many people noted that they themselves could never have afforded this in a similar medical emergency. "If you don't have the money, you just go to a village doctor and try to alleviate the pain," Aihua said. "There isn't anything else you can do."

How, then, do villagers talk about inequalities among themselves as opposed to between villagers and the outside world? A phrase often used to characterize the general state of affairs is "A good father is better than a good education." It embodies the ideas that many people hold in Moonshadow Pond about why and how some people were getting rich in the reform era. Songling's brother, for instance, explained it this way: "If you have a father who can place you in the right place, that's the only way to get a job, and that's how all these cadres place their own sons in good places."

As we have seen, the idea that wealth is often gained as an unofficial perk of an official position was a common one in Moonshadow Pond. Villagers found confirmation for this idea in examples of cadres who helped their kin and prospered, as well as in comparisons with the Maoist past, remembered by Moonshadow Pond residents as a time when cadres were less corrupt and certainly had less chance to profit from their position.

But if nepotism is seen as one route to enrichment, family members don't necessarily see themselves as all sharing in a common economic fate. Beneath many seemingly harmonious relationships, inequalities can also lead to simmering resentment and some recriminations. Aihua usually spoke of Jiawen in positive ways. Both Jiawen and Uncle Wei, Aihua's husband, were closely related. They were both descended from the same brother amongst the five brothers whose collective descendants comprised Team 2. Before building their new houses, they had shared one house in the old part of the village. When Jiawen celebrated his house moving, he employed Uncle Wei as the chief cook for the banquet, even though he had the funds to invite a fancier cook from town.

On the surface, their relationships appeared harmonious and reciprocal despite growing differences in their fortunes. Aihua had suffered a number of economic disappointments. Her eldest son Guobin had a continuing spate of bad luck, despite what most villagers acknowledged was his hardworking and earnest nature. In the 1990s, he had not been chosen as the agricultural technology representative to the township, although he was a skilled farmer and party member. Sneaky's son had been chosen instead. Some of Guobin's earlier ventures had also derailed. A brick kiln factory should have worked because it had been started when his father was the general secretary of the production brigade and he had experience firing bricks. But a worker had been injured and the bricks had been fired wrong. Soon Guobin owed over twenty thousand *yuan* in compensation and had to close the factory. His gambling wife, whom I referred to in chapter 3, hardly improved matters.

One day, in a pique of frustration, Aihua spoke to me about Jiawen. "He looks down on us now, because we are poor and he has money," she complained. "He uses his connections to Jieguo [the police officer] to get things done, and then people use their connections to Jiawen to gain access to Jieguo." I have mentioned Jieguo before. He and his brother had both made use of their own brother's connections to secure good jobs for themselves in the county capital. Given their positions, access to and through them could be very useful and Jiawen was one of the villagers who was very close to them. Aihua then indicated that she and her family were not in on these useful networks that she thought Jiawen provided to others.

Songling could also vent frustration in similar ways. As mentioned earlier, Big Gao, the former village head, was connected to their family as their eldest daughter's father-in-law, as Baoli's good friend, and as the father of Baoli's business partner. As mentioned previously, their families had a long history of mutual help. But one day, Songling complained about the way Big Gao's wife, Yinzhao, acted in her role as mother-in-law. The criticism related directly to comparative differences in wealth between her daughter's husband and Big Gao's other son. "Yinzhao doesn't treat my daughter as well as the other daughter-in-law," Songling complained. "Her eldest son has a good job in the township government, so she gives his wife better treatment."

Likewise the discourse of elders, something I spoke about in chapter 3, often focuses on wealth differences within families and expresses the fear that economic calculation rather than family feeling and filiality will ultimately win the day. I have already mentioned Songling's frequent refrain about pensions—that without one you would be powerless and subject to the whim of your adult children. Aihua's situation, in which one son was unable to support her while the other son often hinted that he couldn't do it all alone, left her in a precarious and dispirited state. Aihua and Uncle Wei took care of their own clothes and medicines on the small two-hundred-*yuan* pension that Uncle Wei received for his army service. They ate with the second son's family but were afraid to make many demands. After everything they had lived through and accomplished during the collective era, life was not easy for them.

As I discussed in chapter 3, a traditional strain in explanations of family tension has been to find its source in the daughter-in-law—an outsider, a woman, and someone who is lower on the totem pole of family hierarchy. Therefore, division in the family between brothers has often been explained as originating with disagreements between their respective wives over how to divide family assets. Now, with the divorce rate rising slowly, I have also heard people talk about the "greed" of women as an explanation for family strains. An expression that means "to covet empty glories" *(tanxu rongxin)* is used as a way to describe the actions of a woman who is tempted by the city and leaves a hard-working rural man. (Men's motivations in divorce are usually not explained as economic.)

But while the family can be construed as a site of economic tension, differentiation, and consequent disappointment, the value of family can also be heralded as a counterpoint to values of wealth. "What use is wealth if you have no descendants?" Songling told me one day. She was discussing the rather bitter fate of a family in Team 1. Their father had started a tanning operation at the beginning of the reform period and made a great deal of money. His three adult sons were equally enterprising. They engaged in multiple ventures from cultivating pomelos to the latest business of the eldest son, raising goats and selling their milk. All the sons had prospered through their ceaseless work, but the eldest son's family had still suffered misfortunes. His one son's first marriage ended in divorce. He remarried, but the couple's infant son died. As such, their family had no descendant in the third generation. Describing this family situation, Songling was implicitly saying that despite their wealth, her own situation was better; hers was a family in the "middle" economically, but with the traditional asset of descendants.

Wealth Has Its Advantages

Despite the discourse about officials discussed earlier, there is also recognition that not all wealth is the result of ill-gotten gain. Some people in the village *are* recognized for prospering because of a particular ability. The founder of the village tannery was one such man who villagers saw as succeeding by dint of hard work and entrepreneurial abilities. Another family, who ran a flourishing business making ritual objects, was also viewed as having earned its wealth rather than gaining it as a perk of power. The village doctor Jiawen went into private practice after decollectivization and prospered greatly. But it was always acknowledged that brigade leaders selected him to study medicine during the collective era precisely because he was considered both smart and studious. As mentioned in chapter 3, his wife, Guizhen, was also considered a very capable midwife.

Of course, material prosperity usually amplifies one's social connections and prestige and Jiawen's case was illustrative in this regard. When Jiawen staged a banquet to celebrate moving into his new house, the wide range of his connections was embodied by the many gifts displayed. These gifts—sofa and chairs, mirrors, coffee tables, and clocks—were displayed and labeled with the donors' names. After the banquet, villagers discussed these gifts, who had presented them and what they gave. Villagers also talked about the many important outsiders who attended the banquet, including cadres from surrounding areas and physicians from the county capital hospital.

Having wealth also makes it possible to organize more frequent or earlier life-cycle celebrations that further enhance one's status. In chapter 3 I mentioned that some couples must delay their wedding banquets because they do not have enough funds. Hence, they may register their marriage and live together for as long as a year or more before they can actually invite people to a banquet. In contrast to delaying a celebration, others are better off financially, and can actually "advance" a banquet celebrating a life-cycle transition. In doing so, they can reap the symbolic and social rewards earlier.

A rather humorous example occurred with respect to the "eightieth" birthday celebration of Uncle Kewen, an elderly man who had once been a worker in the leather factory of Songling's father. Although he lived in the village, he had never been categorized as a peasant because he continued to work in the leather factory near commune headquarters throughout the Maoist period. As a worker, Kewen was one of those privileged few in Moonshadow Pond who could retire with a good pension. He was also the same man who had ostracized his daughter for marrying into a family with overseas Chinese relatives during the Cultural Revolution era. But now he was not only enjoying his pension but also the fruits of connections with his more affluent relatives in Indonesia.

Celebration of birthdays every ten years after the age of seventy is a life-cycle ritual practiced in rural Meixian. However, many people thought Uncle Kewen was actually only seventy-nine and not eighty. Since he had thrived economically, villagers surmised he did not want to delay his birthday celebration. As one villager joked, "If you have money, even thirty or forty is considered old, but without money even eighty is empty!" In other words, it was widely believed that Uncle Kewen accelerated his age because he *did* have money, and wanted to throw a status-enhancing banquet.

Not all commentaries on wealth were quite so sardonic or humorous. Some implied more serious criticisms of the present order. For instance, most villagers thought that the connections and wealth of people like Jiawen insulated them from the law, while ordinary villagers without wealth were often made to pay a heavier price. These ideas were articulated very forcefully during an incident I witnessed in the spring of 1996.

During the New Year celebration period, when families worshipped at their ancestors' graves, an accident occurred. Wind carried off some of the burning paper offerings of one family. Within a few minutes a forest fire had started in the hills. The family escaped down the hill, and soon several hundred volunteers from Moonshadow Pond and surrounding villages were mobilized to stem the advance of the fire. However, by the time the fire was squelched a large area of forest had been destroyed.

In the next few days, the fire and the family that started it were the constant talk of Moonshadow Pond. The family gained their wealth because the father was a contractor, and though they were from Moonshadow Pond they now lived in the county capital. Their economic position figured largely in the talk about this incident. First, people noted that this family had chosen to perform the New Year ancestral worship "late." It was supposed to be completed within two weeks of the Lunar New Year, but this family had waited longer. Many people saw this as reflecting arrogance and selfishness gained from wealth—the idea that now that they had money, they could make their own rules rather than follow convention.

A great deal of discussion also centered on how the family would be punished for starting a forest fire. Certainly, there would be a fine, but how much would it be? Some people asserted that the family would have to give as much as one hundred thousand *yuan* because the fire had burnt several thousand hectares of land. A few days later, a story circulated in the village that the family would be fined thirty thousand *yuan* rather than the one hundred thousand *yuan* people originally expected. And there would be no jail time.

This story produced even more discussion in the village. Many people said that those responsible for starting the fire would certainly have had to go to jail for the offense if they were not wealthy. As evidence for this, they discussed the story of another young man from the village who had accidentally started a forest fire with a cigarette several years earlier. They asserted that he had served two years in prison, and most people said he suffered the penalty because he was poor. (This outcome was not interpreted in the same way by all, however. For instance, Songling declared that if she had a choice she would certainly take prison over a fine, because she would prefer to save her money for her descendants!)

Nonetheless, the idea of justice denied to the poor and deferred for the rich was certainly a common theme in Moonshadow Pond. A particularly horrible story was recited to me about an ordinary peasant woman from another village who went to the market in town to sell fruits and who was beaten by police for selling illegally. She was jailed, and then died in jail as a result of the beating. "Who will dare to take action against the police for this!" one villager exclaimed to me.

The fact that such stories were told and circulated can be seen as an implicit moral criticism of the existing state of affairs, even if they could not always be verified. Another kind of implicit criticism of the present situation was to compare it to Maoist times. But such comparisons, as we shall see, did not indicate an actual desire to return to the policies of that era.

A CONSTRAINED NOSTALGIA

While the inequities of the reform era have led to some unflattering comparisons with the Mao era, it would be wrong to conclude that villagers express an unambiguous nostalgia for that time. Rather, villagers criticize the present by comparing it to specific aspects of the Mao era, but rarely do they suggest that they would like to turn back the clock. As in another southeast Chinese village studied by Hok Bun Ku, the Mao era is usually referenced for purposes of criticizing elements of the present, rather than for seriously suggesting a return to the Maoist order.[17]

A typical example of this kind of nostalgic use of the Mao period to criticize social relations of the present occurred when I was speaking to a man from a neighboring village. At the time, he was struggling to earn a living. He was slowly building his new house brick by brick, but only as fast as he could earn the money to buy the bricks, so the process was frequently stalled and it was far from complete. Ruminating about the changes he had witnessed, he told me, "The former landlords are now doing fine, and the people who were once looked up to because they were poor peasants aren't admired anymore. The people who were your friends are not your friends anymore. If you are poor, you won't want to entertain your former friend because now he might be a big manager. He will give you expensive cigarettes, and you will only be able to give him Meizhou cigarettes [the locally manufactured brand]. But your rich friend won't visit you anyway, because he will be afraid you will want to borrow money!" Using an old aphorism to sum up the situation, he said, "When something happens to the poor family on the busy street, no one inquires, but the rich family on a remote mountain has distant relatives."

Many comparisons of the Mao period and the reform era focused on the issue of official corruption. Many villagers insisted that now, however, corruption was not just for officials, but had become a way of life and that no matter could be attended to without payoffs. For instance, when Aihua sprained her arm and went to the hospital, she launched into a critique of contemporary corruption. "Everywhere you go, you have to give a red envelope now," she said. "When you go to the hospital you don't need to get in line if you give a red envelope. It's even more corrupt now than in the old society!" She continued, "When I was a team leader we couldn't be corrupt. If one of us went astray, we would be cursed. But now if you curse out a cadre, he will just say, 'Why are you annoyed at me?' And then he won't do what you want unless you pay him off."

Such complaints did not mean that people expressed a desire to go back to the living standards of the Mao era, or even to the collective organization of work. "I had to organize the work schedules of one hundred people," Aihua said about her work as team leader. "It was really too much. Now we have relatively more freedom." Uncle Wei added to this by saying, "Every hand has long and short fingers, and no time is completely good or bad. In Mao's time we didn't have much corruption, and now things are very disordered. But now we have more freedom and we can't be lazy."

However, in a discussion I had with a villager in 1996, he decried the corruption of the present and excitedly exclaimed, "We've gone back to the way things were at the end of the Qing dynasty!" He pointed out that village elections, which were supposed to take place, had not yet been implemented in Guangdong. (They were implemented a few years after I spoke with him.) He likened the difficulties of getting change to occur at the local level to food that was caught in the throat and that could not get down to the stomach. He continued, "Education, jobs, and agriculture are the most important things for the government to look at, but none of these things get implemented down to the grassroots. They implemented the birth control plan down to the grass roots though, and this shows they *can* do things if they want to."

What one might call conspicuous consumption was also held up for ridicule at times. The inflation of wedding and funeral expenses, as I have pointed out in previous chapters, did not occur without complaints about the expense, or mild criticism of the desire for status that often motivated it. Other kinds of conspicuous consumption also received comment. The Lunar New Year, for instance, developed into a virtual orgy of fireworks. In the past, each village might put on a public fireworks display during one night of the New Year period, but now private fireworks added to the wildness. Fireworks are not allowed in the county capital, and the New Year is the time almost all family members return to their native villages from cities. This adds extra incentive to make the most of the two-week New Year's celebration in the villages; those with the means set off fireworks every night and seem to be competing for the most magnificent display and the loudest boom.

During the first few nights of New Year in 2007, the fireworks continued into the early hours of the morning each night—literally lighting up the night sky with a constant barrage of sound and light, creating the impression that the village was under attack. But these fireworks are quite expensive and the main actors in this drama tend to be from Moonshadow Pond's wealthier families. One night, while one of Jieguo's adult sons was preparing a particularly large explosion, some of the other neighbors could be heard commenting that blowing up so many fireworks was just like throwing away one's money. I probed a bit further. "They're just showing us that they have enough money to do this," one villager said. Indeed, Jieguo used fireworks as "announcements" on many occasions beyond those that would be expected in yearly or life-cycle rituals. He even set off coils of firecrackers after the New Year's housecleaning, prompting at least one villager to joke that he truly "loved face [mianzi] too much."

In addition to criticism of present-day conspicuous consumption practices, there was also another kind of nostalgia for the Mao period that often came from middle-aged people who were children in the 1960s and 1970s, before the beginning of the reform period. Several people fondly remembered what we might now call "quality time." For instance, Ailing told me once, "When we were children, we all used to eat our dinner outside on the plaza in front of our old houses. We'd just take our chopsticks and a bowl and eat our dinner, then stay outside for the rest of the night and play until bedtime. That was before families had television and everyone just started taking their meals inside their own houses. The children now will never experience this kind of special feeling."

However, for some, the Maoist period was not a point of positive comparison in any respect. As pointed out previously, the class-label system of the Mao era meant that at least some people remembered it for its inequities, since they had received bad class labels. For these people, there was no question of nostalgia for the Maoist class order. One day, Songling and I visited one of the older women in Team 2. She had been team leader for one year before Aihua was selected. As we were leaving the woman's house, Songling commented, "Before, we were victims of her temper. She always gave us the worst jobs because our class status was not good." Although Songling insisted that this was past, she also added that she would always remember how this woman treated her. She used the term *xinli zhidao* (literally, "my mind/heart knows") to talk about this. Hence, while Songling confronted the same issues of inequity and corruption in the present that many other villagers dealt with, her former class status made it unlikely she would use the Maoist period as a means of critiquing the present order.

A DIALOGIC MORALITY

While some villagers have prospered greatly, it is true that the majority of villagers are, as they describe themselves, no longer poverty stricken and yet not wealthy. Expenses such as sending a child to college are beyond the means of most villagers unless they receive financial help, and finding jobs is a continuing issue. As mentioned in chapter 3, most young people leave Moonshadow Pond to find work in cities after graduating from lower middle school. Hence, in articulating moral ideas about how to behave in the new economic order, villagers downplay what most of them are unlikely to achieve—becoming very wealthy—and reinforce ideas of reciprocity or modest living.

I call these particular responses "dialogic morality" because it is a morality that forms in response, or in dialogue, with the current situation. The famous literary theorist M. M. Bakhtin set forth ideas about language as inherently social and contextual when he said, "Any utterance, in addition to its own theme, always responds . . . in one form or another to others' utterances that precede it."[18] Bakhtin's ideas about utterances as explicitly or implicitly a response to some other utterance and therefore inherently dialogic can be applied to the moral ideas of Moonshadow Pond residents that are articulated regarding the reform economy.

This is not to say that the moral responses of Moonshadow Pond residents to the reform economy are new inventions. In fact, most of their ideas in this domain of action draw on traditional aphorisms and concepts. However, these ideas are articulated in response to a particular time and context and hence "in dialogue" with the contemporary situation. In chapter 5, I noted that some villagers still apply collectivist notions with regard to property. But as discussed above, few people express a desire to return to a full-fledged Maoist order in response to the new disparities in wealth. Even if they refer to the Maoist period with nostalgia, as a means of criticizing corruption or income inequalities of the present, they do not portray it as a model for the present.

Rather, faced with the current economic situation, many Moon-shadow Pond villagers articulate a vision of moderation and reciprocity as a foil to the idea of unlimited greed that they see motivating the behavior of cadres and sometimes ordinary fellow villagers. These ideas are expressed in response to a particular dilemma or situation. For example, chapter 5 detailed the ways in which villagers criticize those who they think are playing up to wealthy returnees just for their money. Another kind of criticism is formulated in response to someone accused of neglecting her reciprocal obligations because of a desire for quick monetary gain. For instance, Songling criticized a relative who lived in town but who had still been allocated land from Team 2. When this relative decided she didn't need her share of land, she apparently gave it to Sneaky Tao, so that he could build a bigger house himself. Songling suspected that Sneaky had offered money for the land and criticized her relative for selling to him rather than giving the parcel back to Team 2 so that others might have a chance to use it. In decrying the behavior, Song-ling used the phrase "she recognizes money, but not people" *(ren qian, bu ren ren)*.

Articulating an ideal of modest rather than luxurious living is another way that villagers create a morality in response to the current situation, and this idea is defended as both pragmatic as well as moral. Thus, the aphorism "having a thousand *liang* of silver in the house is not as good as earning a penny per day" is used as a way of saying that steady work is a more appropriate goal than a one-time windfall. Conspicuous consumption, as we have seen, can also be criticized.

People without great wealth can also point to other virtues in summing up their lives, and implicitly or overtly criticize those whose accomplishments are merely having accumulated wealth. For instance, Uncle Wei put it this way, "I don't have wealth to pass on to my sons, but I can pass along my good reputation." By this, he also meant that no one could say his present situation was the result of ill-gotten gains. Of course, one might also say that Uncle Wei had made a virtue of necessity, embracing what cannot be changed, or to use Bourdieu's language, one could call this the "taste for necessity."[19]

It is also true that Uncle Wei's situation was not unique. As a cadre who retired just before the reform period began, he did not have the same opportunities to "cash in" on his position as those cadres who were in office once the reforms were instituted. Indeed, in a study of a north China village, Yunxiang Yan noted that the Mao-era cadres who retired before the reform era were one of the least successful groups economically.[20]

The reform-era cadres, in contrast, had both legal and illegal means of increasing their wealth. They had contacts that they could use to procure materials for new private ventures. They were also in a good position to allocate for themselves the opportunities to lease formerly collective assets. And, of course, they were also able to use their positions to secure payments in return for favors.

THE STORY OF JINTAO'S RING

Despite differences in personal situations, both the newly rich and those who have not fared as well can still best protect their reputations by adhering to the customary idea of remembering moral debt. A story that circulated in the village while I was there worked as an illustrative moral tale in driving this point home. According to the story, a villager named Jintao fled Moonshadow Pond in 1949 because he had fought with the Nationalist Army in the civil war and feared retribution after their defeat. An old woman, who also happened to be Sneaky Tao's paternal aunt, gave the refugee Jintao a gold ring to take with him. Villagers said that the ring she gave to him was worth three thousand *yuan* at the time, and furthermore it was the only item of value he owned when he fled the country. In 1989, after an almost forty-year absence, and after having prospered in Taiwan, Jintao returned to visit Moonshadow Pond. According to the story people told, he woke up one night after his return and thought he saw the old woman's face staring at him. In fact, she had died many years earlier. Nonetheless, on his next visit to Moonshadow Pond in 1996, he acted to rectify the situation and to reciprocate her act of kindness. He knew that this old woman had no children of her own, but Sneaky's younger brother was her "dry son." So in a public ceremony, Jintao presented the old woman's dry son with a gold ring worth five thousand *yuan*.

Acts such as this one, of course, are not meant to address the arrangement of the social order. They are individual acts that illustrate a sense of individual moral obligation and memory. They insulate the actor from the kind of aspersion Songling cast upon her relative—that she recognized money more than people.

Finally, for these acts to be effective, they must be spoken about. Stories must circulate about them, and it is precisely the circulation of these stories that helps to constitute local moral discourse. The anthropologist Tuulikki Pietilä has said, "Acts of giving or not-giving do not establish the moral value of a person and her action in and of themselves; valuation only comes about by means of the talk that accompanies and evaluates those acts and thereby construes their meaning."[21]

When such stories do get told, they demonstrate to the community that the actor is not a person without memory. This symbolism still remains powerful in a local world of continuing social transformation.

Conclusion

Ethnography and Morality

The study of moral discourse by anthropologists can be a particularly delicate enterprise. By its very nature, the word *moral* is weighted down by implications of good versus evil and right versus wrong. But anthropology, by its very nature, is dedicated not to moral judgments about cultures but to the clarification of diverse cultural meanings.

Describing and examining the moral discourse of a culture can be easily misunderstood as a judgment about the "morality" implied by that discourse. This complication may help explain why, according to some ethnographers, the study of moral systems is undeveloped in anthropology as opposed to the examination of other domains of culture. Consider, for instance, this comment by the anthropologist James Laidlaw: "There is no connected history we can tell ourselves about the study of morality in anthropology, as we do for a range of topics such as kinship, the economy, the state, or the body."[1]

However, despite these difficulties, it is essential to study moral discourse in a wide range of cultures and societies. If we fail to do this, we can quickly fall into the trap of completely overlooking a particular culture's ethical code or codes, and from that deduce that there are none, or that they are irrelevant to the way people in that culture act and understand themselves. In the case of China, not only outside observers, but also domestic critics, have often defined the contemporary situation as one without an overarching moral code. Summarizing the social commentary of the Chinese economist He Qinglian, for instance, Liu Binyan and Perry Link observed, "When ordinary people hear stories about greed at the top, they come to feel that it is pointless, and even a bit stupid, for the ordinary citizen to stick to moral behavior. If anything 'trickles down,' in her view, it is cynicism and the abandonment of responsibility."[2] They continue, "She finds the collapse of ethics—not growth of the economy—to be the most dramatic change in China during the Deng Xiaoping era. The challenge facing China is not just 'survival' (which the Chinese government lists as the most basic human right) but 'how to avoid living in an utterly valueless condition.' She does not hold out much hope."[3]

In a recent study of the role of the state in modern China, the historian Patricia Thornton elaborates on the same theme. She notes that both the Qing and Maoist regimes created power for themselves by articulating and enforcing moral standards for the general population (and excluding those who did not comply with these standards). In this way, she says, these regimes made their power appear both "natural and necessary."[4] Contrastingly, she argues that the reform-era state has withdrawn as a moral agent, and that there is a "collective conviction that contemporary society is poised on the brink of moral collapse."[5]

But the very critique of a society or regime as lacking in ethics or a moral code is in itself the implicit acknowledgment that the critic still holds on to one. That this critical activity is engaged in by ordinary citizens, as well as by published social critics, should be evident from the example of Moonshadow Pond residents. The denizens of this village do have expectations about the moral obligations of their fellows—as family, lineage members, team and small-group members, and even as citizens—and their daily discourse and gossip articulate these expectations. These ideas, as I have attempted to illustrate in the previous chapters, are not frozen in time, but evolve over time in their specifics, even as underlying assumptions about moral reciprocity remain.

In the last chapter I called this continued moral response to a changing situation a "dialogic morality" because ideas about the specific content of people's obligations have to be worked out over time, as people respond to the implications of new economic arrangements, social structures, and social mores. Hence, there is always some back and forth, or "dialogue," between the conditions on the ground and people's ideas about necessary obligations and moral conduct. Nonetheless, assumptions about the need to remember and to attempt to reciprocate previous help have remained. As I have shown, villagers continue to judge each other at least partially through this moral lens.

To look outward from Moonshadow Pond for a bit, it seems clear that ideas about moral obligation are far from unimportant in contemporary China; this is highlighted by the fact that these ideas are utilized by so many different actors and for so many different purposes. A particularly chilling example came during the earthquake in Sichuan Province in the spring of 2008. As explained in the international press, the earthquake revealed that the construction of schools was particularly shoddy, and thousands of schoolchildren died in their classrooms, even in schools quite far from the epicenter of the quake. In an attempt to squelch public dissent from parents who connected the fate of their children to these structurally unsound schools, the government issued contracts. Parents who signed received "social aid and special benefits," but in return they vowed to "obey the law and maintain the social order for the postearthquake reconstruction."[6]

The intention of these contracts was clearly to pay off the earthquake victims in return for an agreement not to protest the conditions in the schools. But most interesting for our purposes here is the way these contracts utilized the language of moral debt to obligate the parents, indicating the power that such language still holds. In one middle-school district, the contract to be signed stated, "The Party and the government have reached out their hands to us and mobilized society to help us and alleviate our hardships. In this regard, we sincerely appreciate the help and care from the Party, government, and society!"[7]

Likewise, it is interesting to note that in the nationwide protests during 1989, protesters sometimes specifically disavowed the idea that they were "without *liangxin*" and proposed instead that their actions were for the good of the country.[8] In other words, they did not want it to be said that they were without memory of what the government had done for them.

The ideology of moral debt here articulated with reference to the government parallels that articulated in the days of imperial China, when the emperor was understood as standing in the same relationship to the people as the senior male stood in relationship to his family. In both cases, the senior in the relationship provides gifts that can be reciprocated only by enduring gratitude and memory from the obligated underling.

And yet, as we have seen in this book, the ideology of moral debt is elastic. It works not only to underwrite the obligations of the powerless to the powerful, of juniors to seniors, but it can also work between equals and even create obligations in the other direction—indebting seniors to juniors. In the chapter on family, for instance, we saw not only how adult children were indebted to their parents and in-laws (as they surely were), but how the tables were sometimes turned as parents had to acknowledge and remember their children's contributions to their own well-being. Similarly, in the relationship of officialdom to ordinary villagers, the moral discourse of villagers recognizes that officials may sometimes be obligated to them. As we have seen, the stories villagers tell of contemporary official behavior rarely sound like the language on the earthquake contract cited above. If anything, when it comes to ordinary discourse, officials are more often portrayed as violating rather than fulfilling their obligations to the people by enriching themselves and engaging in corrupt practices.

We need to be clear, however, that despite the national scope and political implications that moral discourse can potentially include within its grasp, in Moonshadow Pond it is usually focused within the boundaries of a much smaller moral community. If rural residents are, in fact, fairly powerless to change actions initiated from the top, they can at least influence the actions of their fellows through the power of talk. As such, moral discourse at the village level is usually about choices within one's reach rather than about those that are beyond one's grasp. Keeping this in mind, a few questions remain that were raised in the introduction, but which we are better able to think about after considering the material in subsequent chapters.

STATUS AND MORALITY, SOCIAL DUTIES VERSUS MORAL ONES

What is an honorable act? As mentioned in the introduction, there is not always an unambiguous separation of social judgments from moral ones. For instance, criticizing someone for not engaging in a socially required act, such as a grand funeral service or wedding, may take on the tones of a moral condemnation in certain settings. Closely connected to this, as I discussed earlier, is the fact that high social status can sometimes influence one's moral standing. A rich or powerful person can "get away with" acts that would be deemed immoral if he had less clout.

How did these issues figure into the moral discourse of Moonshadow Pond villagers? Despite the fairly endless commentary by both Chinese and outsiders on the idea that wealth trumps all in contemporary China, it is clear that in their own discourse about actions, the residents of Moonshadow Pond distinguished between their judgments about people as holders of status-enhancing positions and their judgments about them as people making moral choices. Furthermore, they also clearly separated their judgments about actions required merely by social protocol versus those deemed morally obligatory.

We saw these critical distinctions in the ironic commentaries villagers made about people who do things only for the sake of "face" or *mianzi* in regard to funerals, weddings, and even in the donations of some overseas Chinese to the community. In these cases, the idea that someone acts solely for the purpose of conforming to social convention or to achieve higher worldly status creates spaces for others to poke fun at them.

Further, social status, wealth, and power do not isolate people from moral critique, and in fact may even open them up to greater scrutiny. For instance, as pointed out earlier, cadres and holders of wealth are open to criticism if they are seen as engaging in corrupt behavior. They will also be subject to criticism if, as in the case of Old Guosheng, they are seen as using their wealth to circumvent obligations to live harmoniously with family members and villagers.

Discriminating between status-enhancing acts versus morally necessary ones is closely related to the issue of distinguishing between social custom and moral obligation. This issue is a contested one in the literature on the study of morality cross-culturally; some scholars maintain that the distinction is not clear-cut in all cultures.[9] For instance, in the case of rural China, is a negative judgment about someone who does not perform proper funeral rites for his father a social or a moral critique? Do people who make the judgment distinguish between the two?

In this book I have attempted to show that there is such a distinction in the case of Moonshadow Pond. For instance, we saw in the chapter on funerals that even if an expensive ceremony garnered more status for a family, community members ultimately valued the idea of commemoration itself even more than any particular procedure. Bright Ling was not judged as morally deficient simply because she did not engage in an elaborate funeral ceremony, because the actions she did take were seen as evidence that she was still commemorating her mother. Similarly, we found that the somewhat more modest funeral ceremony undertaken by Red Chong for his father gained him greater respect than the more elaborate ceremonies of a wealthier family, because Red Chong did not mistreat those who helped his family out.

Likewise, while there is great social pressure to have large wedding banquets, this trend is understood precisely for what it is—the pursuit of *mianzi* or status. Registry marriages are not viewed as morally deficient in any way. They are simply viewed as marriage without the status-enhancing event of a banquet.

DOMAINS OF ACTION NOW AND IN THE FUTURE

In the introduction I pointed out that the morality of actions is partially tied to the particular domain in which they occur. For instance, market-based relationships may not be judged by the same moral standards as kin relations. But, of course, it is not always so easy to separate domains of action so cleanly.

In Moonshadow Pond, everyone is technically related through lineage or marriage, and as I have shown, the ideology of lineage is a strong unifier. But, as we have also seen, this does not mean that all relationships can be conducted or evaluated according to the morality of lineage solidarity and obligation. The rhetoric and ideology of lineage solidarity is always competing with other imperatives: the need to make a living, the needs of one's own domestic unit, and the competing demands of one's natal family versus the family of one's marriage in the case of married women. Ironically, the sense of obligation to the old collective structure, voiced by some Moonshadow Pond residents, comprises a set of obligations that does not necessarily contradict lineage solidarity. Since the old production teams so closely paralleled the organization of lineage branches in Moonshadow Pond, solidarity with the members of one's old team is not a far stretch from solidarity within a lineage segment.

Nonetheless, we have seen how the imperatives of many different domains, such as legal statutes or rules of the marketplace, can be influenced by expectations about fulfilling moral obligations. Slippery Cheng's land claim, for instance, may have had a shaky legal foundation, but it was also viewed in a particularly negative light because of his poor treatment of his stepmother. Similarly, Songling's criticism of her relative who "recognized money more than people" was a typical example of the discourse villagers used to fend off the idea that all social ties and obligations can be reduced to market relationships.

But will such ideas fade with the continuing shift of China's population from rural to urban areas and with the decline of agriculture as the economic base of rural life? As indicated in the first chapter, only a small number of Moonshadow Pond residents relied solely on agriculture by 2007, and a growing number, although still a minority, have abandoned agriculture altogether. Many young residents of Moonshadow Pond have migrated for employment to large cities, while others, though continuing to reside in the village, work in the county capital. Do ties of kinship, lineage, and place hold the same meaning to them? Will obligations based on memory be as important in a society where it is possible that you will not interact daily with those who helped you in the past?

On the national level, we have already indicated that the discourse of indebtedness is easily "hijacked" by those who hold political power. But will the language of indebtedness continue to hold power in a society of migrants, a society that becomes more and more urbanized and where social ties may not be as long lasting as in rural areas?

The material in this book cannot possibly be used to answer such a broad question with regard to China as a whole, but it can at least speculate about the future of moral discourse in Moonshadow Pond. In this case, the proximity of Moonshadow Pond to the county capital may actually enable it, in the long run, to retain its identity more easily than villages which are more distant from urban centers. In these more remote villages, employment opportunities are fewer and there are often no other options for the working-age population but to migrate far away to find jobs.

As we saw in chapter 3, even as many young people leave Moonshadow Pond to work in the great metropolises of Guangdong Province, there were others who have found it possible to stay at home—not because they have any intention of farming, but because they can live at home and find work in the urban economy of the county capital. Furthermore, when young workers who have migrated to the larger metropolises do return to Moonshadow Pond over the Lunar New Year holiday, they immediately gather together in groups formed around their shared past—often in associations of classmates from elementary, lower middle, and upper middle schools. We should remember that most rural migrants in China who work in the cities have retained their rural registrations, return home for the Lunar New Year, and may return home for longer periods of time during economic slowdowns in the cities.

Finally, Meixian (Mei County) has great significance throughout the Hakka diaspora in China and worldwide as the "Hakka heartland." For Hakka everywhere, Meixian is constructed as a significant place.[10] Perhaps the special place of Meixian in Hakka identity is another reason why so many young migrants from Moonshadow Pond still express their desire to return to Meixian permanently at some point in their lives.

At the very least, the memories of past experiences are still important for these young people in the formation of their current social relationships. Perhaps the ideology of moral debt, expressed through the multiple uses and meanings of the word *liangxin*, will still hold traction for them in the future.

Notes

1. MOONSHADOW POND

1. On the ideal plan of a Hakka village, and on the importance of *fengshui* location for burying dead and siting residences, see Fang Xuejia, *Kejia Yuanliu Tan Ao* (Guangdong, China: Gaodeng jiaoyu chubanshe, 1994), 193.

2. Stephen Feuchtwang, *An Anthropological Analysis Chinese Geomancy* (Vientiane, Laos: Vithagna, 1974), 2. Feuchtwang writes that *fengshui* "stands for the power of the natural environment, the wind and the airs of the mountains and hills; the streams and the rain; and much more than that: the composite influence of the natural processes. Behind it is a whole cosmology of metaphysical concepts and symbols. By placing oneself well in the environment feng-shui will bring good fortune. . . . Great store is set by the proper placing of landscape features around the site at the appropriate points of the compass."

3. In literary Chinese, this proverb is rendered as *yin shui si yuan*. However, my landlady in Moonshadow Pond stated it in a more colloquial way, *shi shui yao nian shui yuan tou.*

4. Richard Madsen, *Morality and Power in a Chinese Village* (Berkeley: University of California, 1984), 8.

5. In addition to differences in time period and focus, my study is based on fieldwork, while Madsen's was primarily the result of exhaustive interviews of villagers who had fled to Hong Kong. Nonetheless, his work is of critical importance, and is one of the few book-length studies of the issue of moral discourse in rural China to date.

6. The entire area is now referred to as Meizhou and comprises seven counties which are predominantly Hakka. They are Meixian, Wuhua, Dapu, Xingning, Pingyuan, Jiaoling, and Fengshun.

7. Sow-Theng Leong, *Migration and Ethnicity in Chinese History: Hakka,*

Pengmin, and Their Neighbors, ed. Tim Wright (Stanford, Calif.: Stanford University Press, 1997).

8. Myron Cohen. "The Hakka or 'Guest People': Dialect as a Sociocultural Variable in Southeast China," in *Guest People: Hakka Identity in China and Abroad,* ed. Nicole Constable (Seattle: University of Washington, 1996); Sow-Theng Leong, *Migration and Ethnicity in Chinese History* (Stanford, Calif.: Stanford University Press, 1997).

9. For a summary of theories about the emergence of Hakka identity, see Nicole Constable, ed., *Guest People: Hakka Identity in China and Abroad* (Seattle: University of Washington, 1996), and Leong, *Migration and Ethnicity.* Fang Xuejia proposes a different theory about Hakka origins in *Kejia Yuanliu Tan Ao.* He finds that many features of Hakka culture have been influenced by the native non-Han groups that were living in southeast China before the Han migrations to the south. Thus, he argues that Hakka origins can be traced primarily to these native groups.

10. See William Lavely's work on marriage and mobility for more on this. William Lavely, "Marriage and Mobility under Rural Collectivism," in *Marriage and Inequality in Chinese Society,* ed. Patricia Ebrey and Rubie Watson (Berkeley: University of California Press, 1991), 286–312.

11. It was only after 2003 that many of the roads within Moonshadow Pond were paved, part of a province-wide initiative to improve rural roads. Perhaps as travel on village roads becomes easier, the value of a home on the highway will diminish, especially because the highway, an important artery between Meixian, the neighboring county of Pingyuan, and the neighboring province of Jiangxi, is becoming increasingly congested and noisy even during the night.

12. Nicole Constable provides an interesting discussion of the relationship between women's roles and Hakka identity in *Guest People,* pointing out that Hakka in overseas, Taiwanese, and Hong Kong communities, as well as mainland communities, still refer to women's roles as a unique aspect of Hakka identity, even though they live in societies in which women of all ethnic groups increasingly participate in economic activities (27). Whether this reputation of hard work gave Hakka women more power in the family and community is a different issue, an issue which scholars and the Hakka themselves have often debated. For an interesting discussion of this issue, see C. Fred Blake, *Ethnic Groups and Social Change in a Chinese Market Town* (Honolulu: University of Hawai'i Press, 1981), 57. I also discuss it in my own book on the Hakka community in Calcutta, *Blood, Sweat, and Mahjong: Family and Enterprise in an Overseas Chinese Community* (Ithaca, N.Y.: Cornell University Press, 1993).

13. See Fang Xuejia, *Kejia Yuanliu Tan Ao,* and Sow-Theng Leong, *Migration and Ethnicity.*

14. These numbers are based on a survey I conducted in the spring of 2007.

15. These numbers are based on surveys I conducted in the summer of 1997 and the spring of 2007.

16. Arthur Wolf, "Adopt a Daughter-in-Law, Marry a Sister: A Chinese Solution to the Problem of the Incest Taboo," *American Anthropologist* 70, no. 5 (1968): 864–74.

17. The official articulation of this policy was at the Third Plenum of the Eleventh National Party Congress Central Committee.

18. Mao Zedong declared that the Cultural Revolution was over in 1969. But most analysts see its influence as existing until the year of Mao's death in 1976 and therefore date the Cultural Revolution as 1966–76.

19. Meixian Difangzhi Biansuan Weiyuanhui, ed., *Meixian Zhi* [Mei County Gazetteer] (Guangzhou, China: Guangdong Renmin Chubanshe, 1994), 247–48.

20. The average income in the administrative district of which Moonshadow Pond is a part (a two-village district that includes Moonshadow Pond and the neighboring village) went from 3,054 *yuan* in 1996 to 4,022 *yuan* in 2006 (Chengbeixiang ge guanliqu zhuyao jiben qingkuang, 1997, 2007).

21. Many of these families were also those who had received remittances from relatives abroad and were thus somewhat better off.

22. See Alasdair MacIntyre, *After Virtue* (South Bend, Ind.: University of Notre Dame Press, 1981)

23. Arthur Kleinman, "Experience and Its Moral Modes: Culture, Human Conditions, and Disorder," The Tanner Lectures on Human Values, Stanford University, April 13–16, 1998, 363.

24. Ibid., 373.

25. Ibid.

26. Ibid., 359.

27. Madsen, *Morality and Power*, 2.

28. As Mayfair Yang explains in her extensive study of the phenomenon of *guanxi* in contemporary China, *guanxi* is not merely about moral obligation. It also has instrumental components. As such, she says it is "regarded as morally ambivalent." See Yang, *Gifts, Favors, and Banquets: The Art of Social Relationships in China* (Ithaca, N.Y.: Cornell University Press), 71. In addition to Yang, other recent ethnographies on the phenomenon of *guanxi* include Andrew Kipnis, *Producing Guanxi: Sentiment, Self, and Subculture in a North China Village* (Durham, N.C.: Duke University Press, 1997), and Yunxiang Yan, *The Flow of Gifts* (Stanford, Calif.: Stanford University Press, 1996).

29. Andrew Kipnis, " 'Face': An Adaptable Discourse of Social Surfaces," *Positions* 3, no. 1 (Spring 1995): 119–48.

30. H. C. Hu, "The Chinese Concepts of 'Face,' " *American Anthropologist* 46 (1944): 45–64.

31. Steven Parish, *Moral Knowing in a Hindu Sacred City: An Exploration of Mind, Emotion, and Self* (New York: Columbia University Press, 1994), 285.

32. Ibid., 284.

33. Ibid., 289.

34. Bernard Gert, *Morality: Its Nature and Justification* (Oxford: Oxford University Press, 1998), 16.

35. Caroline Humphrey, "Exemplars and Rules: Aspects of the Discourse of Moralities," in *The Ethnography of Moralities*, ed. Signe Howell (London: Routledge, 1997), 26.

36. James Laidlaw, "For an Anthropology of Ethics and Freedom," *Journal of the Royal Anthropological Institute* 8 (2002): 311–32.

37. John Barker, "All Sides Now: The Postcolonial Triangle in Uiahu," in *The Anthropology of Morality in Melanesia and Beyond*, ed. John Barker (Hampshire, UK: Ashgate, 2007), 82.

38. More specifically, some of the conflicting issues addressed by this literature include asking whether subjects profess "an ethic of care and responsibility" that is context-dependent or "an ethic of rights and justice" that is supposed to work from context-free principles (see Kwang-Kuo Hwang's summary of these approaches in Hwang, "Two Moralities: Reinterpreting the Findings of the Empirical Research on Moral Reasoning in Taiwan," *Asian Journal of Social Psychology* 1:211–38). Another issue addressed by this literature is whether subjects distinguish between social duties based on convention and moral duties. See Elliot Turiel, Melanie Killen, and Charles C. Helwig, "Morality: Its Structure, Functions, and Vagaries," in *The Emergence of Morality in Young Children*, ed. Jerome Kagan and Sharon Lamb (Chicago: University of Chicago Press), 155–244; and Richard A. Shweder, Manamohan Mahapatra, and Joan G. Miller, "Culture and Moral Development," in *The Emergence of Morality in Young Children*, ed. Jerome Kagan and Sharon Lamb (Chicago: University of Chicago Press), 1–82.

39. See Pierre Bourdieu's discussion of different kinds of capital in *The Logic of Practice*, trans. Richard Nice (Cambridge: Polity Press, 1990).

40. See Suzanne Brenner, "Why Women Rule the Roost: Rethinking Javanese Ideologies of Gender and Self-Control," in *Bewitching Women, Pious Men: Gender and Body Politics in Southeast Asia*, ed. Michael Peletz and Aihwa Ong (Berkeley: University of California Press, 1995), for a very interesting discussion of dominant and alternative ideologies. Also see Claudia Strauss, "Partly Fragmented, Partly Integrated: An Anthropological Analysis of 'Postmodern Fragmented Subjects,'" *Cultural Anthropology* 12, no. 3 (1997): 362–404, for a very interesting discussion of American ideas about class and politics, and about the ways these integrate contradictory cultural schemas.

41. Although not subscribing to such a distinction himself, Frank Henderson Steward provides a very nice summary of this position in his book *Honor* (Chicago: University of Chicago Press, 1994).

42. Julian Pitt-Rivers, "Honour and Social Status," in *Honour and Shame: The Values of Mediterranean Society*, ed. J. G. Peristiany (Chicago: University of Chicago Press, 1974), 51.

43. See Stanley Brandes, "Like Wounded Stags: Male Sexual Ideology in an Andalusian Town," in *Sexual Meanings: The Cultural Construction of Gender and Sexuality*, ed. Sherry Ortner and Harriet Whitehead (Cambridge: Cambridge University Press, 1987); and Lila Abu-Lughod, *Veiled Sentiments* (Berkeley: University of California Press, 1986), for particularly insightful discussions of the relationship of gender constructions and cultural constructions of honor and status.

44. Nur Yalman, "On the Purity of Woman in the Caste of Ceylon and Malabar," *The Journal of the Royal Anthropological Institute of Great Britain and Ireland* 93, no. 1 (1963): 25–58. As Yalman discusses, the practice of virtual seclusion of unmarried women was enforced by the Nambudiri Brahmins of South India; they preferred nonmarriage rather than marriage to a low-caste man. If men from their own higher caste had sexual relations with low-caste women, however, no problem ensued. The "pollution" of low-caste men was passed on

through women to children, but high-caste men suffered no permanent pollution from sexual relations with low-caste women. Similar beliefs pervaded the racial segregation system in the American South, where lynchings and mob violence against black men often erupted at the mere hint of sexual relations with a white woman. Yet white men could have sexual relations with black women, as long as marriage was not the result.

45. See Mark Juergensmeyer, "What If the Untouchables Don't Believe in Untouchability," *Bulletin of Concerned Asian Scholars* 12, no. 1 (1980): 23–28. Also see Steven Parish, *Hierarchy and Its Discontents* (Philadelphia: University of Pennsylvania Press, 1996), for an interesting discussion of Hindu ambivalence about caste hierarchy.

46. Alan Fiske, "Relativity within the Moose ('Mossi') Culture: Four Incommensurable Models for Social Relationships," *Ethos* 18, no. 2 (1990): 180–204.

47. For an analysis of how villagers operated with a range of moral paradigms during the 1960s, see Madsen, *Morality and Power.*

48. Bradd Shore, "Human Ambivalence and the Structuring of Moral Values," *Ethos* 18, no. 2 (1990): 171.

49. Ibid., 170.

50. Ibid., 171.

51. Ibid., 171.

52. Ibid., 176.

53. Ibid., 177.

54. The literary theorist Bakhtin referred to such contending ideas in one person as an inner "dialogue" (V. N. Volosinov [M. M. Bakhtin], "The Construction of the Utterance," in *Bakhtin School Papers,* trans. Noel Owen, ed. Ann Shukman [Oxford: RPT, 1983], 119). He held that our speech and thought always take the form of questions and answers that respond to our social situation (M. M. Bakhtin, "The Problem of Speech Genres," in *Speech Genres and Other Late Essays,* trans. Vern W. McGee, ed. Caryl Emerson and Michael Holquist [Austin: University of Texas Press], 94). His collaborator V. N. Volosinov pointed out that as we think through issues, our "inner speech . . . immediately assumes the form of questions and answers, assertions and subsequent denials, or to put it more simply, our speech is broken down into separate repliques of varying size; it takes the form of a *dialogue*" (Volosinov, "The Construction," 119).

55. Claudia Strauss and Naomi Quinn, *A Cognitive Theory of Cultural Meaning* (Cambridge: Cambridge University Press, 1997), 44.

56. Patrician Ewick and Susan Silbey, *The Common Place of Law* (Chicago: University of Chicago Press, 1998), 44.

57. Ibid., 40.

58. Strauss and Quinn, *Cognitive Theory of Cultural Meaning,* 53.

59. University of Michigan and Beijing hua tong ren shi chang xin xi you xian ze ren gong si, "Table 1-5: Agricultural population and nonagricultural population by sex and township," Meixian, Guangdong. Township-level data. *China Data Online: Zhongguo Shu Ju Zai Xian* (China: All China Marketing Research Co., 2002).

60. Meixian Difangzhi Biansuan Weiyuanhui, ed., *Meixian Zhi,* 84.

61. For an excellent discussion of the differences between generational cohorts of women in terms of their outlooks on modernity, the revolution, and gen-

der roles, see Lisa Rofel, *Other Modernities* (Berkeley: University of California Press, 1999).

62. See Martin King Whyte, *Small Groups and Political Rituals in China* (Berkeley: University of California Press, 1974).

63. See Daniel Lynch, *After the Propaganda State: Media, Politics, and "Thought Work" in Reformed China* (Stanford, Calif.: Stanford University Press, 1999), 241.

64. Louis Dumont, "Postface: Toward a Theory of Hierarchy," in *Homo Hierarchicus,* ed. XX (Chicago: University of Chicago Press, 1980).

65. Dumont, "Postface," 245.

2. *LIANGXIN*

1. Gary Hamilton, "Introduction," in *From the Soil: The Foundations of Chinese Society,* by Xiaotong Fei, trans. Gary Hamilton and Wang Zheng (Berkeley: University of California Press, 1992), 30.

2. Xiaotong Fei, *From the Soil: The Foundations of Chinese Society,* trans. Gary Hamilton and Wang Zheng (Berkeley: University of California Press, 1992), 69.

3. Ibid., 74.

4. Mayfair Yang, *Gifts, Favors and Banquets: The Art of Social Relationships in China* (Ithaca, N.Y.: Cornell University Press), 68; Yunxiang Yan, *Private Life under Socialism: Love, Intimacy, and Family Change in a Chinese Village* (Stanford, Calif.: Stanford University Press, 2003), 39.

5. Mayfair Yang, *Gifts, Favors, and Banquets,* 109, 70.

6. Yunxiang Yan, *The Flow of Gifts* (Stanford, Calif.: Stanford University Press, 1996), 145.

7. Kwang-Kuo Hwang, "Two Moralities: Reinterpreting the Findings of Empirical Research on Moral Reasoning in Taiwan," *Asian Journal of Social Psychology* 1 (1998): 217.

8. Hwang, "Two Moralities," 217.

9. Richard Madsen, *Morality and Power in a Chinese Village* (Berkeley: University of California Press, 1984), 15.

10. Ibid., 15.

11. Ibid., 18.

12. Charles Taylor, *Modern Social Imaginaries* (Durham, N.C.: Duke University Press, 2004), 7.

13. Another take on these issues comes from discussions in the field of cultural psychology. Some anthropologists and psychologists argue that in cultural contexts where the existing order is seen as sacred, ideas about what people "should" do are necessarily moral, since there is no room for arguing that a specific behavior is necessitated simply because of convention. In a sense, they are arguing that in cultural contexts where the "hermeneutic" notion of morality applies, duty is usually formulated as a moral obligation and there is less room for explaining it as possibly just a matter of following convention (see Richard A. Shweder, Manamohan Mahapatra, and Joan G. Miller, "Culture and Moral Development," in *The Emergence of Morality in Young Children,* ed. Jerome Kagan and Sharon Lamb [Chicago: University of Chicago Press, 1987], 1–82).

14. Taylor, *Modern Social Imaginaries*, 12.

15. Richard Madsen, "The Politics of Revenge in Rural China during the Cultural Revolution," in *Violence in China*, ed. Jonathan Lipman and Stevan Harrell (Albany: SUNY Press, 1990), 180.

16. Ibid., 179.

17. Ibid., 179.

18. Hok Bun Ku, *Moral Politics in a South Chinese Village* (Lanham, Md.: Rowman and Littlefield, 2003); Jing Jun, *The Temple of Memories: History, Power, and Morality in a Chinese Village* (Stanford, Calif.: Stanford University Press, 1996).

19. Xiaoying Wang, "The Post-Communist Personality: The Spectre of China's Capitalist Market Reforms," *China Journal* 47 (January): 7.

20. Ibid., 8.

21. Ibid., 16.

22. Ibid., 9.

23. Jiwei Ci, *Dialectic of the Chinese Revolution: From Utopianism to Hedonism* (Stanford, Calif.: Stanford University Press, 1994), 113.

24. Ibid., 113.

25. Ibid., 204.

26. Ibid., 203.

27. Yunxiang Yan, *Private Life under Socialism: Love, Intimacy, and Family Change in a Chinese Village* (Stanford, Calif.: Stanford University Press, 2002), 234.

28. Ibid., 13.

29. Ibid., 38, 231. We will talk about the revival of traditional forms of death ritual in Moonshadow Pond in more detail in chapter 4.

30. Ibid., 16.

31. Ibid., 234–35.

32. Anita Chan also advances a notion of moral vacuum in her work *Children of Mao* (Seattle: University of Washington Press, 1985).

33. Xin Liu, *In One's Own Shadow: An Ethnographic Account of the Condition of Post-Reform China* (Berkeley: University of California Press, 2000), 182.

34. Xin Liu, *In One's Own Shadow*, 156.

35. It is also important to point out here that while it is true that a person with *liangxin* is one who fulfills obligations in a social world, the category places moral liability on the individual. To go back to an earlier debate about sociocentrism versus individualism in Chinese thought, it is clear that in any actually existing notion of personhood, it is impossible to have one without the other. Although there is certainly greater emphasis on individualism in some cultural systems and on sociocentrism in others, the question is always about the balance between them rather than on whether there is such a thing as a completely individualistic or completely holistic model of personhood (for a more complete discussion of holism versus individualism in Chinese concepts of personhood, see Ellen Oxfeld, "Individualism, Holism, and the Market Mentality: Notes on the Recollections of a Chinese Entrepreneur," *Cultural Anthropology* 7, no. 3: 267–300).

36. For example, see Sarah Allen, *The Way of Water, and Sprouts of Virtue*

(Albany, N.Y.: SUNY Press, 1997). Also see Weiming Tu, " 'The Moral Universal' from the Perspective of East Asian Thought," *Philosophy East and West* 31, no. 3: 259–67, 264.

37. Allen, *Way of Water,* 87.

38. David Hall and Roger Ames, *Thinking from the Han: Self, Truth, and Transcendence in Chinese and Western Culture* (Albany, N.Y.: SUNY Press, 1998), 29.

39. Lung-ku Sun, "Contemporary Chinese Culture: Structure and Emotionality," *Australian Journal of Chinese Affairs* 26 (July 1991): 2.

40. Sun, "Contemporary Chinese Culture," 2.

41. Allen, *Way of Water,* 87.

42. Sun, "Contemporary Chinese Culture," 4.

43. Ambrose King, "Kuan-hsi and Network Building: A Sociological Interpretation," in *The Living Tree,* ed. Wei-ming Tu (Stanford, Calif.: Stanford University Press, 1994), 113.

44. Sun, "Contemporary Chinese Culture," 25.

45. Yunxiang Yan, *Flow of Gifts,* 145, 146.

46. Ibid., 144.

47. There are other ways in Chinese to say what in English we render as "a guilty conscience." But in these cases, the word *liangxin* would not be used. There are many phrases one could use for this phenomenon. One could, for instance, say you were *kuixin,* which literally means one has a guilty heart/mind.

48. Claudia Koonz points out that conscience in the Western tradition is often thought of as an inner voice that tells us how to behave. "Over the centuries, the conscience came to be understood as private and constant. For the Enlightenment philosopher Immanuel Kant, it was one of two poles that held his life in order. 'Two things fill the mind with ever new and increasing admiration and awe . . . the starry heavens above and the moral order within' " (Koonz, *The Nazi Conscience* [Cambridge, Mass.: Harvard University Press, 2003], 4). In contrast, as she also points out, many "others" were often left out of the injunctions of this inner voice. As she states, "Many of the major treatises of the European Enlightenment treat Africans, American Indians, and women as creatures without reason, bereft of fully human status" (Koonz, *Nazi Conscience,* 1).

49. Anita Chan, Richard Madsen, and Jonathan Unger, *Chen Village* (Berkeley: University of California Press, 1984), 209–10.

50. This was a very unusual gift. Coffee is almost never consumed in Moonshadow Pond while tea is ubiquitous. Most likely, it was some form of instant flavored coffee that this particular recipient enjoyed.

51. Charles Stafford, *Separation and Reunion in Modern China* (Cambridge: Cambridge University Press, 2000), 177.

52. Stafford, *Separation and Reunion,* 46.

53. *Yang* meaning to raise children and also to support one's parents. Charles Stafford, "Chinese Patriliny and the Cycles of Yang and Laiwang," in *Cultures of Relatedness: New Approaches to the Study of Kinship,* ed. Janet Carsten (Cambridge: Cambridge University Press, 2000), 42.

54. Ibid., 42.

55. Ibid., 43.

56. See Myron Cohen, *House United, House Divided* (New York: Columbia University Press, 1976); Margery Wolf, *The House of Lim: A Study of a Chinese Farm Family* (New York: Appleton-Century Crofts, 1968).

57. David Sutton, *Remembrance of Repasts* (New York: Berg, 2001), 9.

58. Jing Jun, "Dams and Dreams: A Return to Homeland Movement in Northwest China," in *Living with Separation in China: An Anthropological Account* (London, Routledge and Curzon, 2003), 127.

59. She considered him an uncle (*shufu* or "father's younger brother") because Songling's father and his cousin were descended from two brothers and would have addressed each other as brother.

60. Songling's father said that he gave money in 1949 to local villagers who were Nationalist soldiers and who wanted to flee the country to avoid retribution. But he insisted that he was never a member of any political party.

61. Xin Liu, *The Otherness of Self* (Ann Arbor: University of Michigan Press, 2002).

62. Xiaoying Wang, "The Post-Communist Personality"; Jiwei Ci, *Dialectic of the Chinese Revolution.*

63. Anthony Giddens, *The Consequences of Modernity* (Stanford, Calif.: Stanford University Press, 1990), 113.

64. Ibid., 113.

65. Ibid., 102.

66. Ibid., 118.

67. Ibid., 121.

68. G. William Skinner, "Chinese Peasants and the Closed Community: An Open and Shut Case," *Comparative Studies in Society and History* 13, no. 3 (1971): 270–81.

69. We will deal with the issue of villagers' ideas about the obligations of the state toward them, as well as the state's own use of the language of obligation, in chapter 7 and in the conclusion. What is interesting is that the language of obligation is used both by ordinary people to talk about what the state owes to them and by state and party to make appeals to the loyalty of ordinary people and to enjoin loyalty.

70. Hok Bun Ku, *Moral Politics,* 16.

71. Ibid., 17.

72. Richard Gordon and Carma Hinton, *The Gate of Heavenly Peace* [video-recording] (Brookline, Mass.: Long Bow Group, in association with Independent Television Service, 1995).

73. Clearly, there are shades of gray in many actions which also make them much harder to characterize in terms of memory and obligation. As we pointed out in the first chapter, all moral systems have ambiguity, and moral principles in all cultures may point to contradictory courses of action in any one case. The conflict between family loyalty versus not violating the public trust is just one such example. Some observers might want to explain this particular conflict in China as a conflict between "traditional" virtues versus the principles of modern bureaucracy that demand impartial administration. But we need to keep in mind that even in imperial China, when "traditional" virtues such as filial piety were extolled, entering the bureaucracy was at least theoretically based on merit and

not connections, and administration was also supposed to be based on law and not personal connections (even if the principles behind this law were actually quite different from those of a modern state). So, this contradiction is not a new one and is not best described as a conflict between "modernity" and "tradition."

3. WEIGHTY EXPECTATIONS

1. Margery Wolf, *Women and the Family in Rural Taiwan* (Stanford, Calif.: Stanford University Press, 1972).

2. According to the *Mei County Gazetteer,* three- and even four-generation households were common during the Qing dynasty in Meixian. The gazetteer cites an 1847 survey in which the average population of each Meixian household was 10.78 people. Of course, there is no way to know how reliable this survey was, and the statistics for the next fifty years show fascinating ups and downs. By 1932, the average household size was 4.39, then down to only 3.66 by 1953, back up to 4.21 in 1964, and 4.51 in 1982 (because Mao encouraged births, this was the highpoint). With the implementation of one-child limits for urban areas and two-child limits for rural areas in Guangdong, average household size in Meixian began to decline after this. By 1987, the average rural household size in Meixian was 4.3. See Meixian Difangzhi Biansuan Weiyuanhui, ed., *Meixian Zhi* (梅县志) [Mei County Gazetteer] (Guangzhou, China: Guangdong renmin chubanshe), 1027.

3. Emily Ahern, "The Power and Pollution of Chinese Women," in *Women and the Family in Chinese Society,* ed. Margery Wolf and Roxane Witke (Stanford, Calif.: Stanford University Press, 1975).

4. Yunxiang Yan, *Private Life under Socialism* (Stanford, Calif.: Stanford University Press, 2003), 89, 103, 109.

5. Ibid., 229.

6. Ibid., 115.

7. It is also important to remember as we talk about the rise of conjugality in contemporary rural China, that even in earlier eras, the joint family was never an attainable ideal for many poor peasant families. If more than one son survived into adulthood, it was unlikely that all the brothers would remain together after marriage. Some might migrate in search of work. Or, they might simply split their assets and try to get by in smaller economic units. Of course, the idea that conjugality is on the rise in modern China implies not merely a smaller family size, but also a more intimate and equal relationship within the marriage. For accounts of traditional processes of family division, see Myron Cohen's *House United, House Divided* (New York: Columbia University Press, 1976); and Hugh Baker's excellent summation in *Chinese Family and Kinship* (New York: Columbia University Press, 1979). Margery Wolf's classic *House of Lim* (New York: Appleton-Century Crofts, 1968) is an excellent study of the forces that pull a particular joint family apart in rural Taiwan in the 1960s.

8. Sara Friedman, "The Intimacy of State Power: Marriage, Liberation, and Socialist Subjects in Southeastern China," *American Ethnologist* 32, no. 2 (May 2005): 312–72.

9. Neil J. Diamant, "Re-examining the Impact of the 1950 Marriage Law: State Improvisation, Local Initiative, and Rural Family Change," *China Quarterly* 161 (March 2000): 187.

10. Ibid., 187.

11. Ibid., 177.

12. Jonathan Ocko, "Women, Property, and the Law in the People's Republic of China," in *Marriage and Inequality in Chinese Society,* ed. Rubie Watson and Patricia B. Ebrey (Berkeley: University of California Press, 1991), 314.

13. Yunxiang Yan, *Private Life;* Danyu Wang, "Ritualistic Coresidence and the Weakening of Filial Practice in Rural China," in *Filial Piety,* ed. Charlotte Ikels (Stanford, Calif.: Stanford University Press, 2004).

14. The *New York Times,* for instance, has also reported on this phenomenon. In one Yunnan village visited by a reporter, almost all the able-bodied adults had migrated to the cities to work, leaving grandparents to raise the grandchildren. The article also mentions a successful suit by a widow in Sichuan Province against her adult son and daughter, who had refused to give her a place to live or economic support. Howard French, "Rush for Wealth in China's Cities Shatters the Ancient Assurance of Care in Old Age," *New York Times,* Nov. 3, 2006.

15. Lihua Pang, Alan deBrauw, and Scott Rozelle, "Working Until You Drop: The Elderly of Rural China," *China Journal* 52 (July 2004): 73–96, 75.

16. Ibid., 77.

17. Pang, deBrauw and Rozelle, "Working until You Drop," 90; Ellen Judd, *Gender and Power in Rural China* (Stanford, Calif.: Stanford University Press, 1994); Tamara Jacka, *Women's Work in Rural China* (Cambridge: Cambridge University Press, 1997), 58.

18. See the following chapters in Charlotte Ikels's *Filial Piety* (Stanford, Calif.: Stanford University Press, 2004): Danyu Wang, "Ritualistic Coresidence and the Weakening of Filial Practice in Rural China"; Eric T. Miller, "Filial Daughters, Filial Sons: Comparisons from Rural North China"; and Jun Jing, "Meal Rotation and Filial Piety."

19. Hong Zhang, "Bracing for an Uncertain Future: A Case Study of New Coping Strategies of Rural Parents under China's Birth Control Policy," *China Journal* 43 (July 2005): 53–76, 75.

20. See the following chapters in Deborah Davis and Stevan Harrell, eds., *Chinese Families in the Post-Mao Era* (Stanford, Calif.: Stanford University Press, 1993): Deborah Davis and Stevan Harrell, "Introduction: The Impact of Post-Mao Reforms on Family Life"; Graham E. Johnson, "Family Strategies and Economic Transformation in Rural China: Some Evidence from the Pearl River Delta"; and Mark Selden, "Family Strategies and Structures in Rural North China."

21. Davis and Harrell, "Introduction," 8.

22. Ellen Judd, *Gender and Power in Rural North China* (Stanford, Calif.: Stanford University Press, 1994), 188.

23. Wu Fei, "Gambling for Qi: Suicide and Family Politics in a Rural North China County," *China Journal* 54 (July 2005): 7–28, 17.

24. China has a very strict household registration system in which every cit-

izen has a rural or urban household registration known as a *hukou*. As we discuss in more detail in chapter 7, it is still difficult to officially change one's rural registration to an urban one, even if one works as a migrant in a city. This system was developed in the collective era to control rural to urban migration. Controls over population movement have been lifted, but it is still difficult to change one's official residency.

25. Keith Bradshaw, "Wages Rise in China as Businesses Court the Young," *New York Times*, August 29, 2007.

26. See Arthur Wolf, "Adopt a Daughter-in-Law, Marry a Sister," *American Anthropologist* 70, no. 5 (1968): 864–74; and Margery Wolf, *House of Lim*, for a description of the Taiwanese variant of this practice. In Moonshadow Pond these girls were referred to by two different names, either *tongyang xi*, which we can translate as "adopted daughter-in-law," or *denglang mei*, "girl waiting for her husband." The difference between them is simply that a *denglang mei* was adopted even before her "husband" was born, and as such there might be a considerable age discrepancy between them when they ultimately married. My informants spoke of all these varieties from their own experiences. From now on, we will refer to both of these as "adopted daughter-in-law" unless the situation requires greater specificity. In Moonshadow Pond, some adopted daughters-in-law maintained contact with their natal families. For instance, one elderly woman still gets together with her siblings during Lunar New Year celebrations.

27. Arthur Wolf, "Adopt a Daughter-in-Law."

28. Ibid.

29. The *Gazetteer* points to poverty as a cause of the little daughter-in-law arrangement in Meixian, and although it does not give statistics on its prevalence, it does say that the arrangement was common amongst the poor in pre-revolutionary Meixian (Meixian, *Meixian Zhi*, 1027). Even though this arrangement was legally banned during the Nationalist era, the *Gazetteer* points out that this law was not strictly followed in rural areas (Meixian, *Meixian Zhi*, 1028).

30. An earlier law passed by the Nationalist government had also banned this practice, but the weak hold this government had over many rural areas meant that the practice had continued, at least in Meixian (Meixian, *Meixian Zhi*, 1028). The greater degree of control that the Communist government had in the rural areas might have been one factor in its demise. Nonetheless, older people in the village indicated that, according to their own recollections, the practice had begun to die out in the 1930s and 1940s. So, changes in the economy seemed to have been leading to the end of this practice even before Liberation.

31. These are somewhat different from the ways people talked about marriage in Yunxiang Yan's north China study. Yan noted that villagers created categories for free choice, introduction, and arranged marriages (Yunxiang Yan, *Private Life*, 46). In Moonshadow Pond, arranged and introduction marriages were collapsed into one category.

32. My survey in the spring of 2007 found the following marriage matches since 1996 in Moonshadow Pond: seventeen (15 percent) matches within the township, seventy-one matches (62 percent) within Meizhou, fifteen (13 percent) of the matches from Guangdong Province but outside of Meizhou, and eleven

(10 percent) matches from outside of Guangdong Province. Prior to 1996, only 5.7 percent of all marriages were with people from outside of the Meizhou area.

33. Judd, *Gender and Power,* 191.

34. For instance, see Margery Wolf, *Women and the Family in Rural Taiwan* (Stanford, Calif.: Stanford University Press); Emily Ahern, "The Power and Pollution of Chinese Women," in *Women in Chinese Society,* ed. Roxane Witke and Margery Wolf (Stanford, Calif.: Stanford University Press, 1975).

35. By the mid-nineties, divorce was certainly not unheard of. In the group of thirty-three families that comprised Team 2, for instance, there had been four cases by 1995. When I returned in 2007, two more cases had occurred in the next generation of Team 2. These divorces all sprang from different sources. For instance, Red Chong's wife had simply found another lover, and Red Chong actually felt bad to divorce her at first, because she had helped him build his new house. But then, he told me, it was a question of *mianzi,* because she had cheated on him. Miaoli's sister-in-law had also divorced, but for very different reasons. Money and her husband's incessant gambling were at issue. Finally she moved across the street, and refused to come back (although Miaoli said she was forced to leave). In another case, a wife complained about her husband's drinking, and eventually left him.

"During the time we had the production team," said Aihua, reminiscing about her days as the head of Team 2, "we used to work on couples like this, we did thought work with them" *(sixiang gongzuo).* Referring to the husband with the drinking problem, she said, "I remember working with this couple so many times, and he did improve his behavior. But later on, no one was there [to intervene and try to influence his behavior], and he just got worse."

36. Many of the ideas of the Russian literary theorist Bakhtin, such as "polyphony" and "inner dialogue" are relevant here. See Sue Vice, *Introducing Bakhtin* (Manchester, UK: Manchester University Press, 1997), for a nice summary of his ideas about dialogism and voices. I have also dealt with this issue of contending voices within one individual in an overseas Chinese context (see Ellen Oxfeld, "Individualism, Holism, and the Market Mentality: Notes on the Recollections of a Chinese Entrepreneur," *Cultural Anthropology* 7, no. 3 [August 1992]: 267–300).

37. Rubie Watson has carefully delineated the roles of maids, concubines, and wives in the Hong Kong region of the late imperial and Republican era. As she points out, they entered their respective households in a very different manner. Female servants were indentured, and could only leave after a term of service when their masters married them off or sold them as someone's concubine. Wives, in contrast, were not "bought," but came into the household along with an exchange of gifts between families. Concubines were often "bought," but could establish themselves to a greater degree by giving birth to legitimate heirs. Interestingly, she points out, male servants tended to serve with contracts and pay, and were thus less vulnerable than their female counterparts. See "Wives, Concubines, and Maids: Servitude and Kinship in the Hong Kong Region, 1900–1940," in *Marriage and Inequality in Chinese Society,* ed. Rubie Watson and Patricia Ebrey (Berkeley: University of California Press, 1991).

38. Guangdong per capita net rural income grew from 2,699.24 *yuan* in 1995

to 3,654 *yuan* in 2000. The per capita net income of Moonshadow Pond residents in 1997 was 3,054 *yuan,* just about where one would expect it to fall in that year if it was about average for the province. Per capita income in 2006 for Moonshadow Pond had risen to 4,022. Nonetheless, educational expenses beyond lower middle school are high. The tuition of a student who tested well ran as high as 1,500 *yuan* per year in 2007. But upper middle schools will ask for much more from a child who has not tested well, and this can run as high as ten thousand *yuan.* Despite this, if a child does get through upper middle school and tests into college, parents will do everything to help this child study in college, including borrowing money from friends and relatives. While only nine villagers had completed college in 1997, this number jumped to forty-five by the spring of 2007. Guangdong income source is "Table 10-19: Per Capita Total and Net Income and Their Composition of Rural Households," *Guangdong Statistical Yearbook,* www.gdstats.gov.cn/tjnj/table/10/10_e.htm. The source for Moonshadow Pond is township statistics for 1997 and 2007 and my own survey data.

39. According to the *Guangdong Statistical Yearbook* for 2006, there were 874,686 students in institutions of higher education in Guangdong in 2005. Of these, 400,938—almost half—were female (http://www.gdstats.gov.cn/tjnj/table/18/18_e.htm).

40. See Ellen Judd, "*Niangjia:* Chinese Women and Their Natal Families," *Journal of Asian Studies* 48, no. 3 (1989): 525–44.

41. A "dry son" was a ritualized relationship, but it meant that when someone died, his dry son or daughter would wear the same funeral garb as actual sons or daughters. Some people may also have more extensive relationships with dry sons and daughters, and they may visit during festivals or at other times as well. In the case of Baoli, because he was a "dry son" of Big Gao's mother-in-law, he was able to don the mourning garb of an actual son—which was very important because she had no actual sons to perform the ritual duties required.

42. The third child had somehow been missed by the authorities, since only two children were actually allowed in rural Guangdong at the time.

43. Summarizing a number of wonderfully detailed studies on families in post-Mao China, Deborah Davis and Stevan Harrell conclude in their introduction to *Chinese Families in the Post-Mao Era* (Berkeley: University of California Press, 1993), "The process of family changes, relatively homogeneous in the Maoist period, has become complex and heterogeneous" (17). This heterogeneity is occurring despite the fact that, as Davis and Harrell observe, the birth-planning process has actually imposed a great deal of uniformity on family size (7).

44. Such was the result found in a study by Patricia Beaver, Lihui Hou, and Xue Wang in one pair of northern Chinese townships in "Rural Chinese Women: Two Faces of Economic Reform," *Modern China* 21, no. 2 (April 1995): 205–32.

45. See Govind Kelkar and Yunxian Wang, "Farmers, Women, and Economic Reform in China," *Bulletin of Concerned Asian Scholars* 29, no. 4 (1997): 69–77.

46. See Helen Siu for a discussion of similar trends in the Pearl River Delta, in "Reconstituting Dowry and Brideprice in South China," in *Chinese Families in the Post-Mao Era,* ed. Deborah Davis and Steven Harrell (Berkeley: University of California Press), 165–88.

47. William Lavely, "Marriage and Mobility under Rural Collectivism," in

Marriage and Inequality in Chinese Society, ed. Patricia Ebrey and Rubie Watson (Berkeley: University of California Press), 286–312.

48. Friedman notes the same development in the village she studied in a different area of southeast China. She states that registered couples were legally married, but "lacked the social recognition bestowed by a wedding ceremony" ("The Intimacy of State Power: Marriage, Liberation, and Socialist Subjects in Southeastern China," *American Ethnologist* 32, no. 2 [2005]: 312–72).

49. William L. Parish and Martin King Whyte, *Village and Family in Contemporary China* (Chicago: University of Chicago Press, 1978), 255.

50. Patricia Ebrey, "Introduction," in *Marriage and Inequality in Chinese Society,* ed. Rubie Watson and Patricia Ebrey (Berkeley: University of California Press, 1991), 1-24.

51. See Rubie Watson, "Afterword: Marriage and Gender Inequality," in *Marriage and Inequality in Chinese Society,* ed. Rubie Watson and Patricia Ebrey (Berkeley: University of California Press, 1991), 347–68. As Claude Lévi-Strauss famously asserts, the affinal relationship is the most "elementary structure" of kinship. It is, he argued, the relationship between "wife-givers" and "wife-takers" that created the first set of extrafamilial social relationships. As such, it was the very basis of "civilization" itself. Without this affinal tie, said Lévi-Strauss, we would have "families," but no "society" beyond the family. See Claude Lévi-Strauss, *The Elementary Structures of Kinship,* trans. James H. Bell, John R. von Sturmer, and Rodney Needham (Boston: Beacon, 1969). While subsequent analysts criticized Lévi-Strauss for assuming universal male dominance and the universal exchange of women, few would dispute the importance of the affinal relationship in establishing ties beyond the immediate family and in setting up ongoing systems of exchange in many precapitalist societies.

52. See Rubie Watson, "Class Differences and Affinal Relations in South China," *Man* 16 (1981): 593–615, for an interesting discussion of how affinal relations were utilized more frequently by landlords than by ordinary peasants in the Hong Kong area, and on the ways these relations actually helped maintain the class position of landlords.

53. Representatives of the bride's family arrive shortly before the luncheon banquet and leave later that afternoon. Since 1950, these representatives include the bride's mother, who now gives a red envelope to the son-in-law when he presents tea to her. (The bride's father cannot attend the wedding.) When the bride's mother and other relatives leave later in the afternoon, she may still shed tears, as she did in traditional times. Despite all the changes, she is, after all, moving into a new household.

54. As is explained in more detail in chapter 4, funeral banquets in Moonshadow Pond are now often large and expensive affairs that can add greatly to a family's status. As with wedding banquets, a status-enhancing life-cycle ritual that was once the sole province of the wealthiest is now a more generalized practice.

55. The Marriage Law of 1950 was updated in 1980. According to the law, divorce will be granted only when there is "complete alienation of affection, and when mediation has failed." "The Marriage Law of the People's Republic of China," reprinted in "One Hundred Court Cases on Marriage," *Chinese Sociology and Anthropology* 18, nos. 1–2 (Fall–Winter 1985–1986).

4. EVERLASTING DEBTS

1. In an earlier article, I mistakenly translated this quote to say that the urns were left in the ancestral temple. Later, I realized the person was saying that the urns were left in the hills above the ancestor's houses and I have corrected it here. On my visit to Moonshadow Pond in 2007, I took some pictures of the abandoned urns. Many had been opened and their contents spread around as the quote indicates, but a few had not been touched.

2. In fact, the Chinese have practiced some sort of reburial for over a thousand years. For a discussion of this practice in eleventh-century north China, see Patricia Ebrey, *Confucianism and Family Rituals in Imperial China* (Princeton, N.J.: Princeton University Press, 1991), 69. In southeast China, this kind of reburial is quite common and also has symbolic significance; bones are representative of male substance and therefore the lineage, whereas flesh is seen as female substance. As Goran Aijmer points out, "In a burial, flesh and soft tissues stay in the earth: they become part of the earth and the productive order. . . . In areas such as South-Eastern China, where double burials are practiced, it is essential that the bones should be physically parted from the earth, including the flesh" ("Burial, Ancestors, and Geomancy among the Ma On Shan Hakka, New Territories of Hong Kong," in *Guoji kejiaxue yantaohui lunwen ji/The Proceedings of the International Conference on Hakkaology*, ed. Xie Jian and Zheng Chiyan [Hong Kong: Xianggang Zhongwen Daxue, Xianggang Ya Tai Yanjiusuo, Haiwai Huaren Yanjiushe], 360). The female parts of the dead, the soft tissue, "are by decomposition absorbed by the earth and . . . become components of the productive order" (361). But by the same token, the reburial is also an attempt to "remove the dangerous and polluting corpse from contact with the living and reduce it to clean, everlasting bones. The goal is to reduce the fleshly *yin* elements of the deceased and cordon them off from the living while enhancing the vital *yang* elements in the bones" (Emily Martin, "Gender and Ideological Differences in Representations of Life and Death," in *Death Ritual in Late Imperial and Modern China*, ed. James L. Watson and Evelyn Rawski [Berkeley: University of California Press], 167).

According to James Watson, in Cantonese villages reburial is really a two-step process. The urn is first reburied in the ground, and years later an elaborate tomb is built in which the urn is placed. In Moonshadow Pond, however, the urn was not reburied in the ground. Instead, it was left above ground until the funds could be found for the construction of the tomb in which to place it. This is what created the phenomenon of urns being left in the hills until the funds could later be found to complete the reburial. Watson's account can be found in "Of Flesh and Bones: The Management of Death Pollution in Cantonese Society," in *Village Life in Hong Kong: Politics, Gender, and Ritual in the New Territories*, ed. James Watson and Rubie Watson (Hong Kong: Chinese University Press, 2004).

3. William Jankowiak, *Sex, Death, and Hierarchy in a Chinese City* (New York: Columbia University Press, 1993), 290.

4. Xin Liu, *In One's Own Shadow: An Ethnographic Account of the Condition of Post-Reform China* (Berkeley: University of California Press, 2000); and Helen Siu, "Recycling Rituals: Politics and Popular Culture in Contemporary

Rural China," in *Unofficial China: Popular Culture and Thought in the People's Republic*, ed. Perry Link, Richard Madsen, and Paul Pickowicz (Boulder, Colo.: Westview Press, 1989), 121–37.

5. Eric Hobsbawm and Terence Ranger, ed., *The Invention of Tradition* (Cambridge: Cambridge University Press, 1984).

6. Patricia Ebrey, *Confuciansim and Family Rituals in Imperial China* (Princeton, N.J.: Princeton University Press, 1991); Norman Kutcher, *Mourning in Late Imperial China: Filial Piety and the State* (Cambridge: Cambridge University Press, 1999).

7. Ann Anagnost, "The Politics of Ritual Displacement," in *Asian Visions of Authority: Religion and the Modern States of East and Southeast Asia,* ed. Charles F. Keyes, Laurel Kendall, and Helen Hardacre (Honolulu: University of Hawai'i Press, 1994), 225.

8. Ibid., 228.

9. Prasenjit Duara, "Knowledge and Power in the Discourse of Modernity: The Campaigns against Popular Religion in Early Twentieth-Century China," *Journal of Asian Studies* 50, no. 1 (1991): 67–83.

10. James L. Watson, "The Structure of Chinese Funerary Rites: Elementary Forms, Ritual Sequence, and the Primacy of Performance," in *Death Ritual in Late Imperial and Modern China*, ed. James L. Watson and Evelyn Rawski (Berkeley: University of California Press, 1988), 13; Emily Ahern, *The Cult of the Dead in a Chinese Village* (Stanford, Calif.: Stanford University Press, 1973); Alan Cole, *Mothers and Sons in Chinese Buddhism* (Stanford, Calif.: Stanford University Press, 1998).

11. Cole, *Mothers and Sons.*

12. Ebrey, *Confucianism and Family Rituals,* 14

13. Ibid., 214.

14. Yunxiang Yan, *The Flow of Gifts: Reciprocity and Social Networks in a Chinese Village* (Stanford, Calif.: Stanford University Press). Lien-Sheng Yang, "The Concept of *Pao* as a Basis for Social Relations in China," in *Chinese Thought and Institutions,* ed. John K. Fairbank (Chicago: University of Chicago Press, 1957).

15. Cole, *Mothers and Sons,* 19.

16. Cole, *Mothers and Sons;* Stephen Teiser, *The Ghost Festival in Medieval China* (Princeton, N.J.: Princeton University Press, 1988).

17. Edward L. Davis, *Society and the Supernatural in Song China* (Honolulu: University of Hawai'i Press, 2001), 172.

18. Ebrey, *Confucianism and Family Rituals,* 85.

19. Ibid., 85.

20. Ebrey, *Confucianism and Family Ritual,* 213; Kutcher, *Mourning in Late Imperial China,* 92–93, 95.

21. Donald Munro, "Individualism and Holism: Studies in Confucianism and Taoist Values," in *Individualism and Holism: Studies in Confucian and Taoist Values* (Ann Arbor: Center for Chinese Studies, University of Michigan, 1985).

22. Some authors use the word *guilt* to describe the emotions that offspring would feel upon the death of their parents (see, for instance, Kutcher, *Mourning in Late Imperial China,* 31). The use of this word can be tricky, however, because

there is not an exact Chinese equivalent. The word *neijiu,* which literally means "internal fault," is not always used in the same ways as the English terms *guilt* or *guilty conscience.* Jun Jing discusses this issue extensively and decides to use the word *guilt* when speaking about people's feelings of inadequacy in repaying their ancestors (Jing, *The Temple of Memories: History, Power, and Morality in a Chinese Village* [Stanford, Calif.: Stanford University Press]). In contrast, as explained in chapter 2, my own informants in Moonshadow Pond frequently used the word *liangxin* when speaking of someone who feels, understands, and acts upon his or her obligations. Hence, the word *liangxin* was the critical category used to describe a mourner's feelings, thoughts, and motivations.

23. Kutcher, *Mourning in Late Imperial China,* 48.

24. Cole, *Mothers and Sons.*

25. Cole, *Mothers and Sons;* Margery Wolf, *Women and the Family in Rural Taiwan* (Stanford, Calif.: Stanford University Press, 1972).

26. In his recent book, Alan Cole develops this analysis further. The mother's "good" sexuality or kindness in the form of milk is repaid, while her "bad" sexuality—associated with blood, the vagina, childbirth, and menstruation—"is a sin that must be erased" (*Mothers and Sons,* 231). He ties these physiological distinctions to differences in social roles. Women were revered in their roles as mothers (hence, the "milk debt") but feared in their roles as wives and daughters-in-laws, where their sexuality was seen as having the potential to pull sons away from the joint family. This explains the need to eradicate the pollution associated with their obvious sexuality—the blood of menstruation and childbirth.

27. Watson, "Structure of Chinese Funerary Rites," 8.

28. Wolf, *Women and the Family.*

29. Xuejia Fang, *Kejia yuanliu tan ao* [The Mystery of the Origin of the Hakka] (Guangdong, China: Gaodeng jiaoyu chubanshe, 1994), 232; Cole, *Mothers and Sons,* 87.

30. Emily Ahern, *The Cult of the Dead in a Chinese Village* (Stanford, Calif.: Stanford University Press, 1973), 200.

31. Kutcher, *Mourning in Late Imperial China,* 23.

32. Emily Ahern, *Cult of the Dead;* Maurice Freedman, *Lineage Organization in Southeastern China* (London: Athlone Press, 1958).

33. Watson, "Structure of Chinese Funerary Rites"; Sulamith Heins Potter and Jack Potter, *China's Peasants: The Anthropology of a Revolution* (Cambridge: Cambridge University Press, 1990), 25.

34. Xin Liu, *In One's Own Shadow,* 152–53.

35. Watson, "Structure of Chinese Funerary Rites," 6. Eriberto Lozada upholds Watson's approach in his study of contemporary Catholics in Meixian. Lozada states, "The similarity of Catholic and non-Catholic funerary ritual highlights the strength of orthopraxy as a guiding principle in Chinese society. In fact, because of the shared structure of funerary ritual, the people in Little Rome can be at once Hakka and Catholic" (*God Aboveground: Catholic Church, Postsocialist State, and Transnational Processes in a Chinese Village* [Stanford, Calif.: Stanford University Press, 2001], 149). Lozada argues that the Catholic emphasis on salvation of the soul is clearly different from the Chinese emphasis on continuous exchange with the ancestors. Hence, the similarities between Catholic Hakka funeral ritual

and other Hakka funerals must be explained by an emphasis on form over content. Catholic Hakka villagers used elements of customary Hakka funerals that were already available and tailored these to the Catholic theology. Lozada also reports, however, that food items were presented as offerings at Hakka Catholic funeral services (149) and that Catholic villagers also leave food offerings at the graves of their ancestors each year (144–45). One has to wonder if, despite the theological emphasis on salvation, the ordinary Catholic villagers do not perceive of their actions in terms of repaying their debt to the deceased.

36. See Ebrey, *Confucianism and Family Rituals;* J. J. M. De Groot, *The Religious System of China* (Taipei, Taiwan: Southern Materials Center, 1892/1989), 1:239; Cynthia Brokaw, *The Ledgers of Merit and Demerit: Social Change and Moral Order in Late Imperial China* (Princeton, N.J.: Princeton University Press, 1991).

37. Edward L. Davis, *Society and the Supernatural in Song China,* 174.

38. Timothy Brook, "Funerary Ritual and the Building of Lineages in Late Imperial China," *Harvard Journal of Asiatic Studies* 49, no. 2 (1989): 465.

39. Ibid., 470.

40. Ibid., 484.

41. Martin King Whyte, "Death in the People's Republic of China," in *Death Ritual in Late Imperial and Modern China,* ed. James L. Watson and Evelyn Rawski (Berkeley: University of California Press, 1988).

42. Anagnost, "Politics of Ritual Displacement," 227.

43. Andrew Kipnis, *Producing Guanxi: Sentiment, Self, and Subculture in a North China Village* (Durham, N.C.: Duke University Press, 1997).

44. Jun Jing, *Temple of Memories.*

45. Ibid., 175.

46. Liu Xin, *In One's Own Shadow,* 156.

47. Tomb Sweeping Day, or Qingming Jie, is a festival in the third lunar month when Chinese families traditionally sweep the tombs of their ancestors; Martin King Whyte, "Death in the People's Republic," 314.

48. Whyte, "Death in the People's Republic," 316.

49. Jankowiak, *Sex, Death, and Hierarchy,* 290.

50. Such funerals may also be referred to as *zuo sang shi* (literally, "doing funeral rites"), or *zuo fo shi* (literally, "doing Buddhist rites"). "Doing benevolent acts," however, is the most common way to refer to religious funeral rites as opposed to secular services.

51. Also see Xuejia Fang, *Kejia Yuanliu Tan Ao,* 165.

52. For instance, John Lagerway reports the use of Buddhist monks in Hakka funerals that take place not only in Meixian, but also in Hong Kong and Fujian. He notes that in some Hakka parts of Fujian, the same person may perform both Buddhist and Taoist rituals. When that person performs rituals for the dead, however, he does so in his capacity as an "incense and flower Buddhist" monk (the school of Buddhism prevalent among the Hakka, which combines Buddhist and Confucian influences); John Lagerway, "Taoism among the Hakka in Fujian," in *Guoji kejiaxue yantaohui lunwen ji/The Proceedings of the International Conference on Hakkaology,* ed. Xie Jian and Zheng Chiyan (Hong Kong: Xianggang Zhongwen Daxue, Xianggang Ya Tai Yanjiusuo, Haiwai Huaren Yanjiushe). In

contrast, a number of recent ethnographies of north China, such as Kipnis, *Producing Guanxi,* and Xin Liu, *In One's Own Shadow,* do not mention Buddhist elements of funeral services at all. It is not clear from these texts whether such elements were once important, but not revived after the end of Maoism, or whether they were never an essential component of funeral rites in those areas.

53. This specialist need not be a *fengshui* master, but simply needs to be a layperson with enough knowledge to direct the course of the proceedings. In Moonshadow Pond, this role was performed by a man whose father had been a Buddhist monk. After Liberation, many monks returned to their production teams and married. But in this case, the father was still able to impart considerable knowledge to his son, who was now able to market this for use in local funerals.

54. This was told to me by older residents of Moonshadow Pond. In my earlier research on the Meixian Hakka in Calcutta, I observed that male and female mourners were separated during funeral services. It is likely that since the Calcutta Hakka left China before Liberation, they maintained this earlier element of the ritual. In many other respects, the Calcutta Hakka funerals are quite close to those I observed in Meixian.

55. The *laoren hui,* or council of elders, is a group comprising villagers over the age of sixty. They raise funds to use for trips, celebrations, or to help people in need. In Moonshadow Pond, they do not have a permanent meeting hall, although their members often meet and play mahjong in the courtyard of the main ancestral hall or, more recently, in the building that was once the local school but which has now been closed. In some of the other neighboring villagers, the village elders council has secured a space where elders may meet and spend time together.

56. According to the *Mei County Gazetteer (Meixian Zhi),* the council of elders began to play a role in officiating the funeral only after liberation (*Meixian Zhi,* 1039). The gazetteer also states that the traditional mourning documents (the *aizhang* and the *dianzhang*) were replaced after Liberation by reciting the deceased's life story. In reform-era Moonshadow Pond, this modern eulogy has not replaced the customary mourning documents, nor has it been jettisoned; rather, it has now been integrated into the revived religious rites.

57. See Xuejia Fang, *Kejia Yuanliu Tan Ao,* 165, for more on Hakka popular Buddhism.

58. Myron Cohen, "Souls and Salvation: Conflicting Themes in Chinese Popular Religion," in *Death Ritual in Late Imperial and Modern China,* ed. James L. Watson and Evelyn Rawski (Berkeley: University of California Press, 1988), 180–202.

59. Xuejia Fang, *Kejia Yuanliu Tan Ao,* 167.

60. For an alternative interpretation of the blood-bowl sutra, see Steven P. Sangren, *Chinese Sociologics* (London: Athlone Press, 2000).

61. Weigeng Zhang, ed., *Kejiahua cidian* [Hakka Dictionary] (Guangdong, China: Guangdong renmin chubanshe, 1995), 227.

62. See Shui-cheng Cheng, "Music of the Hakka in Taiwan," in *Guoji kejiaxue yantaohui lunwen ji/The Proceedings of the International Conference on Hakkaology,* ed. Xie Jian and Zheng Chiyan (Hong Kong: Xianggang Zhongwen Daxue, Xianggang Ya Tai Yanjiusuo, Haiwai Huaren Yanjiushe, 1994), 402.

63. Justus Doolittle, *Social Life of the Chinese with Some Account of Their Religious, Governmental, Educational, and Business Customs and Opinions, with Special but Not Exclusive Reference to Fuhchau* (New York: Harper, 1865), 1, 184, 191; J. J. M. De Groot, "Buddhist Masses for the Dead at Amoy: An Ethnological Essay," in *Actes du Sixième Congrès International des Orientalistes* [Proceedings from the Sixth International Meeting of Orientalists], pt. 4, sec. 4. (Leiden: E. J. Brill, 1865); see also Ebrey, *Confucianism and Family Rituals*, 212.

64. *Mei County Gazetteer*, 1039; see also Xuejia Fang, *Village Religion and Culture in Northeastern Guangdong*, Traditional Hakka Society Series, no. 5, International Hakka Studies Association, Overseas Chinese Archives (Paris: École française d'Extrême-Orient, 1997).

65. Kutcher, *Mourning in Late Imperial China*, 92.

66. Alan Klima, *The Funeral Casino: Meditation, Massacre, and Exchange with the Dead in Thailand* (Princeton, N.J.: Princeton University Press, 2002), 252.

67. Ibid., 276.

68. Adam Yuet Chau, *Miraculous Response: Doing Popular Religion in Contemporary China* (Stanford, Calif.: Stanford University Press, 2006), 147.

69. Ibid., 149.

70. Ibid., 150.

71. Xin Liu reports hearing similar comments in the funeral rituals of the north China village that he studied in the 1990s. Describing a funeral procession through the village of Dawa, he describes a woman who called out to the daughter-in-law of the deceased: "Look at you: you weren't crying, in fact you were laughing? Don't pretend any more! You wanted your father-in-law to die, didn't you?" (*In One's Own Shadow*, 155). Liu goes on to explain that the content and form of ritual practices has separated much more greatly in contemporary rural China than in the past (155). Although we might be tempted to say that the kind of ironic detachment and sarcasm that both Moonshadow Pond villagers and those observed in Dawa expressed are a feature of the post-Mao order, there really is no direct evidence that villagers were not equally ironic or capable of poking fun at their ritual expressions in the past.

72. *Haisheng bu xiaoshun, sihou hong guishen* ("Not filial when living, but after death create a sensation by worshipping").

73. Wailing at a funeral that was not for one's own ancestors was described as *jie ren yeniang jiao ziji*, or "borrowing someone else's mother and father and calling them your own."

74. A *jiao* is one tenth of a *yuan* and is therefore more or less the equivalent of a dime to an American dollar.

75. In this case, we should not forget that these funerals also feed a reenergized petty-capitalist economy. Several families in Moonshadow Pond derived good incomes by crafting ritual objects that would be burned as offerings in funerals and other rites. As mentioned above, funerals provided excellent remuneration to monks, as well as helpful added cash for the cooks and other individuals who helped out with the services. Hill Gates (1996) argues that Chinese history is a long dialectic involving the contending demands of a state tributary economy and a petty-capitalist economy. During certain eras, state control is preeminent. These eras are usually followed by a flowering of entrepreneurial ac-

tivity and by vibrant petty-capitalist activity. As such, the reform era in Gates's scheme might be interpreted as just the latest installment of this tributary economy versus petty-capitalist dialectic.

76. Adam Yuet Chau observed a similar phenomenon in the context of rural north China. As he put it, the family is on stage during a funeral, not only in regard to their show of filiality, but in addition, in "relation to . . . kin and community as a generous host" (Chau, *Miraculous Response*, 134).

77. Many people told me stories about the differing kinds of treatment received from those from "good" classes (such as "poor peasants") as opposed to those from "bad" classes (such as "landlords") upon death. Those from bad classes might have no service at all, their closest kin merely taking their coffins up the mountain themselves for burial. However, we should remember that even now there are some categories of people for whom funeral rites are greatly abbreviated. A young person who commits suicide, for instance, would have greatly shortened rites. One reason for this is that only one's descendants can actually attend a funeral as mourners, and this rule would eliminate all of the young person's elder relatives from attending her funeral. Second, suicide is considered extremely inauspicious, and most villagers would fear going to a death rite for a suicide victim.

78. Adam Chau has found a similar continuity of popular religious practice in the village that he studied in north-central China. In this village, there was actually a modest revival of ritual activity during the 1950s, as the area recuperated from war and revolution. Only later, with the beginnings of the Cultural Revolution, was there a more complete interruption of popular religious activity. As such, Chau estimates that not more than a decade passed in this village before the post-Mao revival of popular religion ("The Dragon King Valley: Popular Religion, Socialist State, and Agrarian Society in Shaanbei, North-Central China," PhD diss., Stanford University, 2001, 53).

79. For more information on class differences in the village, see chapter 7.

80. Whyte, "Death in the People's Republic."

81. In fact, not only are the revived death rituals described earlier perceived as primarily the domain of village life and the peasantry, but in addition so is the category of religion itself *(zongjiao)*. Baoli's remark in chapter 1 that intellectuals do not believe in religion is indicative of this attitude.

82. As I will discuss, this explanation has been given by Andrew Kipnis, who sees the revival of popular religion in Chinese rural areas as a way that peasants assert their opposition to state-imposed definitions of "what it means to be a peasant" ("Within and Against Peasantness: Backwardness and Filiality in Rural China," *Comparative Studies in Society and History* 37, no. 1 [1995]: 112).

83. Around New Year's they go to *baichan* ("worship and repent"). Then they go to *qifu* ("raise good fortune"), *nuanfu* ("warm up the fortune"), and *wanfu* ("pay back for the good fortune received"). These are all accompanied by food offerings.

84. Cohen, "Souls and Salvation."

85. Stephen Teiser, *The Ghost Festival in Medieval China*, 381.

86. Cohen, "Souls and Salvation," 199.

87. Ibid.

88. See Teiser, *Ghost Festival in Medieval China;* Steven Sangren, *History and Magical Power in a Chinese Community* (Stanford, Calif.: Stanford University Press, 1987), 176–77. Many scholars use the word *heterodox* in the Chinese context to apply to a religious practice that the state sees as threatening. For those who insist that the word *heterodox* can only be applied to those whom the state sees as threatening state power, Bright Ling's practices during the 1990s when the incidents occurred cannot be so designated. A better example of heterodox in this more narrow sense would be the Falun Gong group, which is indeed viewed by the state as a threat and dealt with very severely.

89. Interestingly, this situation changed dramatically between my 1997 stay in the village and my return ten years later. In the interval, Bright Ling's interest in Buddhism had shifted to the Falun Gong movement, which, as noted earlier, is severely repressed by the Chinese government. Bright Ling lost her job for a time, but then was able to get another government job after renouncing her ties with Falung Gong. As such, one could say she shifted from mere nonconformity with local practice to "heterodoxy."

90. Anagnost, "Politics of Ritual Displacement," 235. Indeed, the latest version of the Chinese constitution protects "freedom of religious worship," while "superstition" is not protected. Of course, the problem with much popular religion is that it falls in what Chau calls "the gray area between legitimate religion and illegitimate, thus illegal, superstition. Who makes the decision to categorize one activity as proper religion *(zhengdang zongjiao huodong)* and another as feudal superstition?" ("The Dragon King Valley," 80).

91. Donald Munro, "Individualism and Holism: Studies in Confucianism and Taoist Values," in *Individualism and Holism: Studies in Confucian and Taoist Values* (Ann Arbor: Center for Chinese Studies, University of Michigan, 1985), 16.

92. Irene Eng and Yi-min Lin, "Religious Festivities, Communal Rivalry, and Restructuring of Authority Relations in Rural Chaozhou, Southeast China," *Journal of Asian Studies* 61, no. 4 (2002): 1263.

93. Jun Jing, *Temple of Memories;* Anagnost, "Politics of Ritual Displacement."

94. Anagnost, "Politics of Ritual Displacement," 233.

95. Andrew Kipnis, "Within and Against Peasantness," 125.

96. Elizabeth Perry, "Trends in the Study of Chinese Politics: State-Society Relations," *China Quarterly,* no. 139 (1994): 704–13.

97. Adam Yuet Chau, "The Dragon King Valley," 81.

98. See Sangren, *Chinese Sociologics;* Cole, *Mothers and Sons.*

99. Louis Dumont, *Homo Hierarchicus: The Caste System and its Implications* (Chicago: University of Chicago Press, 1980), 244.

100. Yunxiang Yan, *The Flow of Gifts,* 145.

5. THE MORAL DILEMMAS OF RETURN VISITS

1. In an earlier article ("Chinese Villagers and the Moral Dilemmas of Return Visits," in *Coming Home? Refugees, Immigrants and Those Who Stayed Behind,* ed. Lynellyn Long and Ellen Oxfeld [Philadelphia: University of Pennsylvania Press, 2004]), I had somewhat different numbers for families with overseas Chi-

nese connections in Moonshadow Pond—twenty-three out of 165 families (14 percent) instead of twenty-one out of 184 families, or 11 percent. The reason for the discrepancy is that after carefully checking my survey, I realized that I had counted a number of separate conjugal families as joint families and hence the total number of families was actually 184 instead of 165. I also took two families off my list after reevaluating their connections to overseas Chinese and concluding that they were too distant.

2. James Watson, *Emigration and the Chinese Lineage* (Berkeley: University of California Press, 1975); Yuen-Fong Woon, "An Emigrant Community in the Ssy-yi Area, Southeastern China, 1885–1949," *Modern Asian Studies* 18 (1985): 273–308; Yuen-Fong Woon, "Social Change and Continuity in South China: Overseas Chinese and the Guan Lineage of Kaiping County, 1949–1987," *The China Quarterly*, no. 118 (1989): 324–44; Madeline Hsu, "Living Abroad and Faring Well: Migration and Transnationalism in Taishan County, Guangdong, 1904–1939," (PhD diss., Yale University, 1995); You-tien Hsing, "Building *Guanxi* Across the Straits: Taiwanese Capital and Local Chinese Bureaucrats," in *Ungrounded Empires: The Cultural Politics of Modern Chinese Transnationalism*, ed. Donald Nonini and Aihwa Ong (New York, Routledge, 1997); Constance Lever-Tracy, David Ip, and Noel Tracy, *The Chinese Diaspora and Mainland China: An Emerging Economic Synergy* (New York: St. Martin's, 1996).

3. Watson, *Emigration and the Chinese Lineage;* Ta Chen, *Emigrant Communities in South China: A Study of Overseas Chinese Migration and Its Influence on Standards of Living and Social Change* (New York: Institute of Pacific Relations, 1940); Yuen-Fong Woon, "An Emigrant Community," and "Social Change and Continuity."

4. Xin Liu, "Space, Mobility, and Flexibility: Chinese Villagers and Scholars Negotiate Power at Home and Abroad," in *Ungrounded Empires: The Cultural Politics of Modern Chinese Transnationalism,* ed. Donald Nonini and Aihwa Ong (New York, Routledge, 1997).

5. Godley's article on the role of returned overseas Chinese in post-1949 China is an exception to this. However, while an excellent summary of the changing role and status of returnees in the PRC, it is broadly focused on the country as a whole, and is not an ethnographic study (Michael Godley, "The Sojourners: Returned Overseas Chinese in the People's Republic of China," *Pacific Affairs* 62, no. 3 [Fall 1989]: 330–52).

6. For references to previous literature on return, including memoirs by returnees, see Ellen Oxfeld and Lynellyn Long, "Introduction," in *Coming Home? Refugees, Migrants, and Those Who Stayed Behind*, ed. Ellen Oxfeld and Lynellyn Long (Philadelphia: University of Pennsylvania Press, 2004).

7. See Donald Nonini and Aihwa Ong, "Chinese Transnationalism as an Alternative Modernity," in *Ungrounded Empires: The Cultural Politics of Modern Chinese Transnationalism,* ed. Donald Nonini and Aihwa Ong (New York: Routledge, 1997); Ronald Skeldon, "The Last Half Century of Chinese Overseas (1945–1994): Comparative Perspectives," *International Migration Review* 29, no. 2 (Summer 1995): 576–79.

8. See Arjun Appadurai, "Disjuncture and Difference in the Global Cultural Economy," *Public Culture* 2, no. 2 (1990): 1–21; James Clifford, "Diasporas,"

Cultural Anthropology 9, no. 3 (1994): 302–38; Linda N. Basch, Nina Glick Schiller, and Christina Szanton Blanc, *Nations Unbound: Transnational Projects, Postcolonial Predicaments, and Deterritorialized Nation-States* (Langhorne, Pa.: Gordon and Breach, 1994); and Nonini and Ong, *Ungrounded Empires,* for discussions of diaspora and transnationalism in terms of the contemporary global economy.

9. Prasenjit Duara, "Nationalists among Transnationals: Overseas Chinese and the Idea of China, 1900–1911," in *Ungrounded Empires: The Cultural Politics of Modern Chinese Transnationalism,* ed. Donald Nonini and Aihwa Ong (New York: Routledge, 1997), 43.

10. Duara, "Nationalists among Transnationals," 42.

11. Yuen-Fong Woon, "An Emigrant Community," 276.

12. Gungwu Wang, "South China Perspectives on Overseas Chinese," *The Australian Journal of Chinese Affairs* no. 13 (January 1985): 69–84, 72.

13. *Mei County Gazetteer,* 1078.

14. See Yuen-Fong Woon, "An Emigrant Community."

15. Godley, "The Sojourners," 333.

16. *Mei County Gazetteer,* 1095.

17. Ibid., 1096.

18. Godley, "The Sojourners."

19. Godley, "The Sojourners"; Yuen-Fong Woon, "Social Change and Continuity."

20. *Mei County Gazetteer,* 1096.

21. Ibid., 1096.

22. Mayfair Yang, *Gifts, Favors and Banquets: The Art of Social Relationships in China* (Ithaca, N.Y.: Cornell University Press, 1994); Yunxiang Yan, *The Flow of Gifts: Reciprocity and Social Networks in a Chinese Village* (Stanford, Calif.: Stanford University Press, 1996); Andrew Kipnis, *Producing Guanxi: Sentiment, Self, and Subculture in a North China Village* (Durham, N.C.: Duke University Press, 1997); You-tien Hsing, "Producing *Guanxi* across the Straits: Taiwanese Capital and Local Chinese Bureaucrats," in *Ungrounded Empires: The Cultural Politics of Modern Chinese Transnationalism,* ed. Donald Nonini and Aihwa Ong (New York: Routledge, 1997).

23. *Mei County Gazetteer,* 84.

24. The primary school in Moonshadow Pond was closed in 2005 due to lower numbers of school-age students (a result of the birth limitation policy). Students in Moonshadow Pond now attend either the primary school in the other village that comprises the administrative district or they must go to the township seat, where there is also a primary school.

25. See Chad Hansen, "Freedom and Moral Responsibility in Confucian Ethics," *Philosophy East and West* 22, no. 2 (1972): 169–82.

26. Hok Bun Ku found a similar phenomenon in the Hakka village he studied and noted that in cases of "instrumental *guanxi*" both the giver and the receiver are negatively evaluated (Hok Bun Ku, *Moral Politics in a South Chinese Village* [Lanham, Md.: Rowman and Littlefield, 2003], 48).

27. Charles Stafford, "Introduction: The Separation Constraint in China," in *Living with Separation in China,* ed. Charles Stafford (London: Routledge, 2003), 7.

28. Ann Anagnost, "Prosperity and Counterprosperity: The Moral Discourse on Wealth in Post-Mao China," in *Marxism and the Chinese Experience,* ed. Arlif Dirlik and Maurice Meisner (Armonk, N.Y.: M. E. Sharpe, 1989).

29. Mayfair Yang, *Gifts, Favors, and Banquets,* 113.

30. In the kula exchange, men participate in exchange networks that trade shell armbands and necklaces. The worth of these objects is accumulated in the identities of previous owners and they cease being valuable if they are ever taken out of the exchange network permanently. See Annette Weiner, *The Trobrianders of Papua, New Guinea* (New York: Holt, Rinehart and Winston, 1988).

31. See Arjun Appadurai, "Disjuncture and Difference in the Global Cultural Economy," in *Modernity at Large: Global Dimensions of Globalization* (Minneapolis: University of Minnesota Press, 1996); and Basch et al., *Nations Unbound.*

32. See James Watson, *Golden Arches East: McDonald's in East Asia* (Berkeley: University of California Press, 1997), on localizing the global.

33. See Eriberto Lozada, *God Aboveground: Catholic Church, Postsocialist State, and Transnational Processes in a Chinese Village* (Stanford, Calif.: Stanford University Press), for an interesting account of how state structures are supported by the practitioners of a transnational religion in a Catholic village in Meixian. In this case, state cadres are well represented at important Catholic ceremonies, such as the opening of a new church in the village. The very process of gaining legitimacy in the eyes of the state by gaining official recognition adds to the state's legitimacy.

34. The return of Gary Locke, former governor of the state of Washington, to his ancestors' village in China is quite interesting in this regard. Locke is a fifth-generation Chinese-American who returned to his ancestral village in the late 1990s. After visiting his ancestors' graves, he was treated to an overwhelming reception and parade. The villagers who were interviewed obviously took great pride in his achievements and pointed out that wherever he went he would always be "one of us" (Rachel Zimmerman, "Chinese Village Swells with Pride as Washington Governor Seeks His Roots on a Pilgrimage," *New York Times,* October 12, 1997).

6. PROPERTY RIGHTS AND WRONGS

1. According to Sally Sargeson, "National laws stipulate that villagers' collectively owned land can only be requisitioned by governments if requisitioning is in 'the public interest.' That caveat offers even less protection in China's transitional economy than it might elsewhere, because governments not only monopolize the transfer of land onto the market, but also own real estate, construction, and industrial ventures, provide public infrastructure, and are major employers. Thus, the entrepreneurial interests of governments are easily conflated with 'the public interest' " (Sally Sargeson, "Full Circle? Rural Land Reforms in Globalizing China," *Critical Asian Studies* 36, no. 4 [2004]: 644). Sargeson goes on to point out that gaining access to such land gives local governments more tax revenue, hence motivating them to foreclose on peasants. As she states, "Lower-level governments earned hundreds of billions of yuan in profit from the taxation and sale of land leases. Escalating fiscal pressure on local budgets in the

late 1990s further increased governments' reliance on land enclosure as a source of revenue" (644).

2. Minnie Chan, "Villagers Order Fujianese to Leave Store They Say Is on Their Farmland: Shopowners Hounded by Locals," *South China Morning Post,* May 14, 2007.

3. Minnie Chan, "Careless Mistake by Officials Nearly Costs Pensioner His Life," *South China Morning Post,* February 4, 2007. Also see Siew Ying Lee, "Learning from Hong Kong to Resolve Land Disputes," *South China Morning Post,* February 4, 2007.

4. Xiaolin Pei, "The Contribution of Collective Land Ownership to China's Economic Transition and Rural Industrialization," *Modern China* 28, no. 1 (2002): 287.

5. Loren Brandt, Ji Kun Huang, Guo Li, and Scott Rozelle, "Land Rights in Rural China: Facts, Fictions and Issues," *The China Journal,* no. 47 (2002): 73.

6. Laurel Bossen, *Chinese Women and Rural Development* (Lanham, Md.: Rowman and Littlefield, 2002); Brandt et al., "Land Rights in Rural China."

7. Although rules regulating the transfer of use rights in the land have become even more lenient since my research took place in Moonshadow Pond, village farmland is still not "private" in the sense that the ownership of the land itself, as opposed to rights to use it, can be permanently transferred away from the collective.

8. Jean Oi and Andrew Walder, "Property Rights in the Chinese Economy: Contours of the Process of Change," in *Property Rights and Economic Reform in China,* eds. Jean Oi and Andrew Walder (Stanford, Calif.: Stanford University Press, 1999), 5.

9. Patricia Ewick and Susan Silbey, *The Common Place of Law* (Chicago: University of Chicago Press, 1998), 40.

10. Ibid., 57.

11. Ibid.

12. Jack Potter and Sulamith Heins Potter, *China's Peasants: The Anthropology of a Revolution* (Cambridge: Cambridge University Press, 1990), 43.

13. Reading accounts of this movement, it is surprising how similar the stories appear, although they originate from disparate parts of the country. These accounts are numerous. A few notable ones are Potter and Potter, *China's Peasants;* William Hinton, *Fanshen: A Documentary of Revolution in a Chinese Village* (New York: Vintage, 1966); Shu-min Huang, *The Spiral Road: Change in a Chinese Village through the Eyes of a Communist Party Leader* (Boulder, Colo.: Westview Press, 1966); Helen Siu, *Agents and Victims in South China: Accomplices in Rural Revolution* (New Haven, Conn.: Yale University Press, 1989).

14. In Moonshadow Pond, as throughout China, these categories literally became inheritable identities, passed down patrilineally. After collectivization these categories no longer had any real relationship to the individual's role in production. Yet they were used as the basis for granting or denying privileges to many individuals until they were rendered illegal in 1978.

15. In addition, there were 1,462 households categorized as rich peasants, 1,024 households categorized as merchants, and 639 households categorized as workers or artisans. See *Mei County Gazetteer,* 239–40.

16. James Watson, "Hereditary Tenancy and Corporate Landlordism in Tra-

ditional China: A Case Study," in *Village Life in Hong Kong: Politics, Gender, and Ritual in the New Territories,* eds. James Watson and Rubie Watson (Hong Kong: Chinese University Press, 2004), 150.

17. *Mei County Gazetteer,* 240.

18. Helen Siu describes a similar attack on estate managers in rural Guangdong. She says, "To avoid implicating and alienating a vast number of people, the cadres were instructed to single out the estate managers, who were often the most influential figures on the local scene. Branded as 'ancestral hall termites' . . . they were accused of embezzling lineage funds and using them for usurious purposes" (Siu, *Agents and Victims in South China: Accomplices in Rural Revolution* [New Haven, Conn.: Yale University Press, 1989], 128).

19. See Dali Yang, *Calamity and Reform in China: State, Rural Society, and Institutional Change since the Great Leap Forward* (Stanford, Calif.: Stanford University Press, 1996), for a particularly solid account of this period.

20. See Dali Yang, *Calamity and Reform in China,* for a good summary of the effects of Great Leap policy on the Chinese countryside.

21. See *Constitution of the People's Republic of China,* 1993 (available at www.qis.net/chinalaw); also see *Law of Land Administration of the People's Republic of China,* 1998 (available at www.chnlaw.com).

22. These six types were *shuitian* (irrigated paddy land), *qiu di* (for other grains besides rice), *han di* (so-called dry land suitable for some crops such as fruit trees), *ziliu di* (the private plots families had already cultivated for their own vegetables since the end of the Great Leap era), *kaihuang di* (wasteland that no one cultivated), and finally *zhuliao di* (pig-feed land).

23. *Zerentian chengbao hetongshu,* 1984, Meixian Shi, Chengbei Qu, Zheshang Xiang, and Xiaping Shengchandui.

24. Bossen, *Chinese Women and Rural Development,* 97.

25. In the upper village this land was dealt with differently and was subdivided amongst each family.

26. Brandt et al., "Land Rights in Rural China."

27. Ibid., 79.

28. See Daniel Kelliher, *Peasant Power in China: The Era of Rural Reform, 1979–1989* (New Haven, Conn.: Yale University Press, 1992), 183–84, for a discussion of the political implications of this issue.

29. See Irene Eng and Yi-min Lin, "Religious Festivities, Communal Rivalry, and Restructuring of Authority Relations in Rural Chaozhou, Southeast China," *Journal of Asian Studies* 61, no. 4 (2002): 1259–86, for a discussion of the role of elders' councils in the fluorescence of popular religious rituals in contemporary rural Guangdong.

30. Says Daniel Kelliher, "Contracts at first restricted rights of alienation. . . . Yet peasants learned almost instantly to commit all these forbidden acts with their contracted land. They leased it, rented it, and sold it. They built homes on it, hired labor to work on it, and used it as security for loans. . . . Within a few years peasants with no more legal title to their farms than a temporary usufruct contract possessed virtually permanent claims on the land. They even gained the right to bequeath the family farm to their children. By the mid-1980s, central

leaders . . . condoned the quick evolution toward a nearly private system of land tenure" (Kelliher, *Peasant Power in China,* 178).

31. See Maureen Fan, "China to Allow Land Leasing, Transfer," *Washington Post,* October 20, 2008.

32. See Yan Yunxiang's description of a bookkeeper, "Calculability and Budgeting in a Household Economy: A Case Study from Rural North China," *Taiwan Journal of Anthropology* 2, no. 1 (2004): 69–92; and Suzanne Brandtstädter's analysis of the transmission of "know-how" in a Fujianese village, "Money Plucked from the Sky: Shrimp Farming, Entrepreneurship, and the Circulation of Know-How in a Fujian Village," *Taiwan Journal of Anthropology* 2, no. 1 (2004): 41–68.

33. Sargeson, "Full Circle," 644.

7. "MONEY CAUSES TROUBLE"

1. Mark Elvin, *The Pattern of the Chinese Past* (Stanford, Calif.: Stanford University Press, 1973), 106.

2. Ibid., 167.

3. Hill Gates, "Money for the Gods," *Modern China* 13, no. 2 (1987): 261.

4. Jonathan Parry, "Introduction," in *Money and the Morality of Exchange,* ed. Jonathan Parry and Maurice Bloch (Cambridge: Cambridge University Press, 1989), 24.

5. Ibid., 26.

6. James L. Watson, "Hereditary Tenancy and Corporate Landlordism in Traditional China," in *Village Life in Hong Kong: Politics, Gender, and Ritual in the New Territories* (Hong Kong: Chinese University Press, 2004), 157–58.

7. Hok Bun Ku describes the revival of lineage rituals and refurbishment of a lineage hall in another Hakka village in Guangdong in *Moral Politics in a South Chinese Village* (Lanham, Md.: Rowman and Littlefield, 2003), 217. Ku also points out that this same phenomenon has been reported by many other ethnographers, including Stephen Feuchtwang, "Religion as Resistance," in *Chinese Society: Change, Conflict and Resistance,* ed. Elizabeth Perry and Mark Seldon (New York: Routledge, 2000), 161–77; Helen Siu, "Recycling Rituals: Politics and Popular Culture in Contemporary Rural China," in *Unofficial China: Popular Culture and Thought in the People's Republic,* ed. Perry Link, Richard Madsen, and Paul Pickowicz (Boulder, Colo.: Westview Press, 1989), 121–37; and Sulamith Heins Potter and Jack Potter, *China's Peasants: The Anthropology of a Revolution* (Cambridge: Cambridge University Press, 1990).

8. A *jin* is equal to half a kilogram and is divided into ten *liang.*

9. See for instance Dorothy Solinger's book *Contesting Citizenship in Urban China: Peasant Migrants, the States, and the Logic of Market* (Berkeley: University of California Press, 1999). Many analysts contend that these rural migrants have "second class" status because they don't have the same access to public services as urban residents. See a discussion in Xiaogang Wu and Donald Treiman, "The Household Registration System and Social Stratification in China: 1955–1996," *Demography* 41, no. 2 (May 2004): 363–84.

10. George M. Foster, "Peasant Society and the Image of the Limited Good," in *American Anthropologist*, new series 67, no. 2 (April 1965): 301.

11. Ibid., 303.

12. Jonathan Unger, *The Transformation of Rural China* (Armonk, N.Y.: M. E. Sharpe, 2002), 29–48.

13. Ibid.

14. Yan Hairong, "Spectralization of the Rural: Reinterpreting the Labor Mobility of Rural Young Women in Post-Mao China," *American Ethnologist* 30, no. 4 (November 2003): 578–96.

15. For an example of the discussion of the rural-urban income disparity in reform China, see Shaoguang Wang, "The Social and Political Implications of China's WTO Membership," *Journal of Contemporary China* 9, no. 25 (2000): 373–405; and Carl Riskin, Renwei Zhao, and Shi Li, eds., *China's Retreat from Equality* (Armonk, N.Y.: M. E. Sharpe, 2001).

16. All brigades *(dadui)* had five officers, and this system continues today, even though the former brigades are not called administrative districts *(guanliqu)*. The officers of the brigades were, and continue to be, a general secretary of the party, a brigade head, an accountant, a women's affairs officer, and a security head.

17. Hok Bun Ku, *Moral Politics in a South Chinese Village* (Lanham, Md.: Rowman and Littlefield, 2003), 147.

18. M. M. Bakhtin, "The Problem of Speech Genres," in *Speech Genres and Other Late Essays,* trans. Vern McGee, ed. Caryl Emerson and Michael Holquist (Austin: University of Texas Press, 1986), 94.

19. Pierre Bourdieu, *Distinction: A Social Critique of the Judgment of Taste,* trans. Richard Nice (Cambridge: Cambridge University Press, 1984), 374.

20. Yunxiang Yan, "The Impact of Rural Reform on Economic and Social Stratification in a Chinese Village," *Australian Journal of Chinese Affairs,* no. 27 (January 1992): 11.

21. Tuulikki Pietilä, *Gossip, Markets and Gender: How Dialogue Constructs Moral Value in Post-Socialist Kilimanjaro* (Madison: University of Wisconsin Press, 2006), 12.

CONCLUSION

1. James Laidlaw, "For an Anthropology of Ethics and Freedom," *Journal of the Royal Anthropological Institute* 8 (2002): 311–22.

2. Quoted in Liu Binyan and Perry Link, "A Great Leap Backward?" *New York Review of Books* 45, no. 5 (October 8, 1998).

3. Ibid.

4. Patricia Thornton, *Disciplining the State: Virtue, Violence, and State-Making in Modern China* (Honolulu: University of Hawai'i Press, 2007), 4.

5. Ibid., 20.

6. "Application for social benefits and special aid by parents whose children died in the 'May 12th' earthquake," http://graphics8.nytimes.com/packages/pdf/world/2008/07/24/24China_doc_contract.pdf.

7. Ibid.

8. See Sue Williams, *China in Revolution,* part 3, "Born under the Red Flag:

Surviving Mao" (Ambrica Productions in Association with WGBH Boston and Channel 4 Television UK, 1997).

9. See in particular an extended discussion of this in Richard A. Shweder, Manamohan Mahapatra, and Joan G. Miller, "Culture and Moral Development," in *The Emergence of Morality in Young Children,* ed. Jerome Kagan and Sharon Lamb (Chicago: University of Chicago Press, 1987).

10. There have been four worldwide conferences on "Hakkaology," the last two taking place in Taiwan (1998) and Hong Kong (1994). Additionally, conferences focused on Hakka culture also convened in Toronto, Canada, in 2004 and 2008.

Chinese Character Glossary

aizhang 哀章
baichan 拜忏
bao 报
bashan, yishui, yitian 八山, 一水,
　一天
bayin 八音
binü 婢女
bu wenming 不文明
bu zhi xiuchi 不知羞耻
chabuduo 差不多
chi ku 吃苦
dadui 大队
da gui suanpan 打鬼算盘
da men 大门
dan 担
danwei 单位
daotou ma 倒头妈
denglang mei 等郎妹
dianzhang 奠章
enqing 恩情
fang 房
feipin 废品
fengshui 风水
fubai 腐败
gan nu'er, gan erzi 干女儿, 干儿子
ganqing polie 感情破裂
gen 根

gongde 功德
Gong Wang 公王
guang zhong qu, an zhong zhuan
　光中去, 暗中转
guanliqu 管理区
guanxi 关系
Guanyin 观音
haisheng bu xiaoshun, sihou hong
　guishen 还生不孝顺, 死后哄
　鬼神
haiwai qiaobao 海外侨胞
han di 旱地
hen si 恨死
hongbao 红包
huadun mei 花顿妹
Huaqiao 华侨
Huaren 华人
Huayi 华裔
hukou 户口
jiao 角
jiefang 解放
jie ru wei 借乳喂
jieshao 介绍
jin 斤
jiuming enren 救命恩人
jiu shehui 旧社会
jiuxi 酒席

ju sha cheng ta 聚砂成塔
kaihuang di 开荒地
laorenhui 老人会
lengqing 冷清
lian 脸
lianai 恋爱
liang 量
liangshi bumen 粮食部门
liangxin 良心
long gu 峇谷
Longshen 龙神
longyan 龙眼
mai lu 买路
M di xiu (Hakka) 唔知羞
mei you liyou 没有理由
mianzi 面子
mixin 迷信
mu 亩
nanba zhuanqian, mama gengtian 男芭赚钱, 妈妈耕田
ni shenti hao ma? 你身体好吗?
ni you xin 你有心
nongmin 农民
nongren 农人
nuanfu 暖福
po si jiu 破四旧
qifu 起福
Qiao Baigong 桥伯公
qinqi 亲戚
qiu di 秋地
quanshi wen 劝事文
qu xifu 娶媳妇
renao 热闹
rende yishi zhi qi, miande baitian zhi you 认得一时之气, 免得百日之忧
ren qian, bu ren ren 认钱, 不认人
ren qi liu cai, shou qi de fu 忍气留财, 受气得福
renqing 人情
sanjiu ku 三救苦
sengjia dizi 僧家弟子
shan guan rending, shui guan cai 山官人丁, 水官财
Sheguan Laoye 社官老爷

shi shui yao nian shui yuantou 食水要念水源头
shili gui 事利鬼
shou ren de qi 受人的气
shuitian 水田
shuizhong bing 水肿病
sixiang gongzuo 思想工作
sujia dizi 俗家弟子
tai ai mianzi 太爱面子
tanwu 贪污
tanxu rongxin 贪虚荣心
t'au sim k'iu (Hakka) 讨心舅
Tushen Baigong 土神伯公
wanfu 完福
wei ren you ji 为仁由己
xiang yi qian 香仪钱
xiao 孝
xin 心
xinli zhidao 心理知道
xisheng 牺牲
xiuxin 修心
xuanchuan 宣传
yang 扬
yin shui si yuan 饮水思源
you ming dengyu ling 有名等于零
you qian zuo guai 有钱作怪
you ren you qian 有人有钱
yuan 元
yue qin yue jian gui 越亲越见鬼
yumei 愚昧
zeren 责任
zhenjing 真经
zhongdeng 中等
zhuidao hui 追悼会
zhuliao di 猪料地
ziji ren 自己人
zi li geng sheng, jian ku fen dou 自力更生, 艰苦奋斗
ziliu di 自留地
zongjiao 宗教
zuo fo shi 做佛事
zuo haoshi 做好事
zuo ren 做人
zuo sang shi 做丧事
zupu 族谱

References

Abu-Lughod, Lila. 1986. *Veiled Sentiments*. Berkeley: University of California Press.

Ahern, Emily. 1973. *The Cult of the Dead in a Chinese Village*. Stanford, Calif.: Stanford University Press.

———. 1975. "The Power and Pollution of Chinese Women." In *Women in Chinese Society*, edited by Margery Wolf and Roxane Witke, 193–204. Stanford, Calif.: Stanford University Press.

Aijmer, Goran. 1994. "Burial, Ancestors, and Geomancy among the Ma On Shan Hakka, New Territories of Hong Kong." In *Guoji kejiaxue yantaohui lunwen ji/ The Proceedings of the International Conference on Hakkaology*, edited by Xie Jian and Zheng Chiyan, 357–72. Hong Kong: Xianggang Zhongwen Daxue, Xianggang Ya Tai Yanjiusuo, Haiwai Huaren Yanjiushe.

Allen, Sarah. 1997. *The Way of Water, and Sprouts of Virtue*. Albany: SUNY Press.

Anagnost, Ann. 1989. "Prosperity and Counterprosperity: The Moral Discourse on Wealth in Post-Mao China." In *Marxism and the Chinese Experience*, edited by Arlif Dirlik and Maurice Meisner, 210–34. Armonk, N.Y.: M. E. Sharpe.

———. 1994. "The Politics of Ritual Displacement." In *Asian Visions of Authority: Religion and the Modern States of East and Southeast Asia*, edited by Charles F. Keyes, Laurel Kendall, and Helen Hardacre, 221–54. Honolulu: University of Hawai'i Press.

Appadurai, Arjun. 1990. "Disjuncture and Difference in the Global Cultural Economy." *Public Culture* 2 (2): 1–21.

Baker, Hugh. 1979. *Chinese Family and Kinship*. New York: Columbia University Press.

Bakhtin, M. M. 1986. "The Problem of Speech Genres." In *Speech Genres and Other Late Essays,* translated by Vern W. McGee, edited by Caryl Emerson and Michael Holquist, 60–102. Austin: University of Texas Press.

Barker, John. 2007. "All Sides Now: The Postcolonial Triangle in Uiahu." In *The Anthropology of Morality in Melanesia and Beyond,* edited by John Barker, 75–92. Hampshire, UK: Ashgate.

Basch, Linda, Nina Glick Schiller, and Christina Szanton Blanc. 1994. *Nations Unbound: Transnational Projects, Postcolonial Predicaments, and Deterritorialized Nation-States.* Langhorne, Pa.: Gordon and Breach.

Beaver, Patricia, Lihui Hou, and Xue Wang. 1995. "Rural Chinese Women: Two Faces of Economic Reform in China." *Modern China* 21 (2): 205–32.

Blake, C. Fred. 1981. *Ethnic Groups and Social Change in a Chinese Market Town.* Honolulu: University of Hawai'i Press.

Bossen, Laurel. 2002. *Chinese Women and Rural Development.* Lanham, Md.: Rowman and Littlefield.

Bourdieu, Pierre. 1984. *Distinction: A Social Critique of the Judgment of Taste.* Translated by Richard Nice. Cambridge, Mass.: Harvard University Press.

———. 1990. *The Logic of Practice.* Translated by Richard Nice. Cambridge: Polity Press.

Brandes, Stanley. 1987. "Like Wounded Stags: Male Sexual Ideology in an Andalusian Town." In *Sexual Meanings,* edited by Sherry Ortner and Harriet Whitehead, 216–39. Cambridge: Cambridge University Press.

Brandt, Loren, Ji Kun Huang, Guo Li, and Scott Rozelle. 2002. "Land Rights in Rural China: Facts, Fictions and Issues." *China Journal* 47: 67–97.

Brandtstäder, Susanne. 2004. "Money Plucked from the Sky: Shrimp Farming, Entrepreneurship, and the Circulation of Know-How in a Fujian Village." *Taiwan Journal of Anthropology* 2, no. 1: 41–68.

Brenner, Suzanne. 1995. "Why Women Rule the Roost: Rethinking Javanese Ideologies of Gender and Self-Control." In *Bewitching Women, Pious Men: Gender and Body Politics in Southeast Asia,* edited by Michael Peletz and Aihwa Ong, 19–50. Berkeley: University of California Press.

Brokaw, Cynthia. 1991. *The Ledgers of Merit and Demerit: Social Change and Moral Order in Late Imperial China.* Princeton, N.J.: Princeton University Press.

Brook, Timothy. 1989. "Funerary Ritual and the Building of Lineages in Late Imperial China." *Harvard Journal of Asiatic Studies* 49, no. 2: 465–99.

Chan, Anita. 1985. *Children of Mao.* Seattle: University of Washington Press.

Chan, Minnie. 2007a. "Villagers Order Fujianese to Leave Store They Say Is on Their Farmland: Shopowners Hounded by Locals." *South China Morning Post,* Monday, May 14, 2007.

———. 2007b. "Careless Mistake by Officials Nearly Costs Pensioner His Life." *South China Morning Post,* February 4, 2007.

Chau, Adam Yuet. 2001. "The Dragon King Valley: Popular Religion, Socialist State, and Agrarian Society in Shaanbei, North-Central China." PhD diss., Stanford University.

———. 2006. *Miraculous Response: Doing Popular Religion in Contemporary China.* Stanford, Calif.: Stanford University Press.

Chen, Ta. 1940. *Emigrant Communities in South China: A Study of Overseas Chinese Migration and Its Influence on Standards of Living and Social Change.* New York: Institute of Pacific Relations.

Cheng, Shui-cheng. 1994. "Music of the Hakka in Taiwan." In *Guoji kejiaxue yantaohui lunwen ji/The Proceedings of the International Conference on Hakkaology*, edited by Xie Jian and Zheng Chiyan, 399–406. Hong Kong: Xianggang Zhongwen Daxue, Xianggang Ya Tai Yanjiusuo, Haiwai Huaren Yanjiushe.

Chengbeixiang ge guanliqu zhuyao jiben qingkuang (成北乡各管理区主要基本情况). 1997, 2007.

China Data Online: Zhongguo Shu Ju Zai Xian (中国数据再现). 2002. China: All China Marketing Research Co.

Ci, Jiwei. 1994. *Dialectic of the Chinese Revolution: From Utopianism to Hedonism*. Stanford, Calif.: Stanford University Press.

Clifford, James. 1994. "Diasporas." *Cultural Anthropology* 9, no. 3: 302–38.

Cohen, Myron. 1976. *House United, House Divided*. New York: Columbia University Press.

———. 1988. "Souls and Salvation: Conflicting Themes in Chinese Popular Religion." In *Death Ritual in Late Imperial and Modern China*, edited by James L. Watson and Evelyn Rawski, 180–202. Berkeley: University of California Press.

———. 1996. "The Hakka or 'Guest People': Dialect as a Sociocultural Variable in Southeast China." In *Guest People: Hakka Identity in China and Abroad*, edited by Nicole Constable, 36–79. Seattle: Seattle University Press.

Cole, Alan. 1998. *Mothers and Sons in Chinese Buddhism*. Stanford, Calif.: Stanford University Press.

Constable, Nicole, ed. 1996. *Guest People: Hakka Identity in China and Abroad*. Seattle: University of Washington Press.

Constitution of the People's Republic of China. 1993. (Adopted at the Fifth National People's Congress and amended at the First Session of the Seventh National People's Congress on March 29, 1993.) Available at www.qis.net/chinalaw.

Davis, Deborah, and Steven Harrell. 1993. "Introduction: The Impact of Post-Mao Reforms on Family Life." In *Chinese Families in the Post-Mao Era*, edited by Deborah Davis and Steven Harrell, 1–24. Berkeley: University of California Press.

Davis, Edward L. 2001. *Society and the Supernatural in Song China*. Honolulu: University of Hawai'i Press.

Diamant, Neil. 2000. "Re-examining the Impact of the 1950 Marriage Law: State Improvisation, Local Initiative and Rural Family Change." *China Quarterly* 161 (March): 171–98.

Donald, Stephanie Hemelryk, and Robert Benewick. 2005. *The State of China Atlas*. Berkeley: University of California Press.

Doolittle, Justus. 1865. *Social Life of the Chinese with Some Account of Their Religious, Governmental, Educational, and Business Customs and Opinions, with Special but Not Exclusive Reference to Fuhchau*. New York: Harper.

Duara, Prasenjit. 1991. "Knowledge and Power in the Discourse of Modernity: The Campaigns against Popular Religion in Early Twentieth-Century China." *Journal of Asian Studies* 50, no. 1: 67–83.

———. 1997. "Nationalists among Transnationals: Overseas Chinese and the Idea of China, 1900–1911." In *Ungrounded Empires*, edited by Donald Nonini and Aihwa Ong, 39–60. New York: Routledge.

Dumont, Louis. 1980. *Homo Hierarchicus: The Caste System and Its Implications*. Chicago: University of Chicago Press.

Ebrey, Patricia. 1991a. *Confucianism and Family Rituals in Imperial China*. Princeton, N.J.: Princeton University Press.

———. 1991b. "Introduction." *Marriage and Inequality in Chinese Society*, edited by Rubie Watson and Patricia Ebrey, 1–24. Berkeley: University of California Press.

Elvin, Mark. 1973. *The Pattern of the Chinese Past*. Stanford, Calif.: Stanford University Press.

Eng, Irene, and Yi-min Lin. 2002. "Religious Festivities, Communal Rivalry, and Restructuring of Authority Relations in Rural Chaozhou, Southeast China." *Journal of Asian Studies* 61, no. 4: 1259–86.

Ewick, Patricia, and Susan Silbey. 1998. *The Common Place of Law*. Chicago: University of Chicago Press.

Fang Xuejia. 1994. *Kejia yuanliu tan ao* (客家源流探奥) [The mystery of the origin of the Hakka]. Guangdong: Gaodeng jiaoyu chubanshe.

———, ed. 1997. *Meizhou heyuan diqu de cunluo wenhua* (梅州河源地区的村落文化)/*Village Religion and Culture in Northeastern Guangdong*. Traditional Hakka Society Series, no. 5. International Hakka Studies Association. Overseas Chinese Archives. Paris: École française d'Extrême-Orient.

Fei, Xiaotong. 1992. *From the Soil: The Foundations of Chinese Society*. Translated by Gary Hamilton and Wang Zheng. Berkeley: University of California Press.

Feuchtwang, Stephen. 1974. *An Anthropological Analysis of Chinese Geomancy*. Vientiane, Laos: Vithagna.

———. 2000. "Religion as Resistance." In *Chinese Society: Change, Conflict and Resistance*, edited by Elizabeth Perry and Mark Seldon, 161–77. New York: Routledge.

Fiske, Alan. 1990. "Relativity within Moose ('Mossi') Culture: Four Incommensurable Models for Social Relationships." *Ethos* 18, no. 2: 180–204.

Foster, George M. 1965. "Peasant Society and the Image of the Limited Good." *American Anthropologist*, new series 67, no. 2 (April): 293–315.

Freedman, Maurice. 1958. *Lineage Organization in Southeastern China*. London: Athlone Press.

Friedman, Sara. 2005. "The Intimacy of State Power: Marriage, Liberation, and Socialist Subjects in Southeastern China." *American Ethnologist* 32, no. 2: 312–72.

Gates, Hill. 1996. *China's Motor: A Thousand Years of Petty Capitalism*. Ithaca, N.Y.: Cornell University Press.

———. 1987. "Money for the Gods." *Modern China* 13, no. 2: 259–77.

Gert, Bernard. 1998. *Morality: Its Nature and Justification*. Oxford: Oxford University Press.

Giddens, Anthony. 1990. *The Consequences of Modernity*. Stanford, Calif.: Stanford University Press.

Godley, Michael. 1989. "The Sojourners: Returned Overseas Chinese in the People's Republic of China." *Pacific Affairs* 62, no. 3: 330–52.

Gordon, Richard, and Carma Hinton. 1995. "The Gate of Heavenly Peace" [video-recoding]. Brookline, Mass.: Long Bow Group, in association with Independent Television Service.

Groot, J. J. M. de. 1885. "Buddhist Masses for the Dead at Amoy: An Ethnological Essay." In *Actes du Sixième Congrès International des Orientalistes* [Proceedings from the Sixth International Meeting of Orientalists]. Part. 4, sec. 4. Leiden, Netherlands: E. J. Brill.

————. 1892/1989. *The Religious System of China.* Vol. 1. Taipei, Taiwan: Southern Materials Center.

Guangdong Statistical Yearbook. 2006. www.gdstats.gov.cn/tjnj/ml_e.htm.

Hamilton, Gary, and Wang Zheng. 1992. "Introduction: Fei Xiaotong and the Beginnings of a Chinese Sociology." In *From the Soil: The Foundations of Chinese Society,* Xiaotong Fei. Translated by Gary Hamilton and Wang Zheng, 1–36. Berkeley: University of California Press.

Hansen, Chad. 1972. "Freedom and Moral Responsibility in Confucian Ethics." *Philosophy East and West* 22, no. 2: 169–82.

Hinton, William. 1966. *Fanshen: A Documentary of Revolution in a Chinese Village.* New York: Vintage.

Hobsbawm, Eric, and Terence Ranger, eds. 1984. *The Invention of Tradition.* Cambridge: Cambridge University Press.

Hsing, You-tien. 1997. "Building Guanxi across the Straits: Taiwanese Capital and Local Chinese Bureaucrats." In *Ungrounded Empires: The Cultural Politics of Modern Chinese Transnationalism,* edited by Donald Nonini and Aihwa Ong, 143–66. New York: Routledge.

Hsu, Madeleine. 1995. "Living Abroad and Faring Well: Migration and Transnationalism in Taishan County, Guangdong, 1904–1939." PhD diss., Yale University.

Hu, H. C. 1944. "The Chinese Concepts of 'Face.'" *American Anthropologist* 46: 45–64.

Huang, Shu-min. 1998. *The Spiral Road: Change in a Chinese Village through the Eyes of a Communist Party Leader.* Boulder, Colo.: Westview Press.

Humphrey, Caroline. 1997. "Exemplars and Rules: Aspects of the Discourse of Moralities." In *The Ethnography of Moralities,* edited by Signe Howell, 25–48. London: Routledge.

Hwang, Kwang-Kuo. 1998. "Two Moralities: Reinterpreting the Findings of the Empirical Research on Moral Reasoning in Taiwan." *Asian Journal of Social Psychology* 1: 211–38.

Jacka, Tamara. 1997. *Women's Work in Rural China.* Cambridge: Cambridge University Press.

Jing, Jun. 1996. *The Temple of Memories: History, Power, and Morality in a Chinese Village.* Stanford, Calif.: Stanford University Press.

————. 2004. "Meal Rotation and Filial Piety." In *Filial Piety,* edited by Charlotte Ikels, 53–62. Stanford, Calif.: Stanford University Press.

Johnson, Graham. 1993. "Family Strategies and Economic Transformation in Rural China: Some Evidence from the Pearl River Delta." In *Chinese Families in the Post-Mao Era,* edited by Deborah Davis and Stevan Harrell, 103–38. Stanford, Calif.: Stanford University Press.

Judd, Ellen. 1989. "*Niangjia*: Chinese Women and Their Natal Families." *Journal of Asian Studies* 48, no. 3: 525–44.

———. 1994. *Gender and Power in Rural North China*. Stanford, Calif.: Stanford University Press.

Juergensmeyer, Mark. 1980. "What If the Untouchables Don't Believe in Untouchability?" *Bulletin of Concerned Asian Scholars* 12, no. 1: 23–28.

Kelkar, Govind, and Yunxian Wang, 1997. "Farmers, Women, and Economic Reform in China." *Bulletin of Concerned Asian Scholars* 29, no. 4: 69–77.

Kelliher, Daniel. 1992. *Peasant Power in China: The Era of Rural Reform, 1979–1989*. New Haven, Conn.: Yale University Press.

King, Ambrose Yeo-chi. 1994. "Kuan-hsi and Network Building: A Sociological Interpretation." In *The Living Tree*, edited by Wei-ming Tu, 109–26. Stanford, Calif.: Stanford University Press.

Kipnis, Andrew. 1995a. " 'Face' An Adaptable Discourse of Social Surfaces." *Positions* 3, no. 1: 119–48.

———. 1995b. "Within and Against Peasantness: Backwardness and Filiality in Rural China." *Comparative Studies in Society and History* 37, no. 1: 110–35.

———. 1997. *Producing Guanxi: Sentiment, Self, and Subculture in a North China Village*. Durham, N.C.: Duke University Press.

Kleinman, Arthur. 1998. "Experience and Its Moral Modes: Culture, Human Conditions, and Disorder." The Tanner Lectures on Human Values. Stanford University, April 13–16.

Klima, Alan. 2002. *The Funeral Casino: Meditation, Massacre, and Exchange with the Dead in Thailand*. Princeton, N.J.: Princeton University Press.

Koontz, Claudia. 2003. *The Nazi Conscience*. Cambridge, Mass.: Harvard University Press.

Ku, Hok Bun. 2003. *Moral Politics in a South Chinese Village*. Lanham, Md.: Rowman and Littlefield.

Kutcher, Norman. 1999. *Mourning in Late Imperial China: Filial Piety and the State*. Cambridge: Cambridge University Press.

Lagerway, John. 1994. "Taoism among the Hakka in Fujian." In *Guoji kejiaxue yantaohui lunwen ji/The Proceedings of the International Conference on Hakkaology*, edited by Xie Jian and Zheng Chiyan. Hong Kong: Xianggang Zhongwen Daxue, Xianggang Ya Tai Yanjiusuo, Haiwai Huaren Yanjiushe.

Laidlaw, James. 2002. "For an Anthropology of Ethics and Freedom." *Journal of the Royal Anthropological Institute* 8: 311–32.

Lavely, William. 1991. "Marriage and Mobility under Rural Collectivism." In *Marriage and Inequality in Chinese Society*, edited by Patricia Ebrey and Rubie Watson, 286–312. Berkeley: University of California Press.

Law of Land Administration of the People's Republic of China. 1997. Revised and adopted at the Fourth Session of the Standing Committee of the Ninth National People's Congress of the People's Republic of China on August 29, 1998. Available at www.chnlaw.com.

Lee, Siew Ying. 2007. "Learning from Hong Kong to Resolve Land Disputes." *South China Morning Post*, February 4, 2007.

Leong, Sow-Theng. 1997. *Migration and Ethnicity in Chinese History: Hakka,*

Pengmin, and Their Neighbors, edited by Tim Wright. Stanford, Calif.: Stanford University Press.

Lever-Tracy, Constance, David Ip, and Noel Tracy. 1996. *The Chinese Diaspora and Mainland China: An Emerging Economic Synergy.* New York: St. Martin's.

Lévi-Strauss, Claude. 1969. *The Elementary Structures of Kinship.* Translated by James H. Bell, John R. von Sturmer, and Rodney Needham. Boston: Beacon.

Liu, Xin. 2000. *In One's Own Shadow: An Ethnographic Account of the Condition of Post-Reform China.* Berkeley: University of California Press.

———. 2002 *The Otherness of Self.* Ann Arbor: University of Michigan Press.

Lozada, Eriberto. 2001. *God Aboveground: Catholic Church, Postsocialist State, and Transnational Processes in a Chinese Village.* Stanford, Calif.: Stanford University Press.

Lynch, Daniel. 1999. *After the Propaganda State: Media, Politics, and 'Thought Work' in Reformed China.* Stanford, Calif.: Stanford University Press.

MacIntyre, Alasdair. 1981. *After Virtue.* South Bend, Ind.: University of Notre Dame Press.

Madsen, Richard. 1984. *Morality and Power in a Chinese Village.* Berkeley: University of California Press.

———. 1990. "The Politics of Revenge in Rural China during the Cultural Revolution." In *Violence in China: Essays in Culture and Counterculture,* edited by Jonathan Lipman and Steven Harrell, 203–26. Albany: SUNY Press.

"Marriage Law of the People's Republic of China." 1980. Adopted by the Fifth People's Congress at Its Third Session on September 10, 1980. Reprinted in "One Hundred Court Cases on Marriage." *Chinese Sociology and Anthropology* 18, nos. 1–2 (Fall–Winter 1985–86).

Martin, Emily. 1988. "Gender and Ideological Differences in Representations of Life and Death." In *Death Ritual in Late Imperial and Modern China,* edited by James L. Watson and Evelyn Rawski, 164–79. Berkeley: University of California Press.

Meixian Difangzhi Biansuan Weiyuanhui, ed. 1994. *Meixian Zhi* (梅县志) [Mei County Gazetteer]. Guangzhou, China: Guangdong Renmin Chubanshe.

Miller, Eric T. 2004. "Filial Daughters, Filial Sons: Comparisons from Rural North China. In *Filial Piety,* edited by Charlotte Ikels, 34–52. Stanford, Calif.: Stanford University Press.

Munro, Donald. 1985. "Introduction." In *Individualism and Holism: Studies in Confucian and Taoist Values,* edited by Donald Munro, 1–34. Ann Arbor: Center for Chinese Studies, University of Michigan.

Nonini, Donald, and Aihwa Ong, 1997. "Chinese Transnationalism as an Alternative Modernity." In *Ungrounded Empires,* edited by Donald Nonini and Aihwa Ong, 3–36. New York: Routledge.

Ocko, Jonathan. 1991. "Women, Property, and the Law in the People's Republic of China." In *Marriage and Inequality in Chinese Society,* edited by Rubie Watson and Patricia Ebrey, 313–46. Berkeley: University of California Press.

Oi, Jean, and Andrew Walder. 1997. "Property Rights in the Chinese Economy: Contours of the Process of Change." In *Property Rights and Economic Reform in China,* edited by Jean Oi and Andrew Walder, 1–26. Stanford, Calif.: Stanford University Press.

Oxfeld, Ellen. 1992. "Individualism, Holism, and the Market Mentality: Notes on the Recollections of a Chinese Entrepreneur." *Cultural Anthropology* 7, no. 3: 267–300.

———. 1993. *Blood, Sweat, and Mahjong: Family and Enterprise in an Overseas Chinese Community*. Ithaca, N.Y.: Cornell University Press.

———. 2004a. "Chinese Villagers and the Moral Dilemmas of Return Visits." In *Coming Home? Refugees, Immigrants and Those Who Stayed Behind*, edited by Lynellyn Long and Ellen Oxfeld. Philadelphia: University of Pennsylvania Press.

———. 2004b. " 'When You Drink Water, Think of Its Source': Morality, Status, and Reinvention in Rural Chinese Funerals." *Journal of Asian Studies* 63, no. 4: 961–90.

Pang, Lihua, Alan deBrauw, and Scott Rozelle. 2004. "Working Until You Drop: The Elderly of Rural China." *China Journal* 52: 73–96.

Parish, Steven. 1994. *Moral Knowing in a Hindu Sacred City: An Exploration of Mind, Emotion, and Self*. New York: Columbia University Press.

———. 1996. *Hierarchy and Its Discontents: Culture and the Politics of Consciousness in Caste Society*. Philadelphia: University of Pennsylvania Press.

Parry, Jonathan. 1989. "Introduction." In *Money and the Morality of Exchange*, edited by Jonathan Parry and Maurice Bloch, 1–32. Cambridge: Cambridge University Press.

Pei, Xiaolin. 2002. "The Contribution of Collective Land Ownership to China's Economic Transition and Rural Industrialization." *Modern China* 28, no. 1: 279–314.

Perry, Elizabeth. 1994. "Trends in the Study of Chinese Politics: State-Society Relations." *China Quarterly* 139: 704–13.

Pietilä, Tuulikki. 2006. *Gossip, Markets, and Gender: How Dialogue Constructs Moral Value in Post-Socialist Kilimanjaro*. Madison: University of Wisconsin Press.

Potter, Sulamith Heins, and Jack Potter. 1990. *China's Peasants: The Anthropology of a Revolution*. Cambridge: Cambridge University Press.

Riskin, Carl, Renwei Zhao, and Shi Li, eds. 2001. *China's Retreat from Equality*. Armonk, N.Y.: M. E. Sharpe.

Rivers, Julian Pitt. 1974. "Honour and Social Status." In *Honour and Shame: The Values of Mediterranean Society*, edited by J. G. Peristiany, 19–78. Chicago: University of Chicago Press.

Rofel, Lisa. 1999. *Other Modernities*. Berkeley: University of California Press.

Sangren, P. Steven. 1987. *History and Magical Power in a Chinese Community*. Stanford, Calif.: Stanford University Press.

———. 2000. *Chinese Sociologics*. London: Athlone Press.

Sargeson, Sally. 2004. "Full Circle? Rural Land Reforms in Globalizing China." *Critical Asian Studies* 36, no. 4: 637–56.

Seldon, Mark. 1993. "Family Strategies and Structures in Rural North China." In *Chinese Families in the Post-Mao Era*, edited by Deborah Davis and Steven Harrell, 139–65. Stanford, Calif.: Stanford University Press.

Shweder, Richard A., Manamohan Mahapatra, and Joan G. Miller. 1987. "Culture and Moral Development." In *The Emergence of Morality in Young Children,* edited by Jerome Kagan and Sharon Lamb, 1–82. Chicago: University of Chicago Press.

Siu, Helen. 1989a. "Recycling Rituals: Politics and Popular Culture in Contemporary Rural China." In *Unofficial China: Popular Culture and Thought in the People's Republic,* edited by Perry Link, Richard Madsen, and Paul Pickowicz, 121–37. Boulder, Colo.: Westview Press.

———. 1989b. *Agents and Victims in South China: Accomplices in Rural Revolution.* New Haven, Conn.: Yale University Press.

———. 1993. "Reconstituting Dowry and Brideprice in South China." In *Chinese Families in the Post-Mao Era,* edited by Deborah Davis and Steven Harrell, 165–88. Berkeley: University of California Press.

Skeldon, Ronald. 1995. "The Last Half Century of Chinese Overseas (1945–1994): Comparative Perspectives." *International Migration Review* 29, no. 2 (Summer): 576–79.

Skinner, G. William. 1971. "Chinese Peasants and the Closed Community: An Open and Shut Case." *Comparative Studies in Society and History* 13, no. 3: 270–81.

Stafford, Charles. 2000a. *Separation and Reunion in Modern China.* Cambridge: Cambridge University Press.

———. 2000b. "Chinese Patriliny and the Cycles of Yang and Laiwang." In *Cultures of Relatedness: New Approaches to the Study of Kinship,* edited by Janet Carsten, 37–54. Cambridge: Cambridge University Press.

———. 2003. "Introduction: The Separation Constraint in China." In *Living with Separation in China,* edited by Charles Stafford, 1–26. London: Routledge.

Steward, Frank Henderson. 1994. *Honor.* Chicago: University of Chicago Press.

Strauss, Claudia. 1997. "Partly Fragmented, Partly Integrated: An Anthropological Analysis of 'Postmodern Fragmented Subjects.'" *Cultural Anthropology* 12, no. 3: 362–404.

Strauss, Claudia, and Naomi Quinn. 1997. *A Cognitive Theory of Social Meaning.* Cambridge: Cambridge University Press.

Sun, Lung-ku. 1991. "Contemporary Chinese Culture: Structure and Emotionality." *Australian Journal of Chinese Affairs* 26 (July): 1–41.

Taylor, Charles. 2004. *Modern Social Imaginaries.* Durham, N.C.: Duke University Press.

Teiser, Stephen F. 1988. *The Ghost Festival in Medieval China.* Princeton, N.J.: Princeton University Press.

———. 1995. "Popular Religion." *Journal of Asian Studies* 54, no. 2: 378–95.

Thornton, Patricia. 2007. *Disciplining the State: Virtue, Violence, and State-Making in Modern China.* Honolulu: University of Hawai'i Press.

Tu, Weiming. 1981. "The 'Moral Universal' from the Perspective of East Asian Thought." *Philosophy East and West* 31, no. 3: 259–67.

Turiel, Elliot, Melanie Killen, and Charles C. Helwig. 1987. "Morality: Its Structure, Functions, and Vagaries." In *The Emergence of Morality in Young Children,* edited by Jerome Kagan and Sharon Lamb, 155–244. Chicago: University of Chicago Press.

Unger, Jonathan. 2002. *The Transformation of Rural China*. Armonk, N.Y.: M. E. Sharpe.

Vice, Sue. 1997. *Introducing Bakhtin*. Manchester, UK: Manchester University Press.

Volosinov, V. N. (M. M. Bakhtin). 1983. "The Construction of the Utterance." In *Bakhtin School Papers*. Translated by Noel Owen, edited by Ann Shukman, 114–38. Russian Poetics in Translation, vol. 10. Oxford: RPT Publications in association with the Department of Literature, University of Essex.

Wang, Danyu. 2004. "Ritualistic Coresidence and the Weakening of Filial Practice in Rural China." In *Filial Piety: Practice and Discourse in Contemporary Asia*, ed. Charlotte Ikels, 16–33. Berkeley: University of California Press.

Wang, Gungwu. 1985. "South China Perspectives on Overseas Chinese." *Australian Journal of Chinese Affairs*, no. 13 (January): 69–84.

Wang, Shaoguang. 2000. "The Social and Political Implications of China's WTO Membership." *Journal of Contemporary China* 9, no. 25: 373–405.

Wang, Xiaoying. 2002. "The Post-Communist Personality: The Spectre of China's Capitalist Market Reforms." *China Journal*, no. 47 (January): 1–18.

Watson, James. 1975. *Emigration and the Chinese Lineage*. Berkeley: University of California Press.

———. 1988. "The Structure of Chinese Funerary Rites: Elementary Forms, Ritual Sequence, and the Primacy of Performance." In *Death Ritual in Late Imperial and Modern China*, edited by James L. Watson and Evelyn Rawski, 3–19. Berkeley: University of California Press.

———. 1997. *Golden Arches East: McDonald's in East Asia*. Stanford, Calif.: Stanford University Press.

———. 2004a. "Hereditary Tenancy and Corporate Landlordism in Traditional China: A Case Study." In *Village Life in Hong Kong: Politics, Gender, and Ritual in the New Territories*, edited by James Watson and Rubie Watson, 145–68. Hong Kong: Chinese University Press.

———. 2004b. "Of Flesh and Bones: The Management of Death Pollution in Cantonese Society." In *Village Life in Hong Kong: Politics, Gender, and Ritual in the New Territories*, edited by James Watson and Rubie Watson, 355–90. Hong Kong: Chinese University Press.

Watson, Rubie. 1981. "Class Differences and Affinal Relations in South China." *Man* 16: 593–615.

———. 1991a. "Afterword: Marriage and Gender Inequality." In *Marriage and Inequality in Chinese Society*, edited by Patricia Ebrey and Rubie Watson, 347–68. Berkeley: University of California Press.

———. 1991b. "Wives, Concubines, and Maids: Servitude and Kinship in the Hong Kong Region, 1900–1940." In *Marriage and Inequality in Chinese Society*, edited by Patricia Ebrey and Rubie Watson, 231–55. Berkeley: University of California Press.

Weiner, Annette. 1988. *The Trobrianders of Papua, New Guinea*. New York: Holt, Rinehart and Winston.

Whyte, Martin King. 1974. *Small Groups and Political Rituals in China*. Berkeley: University of California Press.

———. 1988. "Death in the People's Republic of China." In *Death Ritual in Late*

Imperial and Modern China, edited by James L. Watson and Evelyn Rawski, 289–316. Berkeley: University of California Press.

Wikan, Unni. 1984. "Shame and Honour: A Contestable Pair." *Man* 19: 635–52.

Williams, Sue. 1997. *China in Revolution, Part 3.* ("Born under the Red Flag—Surviving Mao.") Ambrica Production in association with WGBH Boston and Channel 4 Television, UK.

Wolf, Arthur. 1969. "Adopt a Daughter-in-Law, Marry a Sister: A Chinese Solution to the Problem of the Incest Taboo." *American Anthropologist* 70, no. 5: 864–74.

Wolf, Margery. 1968. *The House of Lim: A Study of a Chinese Farm Family.* New York: Appleton-Century Crofts.

———. 1972. *Women and the Family in Rural Taiwan.* Stanford, Calif.: Stanford University Press.

Woon, Yuen Fong. 1985. "An Emigrant Community in the Ssy-yi Area, Southeastern China, 1885–1949." *Modern Asian Studies* 18: 273–308.

———. 1989. "Social Change and Continuity in South China: Overseas Chinese and the Guan Lineage of Kaiping County, 1949–1987." *China Quarterly* 118: 324–44.

Wu, Fei. 2005. "Gambling for Qi: Suicide and Family Politics in a Rural North China County." *China Journal* 54: 7–28.

Yalman, Nur. 1963. "On the Purity of Woman in the Caste of Ceylon and Malabar." *Journal of the Royal Anthropological Institute of Great Britain and Ireland* 93, no. 1: 25–58.

Yan, Hairong. 2003. "Spectralization of the Rural: Reinterpreting the Labor Mobility of Rural Young Women in Post-Mao China." *American Ethnologist* 30, no. 4 (November): 578–96.

Yan, Yunxiang. 1992. "The Impact of Rural Reform on Economic and Social Stratification in a Chinese Village." *Australian Journal of Chinese Affairs,* no. 27 (January): 1–23.

———. 1996. *The Flow of Gifts: Reciprocity and Social Networks in a Chinese Village.* Stanford, Calif.: Stanford University Press.

———. 2002. *Private Life under Socialism: Love, Intimacy, and Family Change in a Chinese Village.* Stanford, Calif.: Stanford University Press.

———. 2004. "Calculability and Budgeting in a Household Economy: A Case Study from Rural North China." *Taiwan Journal of Anthropology* 2, no. 1: 69–92.

Yang, Dali L. 1996. *Calamity and Reform in China: State, Rural Society, and Institutional Change since the Great Leap Forward.* Stanford, Calif.: Stanford University Press.

Yang, Lien-sheng. 1957. "The Concept of *Pao* as a Basis for Social Relations in China." In *Chinese Thought and Institutions,* edited by John K. Fairbank, 291–309. Chicago: University of Chicago Press.

Yang, Mayfair Mei-hui. 1994. *Gifts, Favors, and Banquets: The Art of Social Relationships in China.* Ithaca, N.Y.: Cornell University Press.

Zerentian chengbao hetongshu (责任田承包合同书). 1984. Meixian Shi, Chengbei Qu, Zheshang Xiang, and Xiaping Shengchandui (梅县市, 城北区, 扎上乡, 下坪生产队).

Zhang, Hong. 2005. "Bracing for an Uncertain Future: A Case Study of New Coping Strategies of Rural Parents under China's Birth Control Policy." *China Journal* 43: 53–76.

Zimmerman, Rachel. 1997. "Chinese Village Swells with Pride as Washington Governor Seeks His Roots on a Pilgrimage." *New York Times*, October 12, 1997.

Index

TEXT
10/13 Sabon

DISPLAY
Sabon

INDEXER
Thérèse Shere

CARTOGRAPHER
Bill Nelson

COMPOSITOR
Integrated Composition Systems

PRINTER AND BINDER
Sheridan Books, Inc.